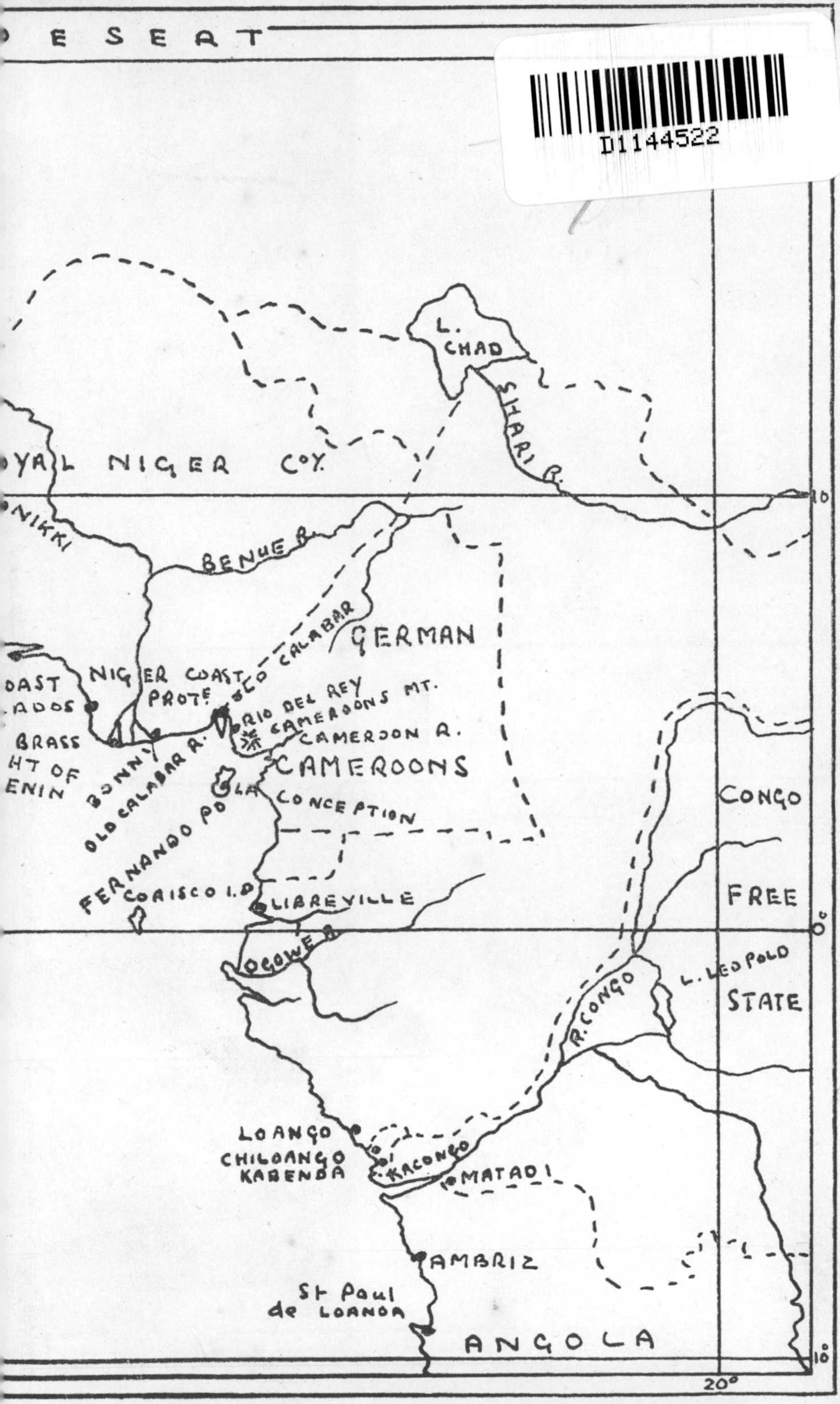

DESERT
L. CHAD
SHARI R.
ROYAL NIGER COY.
NIKKI
BENUE R.
OLD CALABAR
GERMAN
NIGER COAST PROTE
COAST
LAGOS
BRASS
BIGHT OF BENIN
BONNY
OLD CALABAR R.
RIO DEL REY
CAMEROONS MT.
CAMEROON R.
CAMEROONS
FERNANDO PO
LA CONCEPTION
CONGO
FREE
STATE
CORISCO I.
LIBREVILLE
OGOWE R.
R. CONGO
L. LEOPOLD
LOANGO
CHILOANGO
KABENDA
KACONGO
MATADI
AMBRIZ
St Paul de LOANDA
ANGOLA
10°
0°
20°

MARY KINGSLEY

Juliet Pannett.

Mary Kingsley

by

CECIL HOWARD

HUTCHINSON OF LONDON

HUTCHINSON & CO. (*Publishers*) LTD
178–202 Great Portland Street, London, W.1

London Melbourne Sydney
Auckland Bombay Toronto
Johannesburg New York

First published August 1957
Second impression September 1957

*Set in eleven point Garamond, one point
leaded, and printed in Great Britain
by The Anchor Press, Ltd.,
Tiptree, Essex*

To my brother

H. E. HOWARD

in gratitude

ACKNOWLEDGEMENT

I wish to thank Mr C. R. Holt for giving me permission to read and to refer to Mary Kingsley's letters to his grandfather, Mr John Holt of Liverpool.

C. H.

CONTENTS

7

INTRODUCTION

The Kingsleys, a typical English middle-class family, produced two or three striking figures in the last half of the nineteenth century. The best known is Charles, Rector of Eversley, author of *Yeast*, *Hereward the Wake*, *The Heroes*, *The Water Babies*, and a number of other books. He belonged to the school of Christian Socialists, devoted himself to attacking the social evils of his time, and was sufficiently liberal-minded to become a friend of Darwin and Huxley. His name is still a household word.

His youngest brother, Henry, wrote novels too; his work was highly thought of, and there are those who consider that he was a more gifted writer than Charles. He fell on hard times, and died young; his name is rarely heard nowadays.

The most remarkable member of the family was undoubtedly Mary Henrietta Kingsley, the daughter of a third brother, George. In the eight years after the death of her parents in 1892, she made a great name for herself as African traveller, writer, and publicist. To study primitive religious beliefs, she made expeditions into the most dangerous parts of equatorial West Africa, and on her return from her second journey, in 1895, she became a figure of national importance. Thousands read her books, and flocked to hear her lectures, while even the forceful Joseph Chamberlain, then at the height of his power, asked for her advice on the administration of our West African dependencies.

In the 'nineties the Great Powers of Europe were engaged in 'the scramble for Africa', and vast new territories were annexed by England. Though Mary Kingsley is almost forgotten today, and her books have been out of print for fifty years, she exerted a unique and entirely beneficial influence at this critical time. More than any other public figure, she helped to create the sympathetic atmosphere in which, on the whole, these lands have been developed. Stanley, with whip and rifle, had just forced a way from east to west of the Continent, and had returned to paint a dark picture of the people who lived there. Missionaries horrified their supporters by tales of slave-raiding, infant marriage,

9

cannibalism, and human sacrifice. There was thus a serious danger that the British public would come to believe that the African was inherently evil, and would insist on a policy of ruthless repression. Mary Kingsley, having lived alone and unarmed among the most ferocious tribesmen, insisted, on her return to England, that the negroes of West Africa were, 'taken all round, gentle, kindly, hospitable, willing, cheerful, and strong'. She spoke out boldly, and was not afraid to stand up to Colonial Governors or even Joseph Chamberlain himself.

Though she loved danger and longed to return to 'skylark and study' in West Africa, she conceived it to be her duty to stay in England and fight for the preservation of African law and institutions. Five exhausting years—from 1895 to 1900—were spent in trying to convince our rulers that unless fundamental changes were made in Colonial Administration, our new colonies might become as great a failure as the West Indian Islands. Then, when she thought that she had failed in all that she had set out to do, she volunteered to go to South Africa, and died there nursing Boer prisoners.

Even if she had not become the champion of the African, Mary Kingsley would deserve to be remembered as one of the outstanding women of Victorian England. Her fearlessness challenged comparison with that of our greatest explorers; her understanding of African thought processes and religious ideas was deep and penetrating. When she came to recount her experiences, her modesty, humour, and originality of thought and expression combined to produce one of the most entertaining travel books in the English language.

I

EARLY LIFE AND FAMILY

MARY HENRIETTA KINGSLEY was born in Islington on November 13th, 1862, into an eccentric, middle-class family. She was the eldest child of Dr. George Henry Kingsley, the brother of Charles, the well-known novelist. Two years previously he had married Mary Bailey, and Mary was their first child. The doctor was a strange man, quick-tempered, self-indulgent, passionately devoted to travel. His marriage to Mary Bailey in 1860 made little difference to his way of life: he felt that he had done his duty if he spent two or three months of the year at home, leaving his wife to look after his affairs and to bring up his daughter in his absence. The birth of a son a few years later caused no change to his bizarre, self-regarding existence.

His absence had a marked effect upon his wife and daughter. Mrs Kingsley was capable of running his house, and seems to have accepted without complaint all the responsibilities which he thrust upon her; yet, as the years went by, her health began to suffer from the strain under which she lived. She worried about her husband's safety: sometimes, when she knew that he was travelling in dangerous places, she had no news from him for months on end. In a constant state of anxiety, she seemed to lose all pleasure in life, and began to confine herself more and more within the small family circle, seeking her sole relaxation in reading. She shunned her former friends and acquaintances, and went out among her neighbours only when they wanted her help.

There is a suggestion of neurosis in the way she withdrew herself from the outer world and so, perhaps unconsciously, began to forge the chains which bound Mary to her until the day of her death. Certainly the child grew up with the fixed idea that her primary duty was to serve others, and that only when her

mother or brother had no further need for her could she attend
to her own affairs.

Mary was warm-hearted, spirited, and eager to make friends.
Later, she enjoyed the company of ships' pursers, bush traders,
and even cannibals, but the seclusion of her early years had
its effect. She grew up shy and awkward in the company of people
of her own class; she never felt completely at home in the drawing-
rooms of London. Her chance to learn how to move easily
and naturally in society came too late.

Nor was this the only effect of a lonely youth. She built
up barriers against the outside world; she came to regard herself
as one apart, one who somehow lacked the warm human qualities
which would lead people to love her for her own sake. Never, she
felt, could she have a real friend. This feeling of isolation gave
to her nature, which was essentially lively and gay, a tinge of
deep melancholy.

When Mary was a year old, the family moved to a little
house in Highgate, with lanes on two sides, and a big garden.
It stood next door to a Baptist church, and strangers often
mistook it for the manse. The people who lived in the 'Terrace'
nearby were convinced that this isolated house was the centre of
operations of burglars and thieves who were reputed to lurk in
the lane by the Kingsleys' long garden. They hinted darkly that
one day Mrs Kingsley and her children would be found with
their throats cut. No robber ever dared to break in, however;
they may have been scared by the dogs which Mrs Kingsley
always kept, or by the knowledge that she was an excellent
shot with a revolver—in itself an unusual accomplishment
in a quiet Victorian lady.

Though the neighbours may have thought that the Kingsleys
led a dangerous life, Mary was aware only of its monotony.
She had to do her share of household work from the earliest
age, and by the time that she was ten she was held responsible
for the general tidiness of the house. Her only helper was an
elderly, hymn-singing maid, Mrs Barrett, who did her best to
liven things up by blowing the soot out of the copper flue in the
kitchen periodically with charges of her master's gunpowder.
She was a poor substitute for friends of Mary's own age.

Every year Dr. Kingsley returned, bringing more trophies
with him, and Mary's task became more and more difficult.

All over the house were curiosities from strange places 'battling for space with the Transactions of half a dozen learned societies and books innumerable on all manner of strange subjects, as joyously as trees battle for life-space in a tropical forest; so that when at length a chair had been disencumbered of Darwin on *The Expression of the Emotions*, the *Kabbala Denudata*, *Tristram Shandy*, the professional jacket of a Sioux medicine man, Lotze's *Microcosmos*, Mr Sponge's *Sporting Tour*, Fitzgerald's *Omar Khayyam*, and Philemon Holland's *Pliny*, or some similar assortment . . .' there was a good chance that the visitor who sat down unwarily might encounter 'the sting of a great black Trygon from the Hauraki Gulf, or a stone axe from that region, or an equally crisp thing—a Red Indian iron ornament, or a set of arrow heads'.

Henry Kingsley, the younger brother of George and Charles, was the only regular visitor. He had established a claim to the attic, and was often to be found there, sitting in a fog of tobacco smoke, working hard at his latest novel or play. It was a peaceful haven compared with the house in Kentish Town where he lived. On fine afternoons he left his attic and came down on to the lawn, for no Kingsley could resist the call of the sun, and there he would sometimes pause from his work to tell his niece hair-raising tales of the five wild years that he had spent in Australia after he had come down from Oxford. He had gone out to prospect for gold, failed to make even a living, and finished up as a mounted policeman. He had met some of the roughest of bush-rangers, and Mary listened to his tales wide-eyed.

Mary had no conscious desire for friends. When her household tasks were done, she turned eagerly to the books in her father's library. They covered a wide range, and Mary at first found pleasure and escape by reading Smollett's works, old books of the West Indies—where some of her paternal grandmother's ancestors had been planters in the eighteenth century—and stories of the buccaneers such as Johnson's *Robberies and Murders of the Most Notorious Pyrates*. She was not one, however, who could live in a world of fantasy. Though imaginative, she had an active and critical mind and as she grew up she started to read books on natural history, medicine, and the sciences. Those on medicine were doubtless adequate, but she was to suffer a bitter disappointment as a result of her scientific studies. She tells the

story of how, after reading chemistry for months, she happened
to be introduced to an expert, and tried her knowledge on him:
'he said he had not heard anything so ridiculous for years, and
recommended I should be placed in a museum as a compendium
of exploded chemical theories'.

This hurt her feelings very much, but, though she cried
bitterly, she did not give up. She was determined to learn, and
asked for help from her parents. They were not very sympathetic;
in the 'seventies it was not considered at all necessary for a
young lady to concern herself with science. They did, however,
buy for her Craig's *Pursuit of Knowledge Under Difficulties*. From
this compendium she learnt 'how men had invented the steam
engine from observing the habits of tea-kettles, and mastered
exceedingly difficult dead languages from merely finding a leaf
of a book, written therein, in a dust-bin, and subsequently had
attained such eminence in their respective walks of knowledge
that Europe trembled at their names'. Reassured, she made up
her mind to find out things for herself.

She was not satisfied with theory; she wanted to experiment.
A popular journal of the time, *The English Mechanic*, provided just
the kind of information and practical advice she needed, and
throughout her 'teens she looked eagerly forward to the day of
its publication. A burst pipe, or a faulty stove, or a necessary job
of carpentry gave her a chance to put its teaching to the test,
and though she made mistakes, she learned how to use her hands
—an invaluable preparation for the time when she would be in
Africa, far from any help.

She had to teach herself elementary mathematics, but her
parents were persuaded to find her a tutor in German. Later,
she learned the language more thoroughly when she went to
Germany for a few months to study medicine. Yet, in the main,
she had to educate herself, slowly and laboriously, and she
could not help being jealous and hurt when she saw that her
father thought nothing of spending hundreds of pounds on
her young brother's schooling at the same time as he treated her
demands with amused indifference.

In 1879 the family moved from Highgate to Bexley Heath
in Kent, for the sake of Mrs Kingsley's health, which was causing
alarm. Her obsessive nature, however, had fastened itself on the
fear that her husband would be killed on one of his dangerous

journeys; since he refused to stay at home, the change of district brought no relief.

Mary at seventeen has been described by one of her father's friends as 'a thin, pale girl of middle height, with straight fair hair and blue eyes, quiet and of domestic habits'. Upon her now devolved the task of caring for a sick mother and a delicate brother. The house they lived in was somewhat dilapidated, and in this country district she found her textbook, *The English Mechanic*, more essential than ever. Most of her time was taken up in running the house, but she spent the few hours that were left reading all she could find on ethnology and anthropology. For relaxation, she turned again to her old travel books, often disregarding her mother's complaints and reading far into the night.

She read as many people do who are both imaginative and concrete-minded. She could become absorbed in the adventures of an explorer even if he told his tale without literary skill. She did, however, demand an observant eye and detailed descriptions of what he saw, and often found her greatest enjoyment in reading the long passages, quite irrelevant to the main story, in which Jobson or Dampier would turn aside to give naive accounts of monstrous beasts or strange happenings. To these seventeenth- and eighteenth-century writers Mary owed a great deal. From them she learnt to look at the African with curious but unbiased eyes. They had not been shocked by anything they saw: neither was she.

For seven years Mary lived at Bexley Heath. The only excitement in her life was caused by the return, often unexpected, of her father; the only human interest, in reading the vivid letters which he wrote from ships' cabins, from Rocky Mountain huts, or from ramshackle inns in the Middle West of the States. He came to stand for all that she most admired: adventure, courage, strange lands.

2

GEORGE HENRY KINGSLEY

DR. GEORGE HENRY KINGSLEY was a selfish, fiery, gifted man, with a touch of the crank and a touch of the hero. For a girl like Mary, he was impossible to resist. She worshipped him. The time when she was not reading his letters, listening to his views, or, later, helping him in his work, seemed to her merely so much time wasted. No man ever fully supplanted him in her affections or earned the devotion and admiration she gave to him.

When she was young his homecoming, although exciting, was not without its dangers. He had a 'volcanic' temper and Mary was the one upon whom it was most liable to erupt. He could not bear noise. Both Mrs Barrett and the old gardener who worked for him were aware of this and took care not to make a sound: the former trying hard 'to avoid her pet accident, namely falling downstairs with a dustpan, scrubbing brush, pail, and a shriek: she greased the bearings of the kitchen sink assiduously, and never sang more than a line and a half of a hymn', while the latter found such quiet ways of passing the time as sleeping for a whole afternoon among the artichokes or talking with another gardener over the hedge.

Mary was not so successful. At Highgate her favourite pets were a pair of fighting cocks, and though it is true that they delighted the doctor on one occasion by driving the postman to seek refuge in the coal cellar, there were times when they infuriated him. They made a point of strutting before his study window when they crowed their loudest. Mary was blamed for not keeping them shut up in their run at the bottom of the garden. Though she had learned how to prevent them from fighting—for she hated any sport which involved cruelty to bird or beast—she never succeeded in keeping them away from her father.

Her love for practical experiments sometimes led to clashes. She had always been impressed by Mrs Barrett's explosions, and on one occasion, when she was about twelve, she decided to try her hand. Her father had brought home a tin of gunpowder which he described as very strong. She had been reading about military mines and thought this was an excellent opportunity to make one. When she touched it off at the bottom of the garden a startling explosion blew a tub of manure water over the household blankets hanging on a nearby clothes-line. This brought down on her 'the usual prophecies of an awful end, and an immediate personal chastisement into the bargain'.

Because she was in charge of general tidiness, she was always blamed when anything was mislaid—a not infrequent occurrence in that household. She also offended her father with her racy and picturesque language, for, from the earliest age, she showed a marked preference for strong expressions. After all, her father in one of his rages was not a man who paused to choose his words, and he was her model. Naturally, however, in his calmer moments he was shocked at his young daughter's vocabulary.

Sometimes trouble was caused by Mary's fancy for decorating empty fire-grates with willow shavings topped with gold paper. The doctor was a great smoker and rarely gave a thought to where he flung his matches once his pipe was drawing. He blamed Mary when one of them landed in the fireplace and started a blaze. On these occasions Mrs Kingsley made matters worse by pointing out to her husband that he was entirely to blame; he should be careful where he threw his matches, and keep a check on his swearing when his daughter was present.

The similarity of taste between father and daughter also led to friction. A case in point was the interest they both took in a new book on science, *Solar Physics*. Mary was reading it when she heard her father recommend it to one of his friends and promise to send it round to him in the morning. Since she had no intention of parting with the book until she had finished it, she promptly hid it. She was too truthful to say that she did not know where it was, and too obstinate to hand it over. George Kingsley raved and shouted—all to no purpose.

These clashes, however, never lasted long, nor did they leave any unpleasantness behind them. Her father's fury was truly frightening while it lasted; mercifully it was brief. So long as she dodged the books which were hurled at her and kept quietly out of the way for a few hours, all was well again. As the years passed, however, Dr. Kingsley's regard and affection for his daughter steadily grew, for he realized her worth of character and so came to treat her more and more as a friend and confidant. Some of his longest letters were written to her, for he knew that she would appreciate his accounts of hunting and his detailed descriptions of the ways of primitive peoples. He referred to her sarcastically as 'the learned one' in his letters to his wife, yet he was clearly impressed by her powerful character and touched by her devotion.

From the earliest age George Kingsley had craved for travel and a life of adventure. Born in 1826 at Barnock Rectory, Northamptonshire, he had spent his boyhood first at Clovelly, and later at Chelsea. His father, the rector, was a brave and hardy man who won the love and respect of the fishermen on this rough Devon coast as much by his fearlessness in the face of danger as by his care of their souls. He must have sympathized with the bold spirit shown by each of his four sons—a spirit which was to drive all of them, though in vastly different ways, to lives of adventure.

Gerald, the eldest, became a naval officer and died at his post on a disease-ridden ship in the Gulf of Carpentaria. Charles found adventure in his fight against the evils of poverty and oppression which he saw everywhere around him, and from which he sought relief by writing of such heroes as Hereward the Wake or Amyas Leigh. Henry, the youngest son, who was born in 1830, after his five rough-and-tumble years in Australia, settled down to write sixteen novels and plays between 1863 and 1876. *Geoffrey Hamlyn* and *Ravenshoe* brought him good reviews and recognition, but he found it increasingly difficult to make a living by his pen, and towards the end fought a grim battle against poverty and the deadly disease—cancer of the throat—which was to kill him in 1876.

George, like his brothers, had grown up to love nature and to dream of strange adventures. His desires were fed by the books in his father's library:

venerable treatises on natural history, embellished with fantastical illustrations dating from that happy age when the artistic imagination

wandered free in a paradise that was untainted by the presence of that
serpent Scientific accuracy: records relating to the West Indian Islands
and the golden Spanish Main; books that had been collected by their
mother's ancestors who were for generations planters in Barbados and
Demerara. Histories of the globe, and lordly folios on whose maps full
many a sturdy coast-line dwindled into dots. . . . Volume on volume
of famous voyagers—Dampier, Rogers, Shelocke, Byron, Cook and
grand old Esquemeling—the Froissart of the Buccaneers . . .

Life at Clovelly had been tolerable, with the sea at hand,
excellent trout fishing, and fine scenery. This came to an end when
their father accepted the living at Chelsea. The rectory and the
church were planted in the midst of mean alleys, squalid courts,
and primitive lanes. George felt that he had to escape. He was
at this time a medical student, but the moment term was over
he took a rucksack, setting out to tramp in Germany, or Switzer-
land or Austria. For the rest of his active life he sought happiness
in fleeing from the dull, matter-of-fact towns of England, escap-
ing, too, from all the duties and ties which life in one of them
involved.

Until 1847 he had to be satisfied with his long rambles on
the Continent. In that year he became a qualified doctor, and
went to Paris to continue his studies. His liberal sentiments—
evident only in his youth—led him to take his place at the barri-
cades by the side of the citizens who ultimately overthrew Louis
Philippe in 1848. On his return to England he faced the un-
welcome prospect of a monotonous life as a medical practitioner.
But he was lucky. In 1850 he became private physician to the
first Marquess of Ailesbury, and he afterwards attended in a
similar capacity the Dukes of Norfolk and Sutherland, and the
first and second Earls of Ellesmere. He had leisure and the
opportunity to enjoy his favourite pastimes of fishing and
hunting and to indulge his lively mind in what could have been
only a superficial study of literature and science.

He became a Fellow of the Linnean Society and of the Royal
Microscopical Society. He made plans to write a historical novel,
to publish a catalogue of Elizabethan drama with biographies of
each writer, and to compile a popular anthology of early songs
and poetry. In a letter to George A. Macmillan, his publisher, he
explained why none of these projects ever matured:

I am here, slaughtering salmon, stags, and fowl at a most fearful rate. I am either IN the river or on the hill from six in the morning till nine at night, so you can readily imagine that I have no time left for mental work; indeed I am so utterly insane about questions of wild Highland sport that I can produce, think and dream of nothing else.

From the start he was essentially a man of action rather than of ideas, and such he remained throughout.

It has been seen that his marriage to Mary Bailey in 1860 made no difference to the doctor's way of life. Indeed, after the death of the second Earl of Ellesmere in 1862, he eagerly accepted an invitation from the captain of H.M.S. *St. George* to join him on a cruise in the Mediterranean. He found this so delightful that he returned the following year and visited the Balearics. On his way there, he saw Naples, called on Garibaldi on Caprera, and enjoyed a short cruise in the Duke of St. Albans' yacht.

From Syracuse he wrote a letter to his wife. It was typical of many that were to follow during the next twenty years:

You must not be surprised to see where I have got to. I had an offer of a cruise from the Duke of St. Albans, and so came round here. Lucky for us that we are here, for we were very nearly lost on the night we sailed. I was suddenly awakened by being thrown out of my bunk, and, on opening the cabin door, found that we were, apparently, upsetting. It was no easy work getting up the companionway, for the ladder was very nearly where the handrail should have been. We had been struck, without a moment's warning, by one of those fearful Mediterranean white squalls. On deck there was a terrible scene, the wind howling fearfully, the sea perfectly white with foam, and the ship tearing like a mad thing through the water, which was surging halfway up the deck. We thought that it was, literally, all over with us, but at last she righted again. We lost two boats, but, fortunately, none of the crew. . . .

This could hardly have been a reassuring letter for his young wife, nursing her year-old baby; worse was to follow, for the doctor soon found a chance to extend his travels. In 1867 he became attached to the young Earl of Pembroke and for three years they cruised together in the Pacific in the *Albatross*, a small coasting schooner which the Earl had fitted up as a yacht.

Their experiences amongst the islands are told in *South Sea Bubbles: by the Earl and the Doctor*. Some of the more interesting chapters of this book were written by George Kingsley, whose light-hearted style, full of asides and whimsical fancies, must have served as a model to Mary when she came to write of her travels.

Sometimes Mrs Kingsley had to wait months for a letter. When at last she heard from him, she found, amongst descriptions of superb scenery, of handsome and friendly islanders, of strange birds, animals, and fish, alarming references to the dangers of yachting in those inadequately charted waters, and of being eaten by the inhabitants of the remoter islands. The *Albatross* ended her days on a coral reef off Nukumbasanga, in the Ringgold Group, and the crew lived for nine days on the rain-swept island, in hourly fear of an attack by cannibals. Eventually they put to sea in the ship's boats which had been saved from the wreck, and after hours of rowing, sailing, and baling they were picked up by a British ship.

The doctor returned home for several months when Mary was eight years old. But the cruise in the Pacific had merely whetted his appetite. In 1870 Lord Dunraven planned a prolonged hunting expedition to North America, and offered Dr. Kingsley a post as travelling companion and physician to the party. He accepted with alacrity and spent the greater part of the next five years with his employer in Canada and the United States. The hunting and fishing were much to the doctor's taste, though, as he declared in an article to the *Field*, he suffered one great disappointment: 'Possibly were I a sportsman, I would prefer galloping in the midst of a herd of poor blundering brutes, plugging one after another . . . with a Springfield, and leaving a long line of carcases behind me to rot on the plain. It is a thing to do once; but for sport, No, sir! . . .' He and Dunraven soon gave up hunting buffalo and went in search of more dangerous game: caribou, moose, and the savage bears of the Rockies. Nor did he fail to give a graphic account, in one of his letters to his wife, of his narrow escape from death when stalking a grizzly.

The 'seventies were a time of ferocious Indian warfare. Dunraven and his party were hunting well within the danger zone. With little imagination, George sent to his wife a detailed description of what they might meet:

We rather expected an Indian fight the other day whilst we were away on the North Platte in a country far north of that in which we hunted last year, which has rarely been visited. I think that the Indians saw the hunting; at any rate, a few miles off the oddest puffs of smoke began to rise in the air, one after another, in a line of, perhaps, two miles in length. . . . The next day we moved up the stream twenty miles, and, just as I had killed a buck, I saw opposite to me and two miles off, the same number of puffs of smoke arise as before, showing that the brutes had been watching me steadily and had gone up abreast of our party! However, I fancy they thought we were too strong for them, and we got in yesterday with our scalps on. This is the last bit of Indian danger we are likely to have; and I for one am not sorry, for there is a certain feeling of anxiety about the top of one's head when one walks about with one's life in one's hand.

In another long letter home, George sang the praises of William Cody, later to be famous under the name of Buffalo Bill, whom Dunraven had hired as his chief huntsman. The doctor was intrigued by this professional hunter whom he had not believed existed outside Fenimore Cooper's novels. Cody and his assistant had the strangest feelings towards Indians:

though when on the warpath, they would no more hesitate to shoot down an Indian off his reservation, than they would hesitate to throw a stone at a felonious chipmunk, they have a sympathy and tenderness towards them infinitely greater than you will find among the greedy, pushing settlers, who regard them as mere vermin who must be destroyed for the sake of [their] lands.

The doctor rather agreed with the settlers:

I really fear that they [the Indians] will have to be wiped out if they will not settle and be civilized—and they won't! The world cannot afford to give up enormous tracts of valuable land in order to enable a few bands of wandering savages to live in idleness. . . .

The worst shock that Mrs Kingsley ever had came when her husband was in North America. A letter arrived informing her that Lord Dunraven and his party were about to join General Custer, who was leading an American armed force against Big Chief Sitting Bull. Next, she read in the papers of the disaster at Little Big Horn, where the general and the whole of his force were ambushed and shot down in June 1876. A dreadful period of anxiety followed: then came a letter saying that providentially bad weather had prevented Dunraven from joining Custer at all.

Later letters from the doctor show that he was beginning to realize that he was growing too old for such a strenuous life. The hunting trips in bitterly cold weather, often with no protection save flimsy tents, the long days in the saddle, and the struggles with rapids, were too tiring for a man who was past fifty. Regretfully, he had to abandon the life of the hunter. But this was by no means the end of travel. He revisited the States, crossed Newfoundland, was away on Frobisher's Straits, visited Cape Colony and Japan, and went round the world. But none of these things was exciting enough for George Kingsley, and he looked regretfully back to the days he had spent with Pembroke and Dunraven.

The doctor had never been merely a man of action: his interests were wide and varied and his pen constantly in his hand to record and to comment on what he saw. When he could no longer spend the greater part of his time in adventures abroad, he began to add to his voluminous notes with the idea of writing a book on the customs and laws of primitive peoples. He had left it too late, however. He had failed to carry through the ambitious literary projects of his early manhood and there was little chance that he would now succeed.

From the time she was about sixteen, Mary had been fitting herself to become her father's helper and companion. She had inherited his restless nature and love of adventure, but her sense of duty had kept her at home looking after her mother, who, not surprisingly, had become a neurasthenic invalid. She was, nevertheless, free to follow her father in his intellectual pursuits. Her study of German had been undertaken primarily to enable her to read standard works on anthropology, and she now began to collect for him accounts given by travellers of sacrificial rites, and opinions expressed on the subject by German authors. Without these years of study she could never have written with such penetration of the primitive societies in West Africa.

In 1886 her younger brother, Charles, entered Christ's College, at Cambridge, to read law. In order to be near him, the family left Bexley Heath and took a house there in Mortimer

Road. Her father, still lively and vivacious and a brilliant conversationalist, soon attracted a circle of friends and acquaintances
connected with academic life. A new world opened out for
Mary. For the first time she knew the pleasures of intelligent
company. She was encouraged and stimulated: there was no
longer any danger of her becoming a 'compendium of exploded
theories'.

The doctor now had to be content for the most part with
life at home, and Mary found his company exciting. His temper
was still uncertain, and could easily be roused, especially by
'Mr Gladstone in print or a Roman Catholic priest in the flesh'.
The *Telegraph*, which often supported Mr Gladstone's policy,
was frequently torn to shreds or thrust bodily into the fire;
but when Mary and her mother agreed to replace it by the more
conservative *Standard* they found that they had made things
worse. The doctor was so struck with the truth of its criticisms
of Gladstone's government that his fury at the Prime Minister's
betrayal of the Empire knew no bounds.

It is interesting to see how far Mary agreed with her father's
views. He was her hero, the pivot of her life, and represented all
that she longed to be, yet she steadfastly refused to shut her
eyes, as he did, to the evils of colonial rule. To him, England
was 'the incarnation of fearlessness, justice and honour', and
the Englishman had almost a divine right to rule wherever he
could establish himself. She, on the other hand, though prepared
to admit that English administrators were honest and well
intentioned, was firmly convinced that they were too aloof or too
ignorant to promote the welfare of the peoples whom they ruled.
Their mistakes often led to loss of men and money. Until these
officials were forced to study primitive laws and customs, British
rule would continue to be based on insecure foundations.

She, like her father, was completely without sentimentality.
They would probably have agreed that the Red Indians of
North America must either learn the ways of civilized men or
be exterminated. Justice and honour they both understood, but
they had no sympathy with those who claimed to be doing
good while in fact they were forcing primitive people to adopt a
way of life which was not suited to them. Dr. Kingsley had seen
the results of this in the islands of the South Seas: there, Christian
missionaries had established a petty tyranny and had done their

utmost to turn the friendly, carefree, amoral islanders into sombre puritans. Until the day of his death, he detested them and all their works.

Mary came to hold very similar views on the West African Missions, but her friendship and respect for some of the more intelligent missionaries saved her from the unbalanced bitterness of her father. It is a measure of her quality that she could publicly disagree with them, yet remain their friend.

Mary lacked the hard core of selfishness which characterized her father. Though she loved and respected him, she was not blind to this great weakness. She did not blame him for shirking his family responsibilities, or for abandoning a promising career as a physician, nor did she think less of him for failing to leave behind any written work of importance. She was convinced, however, that her mother's ill-health and early death were largely due to her constant anxiety on his account. She was even irritated at times at the way in which he 'used to reconcile and explain it to himself, that because he had a wife and family it was his dire and awful duty to go and hunt grizzly bears in a Red Indian infested district and the like'. But for her it was sufficient explanation that he was driven by an inner urge to see strange places, and that he 'loved the bright eyes of danger'.

Though she deeply regretted that he, with his wealth of experience and scholarship, should have left no work of importance, she put this down to his pride and his depth of knowledge, which would not permit him to publish a work which in any way fell short of perfection. Seven years after his death her considered opinion of him was that he had lived 'the very happy life of a noble, perfect English gentleman—a man who all his life long, wild as the circumstances of it had often been, never did a mean act or thought a mean thought, and never knew fear'.

He satisfied the deepest need in this unusual woman—the need to feel passionate respect. 'They are brave and so you can respect them, which is an essential element in a friendly feeling,' she wrote of her favourite tribe, the Fans. This quality which she sought, led her, the moment she was free, to find a pretext for going to live amongst the most remote and dangerous tribesmen of West Africa.

3

CAMBRIDGE

THOUGH the Kingsleys' rather gaunt, bow-windowed house overlooking Parker's Piece saw plenty of company in the next few years, Mary's domestic duties grew heavier. Her brother was delicate, and, in spite of the anxious care with which she looked after him, he was often ill. Mrs Kingsley's misanthropy remained unaffected although her husband had given up his wanderings. She had lived alone for over twenty years, and visitors disturbed her. Finally, George Kingsley at sixty was beginning to feel the effects of years of rough living.

Yet life was more tolerable here than at Bexley Heath. Though the family was not affluent, the doctor had been well paid by his noble clients and could afford to live in some comfort now that he had retired. The years had mellowed him a lot and he was surprisingly happy in Cambridge. He was soon keenly interested in University sport. Long summer days were spent watching cricket at Fenner's, though sometimes he would cross the road to venture amongst the games on Parker's Piece. There, cricket balls hurtling through the air from all quarters gave him a pleasant sense of living dangerously once more. In the spring he lingered so long on the towpath beside the Cam, watching the training and racing of the College eights, that Mary had to warn him that the cold east winds and the river mists were dangerous to a man who suffered from rheumatism.

Mary now had many acquaintances and several friends, but she was intimate with few outside the family. At twenty-four, though eager to find time to listen to the exciting conversation in the drawing-room, she attracted little attention. Her brilliant father was the magnet which drew visitors, and the shy, studious young woman, so often called away to attend to household tasks, remained very much in the background. Her sudden rise to fame within a few years of her parents' death must have come as a great surprise to the academic and professional men and women who had met her at the house in Mortimer Road.

Mary claimed that she had never been in love: in a rare moment of confidence she made this confession to Stephen Gwynn whom she had come to know well on her return from Africa in 1895. It was unusual for her to give even a hint of her personal feelings: she did so on this occasion only to excuse herself from a discussion of the love scenes in a novel he had sent for her to criticize. She said that she knew nothing of love save at second hand, for of course she had read of it and seen its effects upon her friends. Because she had never loved anyone in this way, nor been the object of such love, she was convinced that there was something lacking in her character. She made the humble claim, however, that this deficiency left her free to undertake tasks which bored other people.

Perhaps Mary was too preoccupied with nursing her mother and hero-worshipping her father to give any thought to men of her own age. She was kind, loyal, sympathetic, and very lovable; yet she had few of the arts and graces which first attract young men. She could be gay and light-hearted in the right company, but perhaps the blue eyes looked too frankly from under the high brow, with the hair above parted severely in the middle; the mouth was too firm, hinting only at a sense of humour; and the jaw showed strength that might be admired but could hardly be found attractive. Only a man very much in love could have broken through the barriers which this sensitive young woman had built to protect herself from a strange world.

She had friends and relations who would have helped if she had been prepared to play her part. Young men were introduced to her, and her cousins led her off to parties. But she was convinced that she was in some way different from the light-hearted, flirting girls whom she saw around her, and was quite content to entertain and amuse her companions with her vivid, humorous conversation. One young man, who could not make up his mind which of her attractive cousins he wished to marry, spent a great deal of time in her company. Neither of the girls showed any signs of jealousy, for they were certain that he was quite safe in her hands.

Her health and spirits gradually revived in Cambridge. In spite of having to run the house, she began to enjoy herself, even spending a week in Paris with one of her father's friends. But the time when she could relax was brief. Soon after her return from abroad the prison gates were shut on her more firmly than ever. Her mother's illness became acute, and Mary was the only one who could look after her and soothe her in her terrible suffering. For four years she devoted herself entirely to this task, frequently sitting up with her at night, and being always at hand during the day.

She had very little help from those closest to her. Her brother, who was never in the best of health, was not a man to put himself to any inconvenience; he had grown used to seeing Mary looking after everyone, and took it for granted that she would always do so. In this, he resembled his father. The latter may, in Mary's words, have possessed 'an infinite gentleness with weak things, a vigorous hatred for those who inflicted suffering unnecessarily on man or beast, that came from a sympathy which made him feel the extent of that suffering', but as a practical helper he was of little value. The previous ten years, when his wife's illness was developing, he had spent as far from England as possible, and it was unlikely that he would be deeply affected, or become less self-centred, at his time of life.

Indeed, he was shortly to contribute to Mary's unhappiness. A medical friend, Sir William Gull, being ill, asked him to take charge of a case for him. To do this, George Kingsley had to go out in all weathers and as a result he contracted rheumatic fever. He was nursed with great care and appeared to have recovered. To aid his complete cure, he embarked on a voyage round the world, once more leaving Mary entirely responsible for her mother. When he did return to Cambridge it was found that his heart had been permanently weakened and he too had need of his daughter's care and attention.

Of this dreadful period in her life, Mary wrote, 'It was years of work and watching and anxiety, a narrower life in home interests than ever, and a more hopelessly depressing one, for it was a losing fight with death the whole time.' The end of her long servitude came in 1892. On the second of February, on going up to her father's room to take him his morning post, she found him dead. His heart had failed and he had died peacefully in his sleep. She was stunned, for he had been in better spirits for some time before his death, and she had had no warning of the blow that was to fall. Her grief was deep and lasting. The death of the man whom she had loved and admired above all, and whose deeds and presence had given colour to her life, brought an anguish and a sense of desolation almost too intense to bear.

Her devotion to her mother never wavered, and while she made all the arrangements for her father's funeral and for the settling of his estate, she still found time to spend hours in the sick-room. It was only when, five weeks later, her mother died too, that Mary had time to think of herself, and to wonder what she was to do. She had suddenly lost all that had given purpose to her life.

And then, when the fight was lost, when there were no more odd jobs anyone wanted me to do at home, I, out of my life in books, found something to do that my father had cared for, something for which I had been taught German, so that I could do for him odd jobs in it. It was the study of early religion and law, and for it I had to go to West Africa, and I went there, proceeding on the even tenour of my way, doing odd jobs and trying to understand things, pursuing knowledge under difficulties with unbroken devotion.

It was characteristic of her that when her old way of life was shattered, she did not give way to despair. She could see no way to rebuild her life; she felt herself incapable of experiencing another deep attachment, yet she was determined to do something of value. The job really did not matter, provided it was worth doing and led her out of England. Charles, her brother, had first claims on her time: she would look after him as long as he needed her. The moment she was free, however, she meant to get away from the suburban life which irked her just as it had irked her father.

George Kingsley left between eight and nine thousand pounds to his wife when he died, and this money, together with her small private estate, now belonged to Charles and Mary. Provided that they were prudent, they had enough to live on without working: they could even afford an occasional extravagance. When, later, Mary went to Africa, she limited her expenditure very carefully, sleeping in African huts to avoid the expense of camping gear and porters to carry it, and eating African food. To help still further to keep the cost down she took pains to become an expert trader, buying rubber and ivory to sell again on the Coast. She estimated that her second journey cost her three hundred pounds.

After her return, of course, she earned far more money. Royalties from her book, *Travels in West Africa*, brought in over five hundred pounds in 1897, and fees from articles and lectures must have amounted to another three or four hundred pounds. She valued her independence so highly, however, that she declined three lucrative offers: one, to join an expedition to central East Africa; another to investigate the gum trade in West Africa, and a third to visit China with all expenses paid and a fee of one thousand pounds.

Before she was fit to undertake any new task, she needed rest and a change of scene, for her health and spirits had been affected by the long strain of nursing her parents. She shunned the health resorts of England or of the Continent and took ship to the Canaries. As the *Castle* liner on which she was a passenger approached the islands, she saw from the deck the Peak of Tenerife standing out a deep purple against a green sky, separated from the sea by masses of pink and gold cumulus. In a short while the mountains of the Grand Canary came into sight and Mary gazed spellbound at the yellowish-red peaks and the 'lovely lustrous blue' of the 'air which lies among their rocky crevices and swathes their softer sides'. She had the strange fancy that if she could only have collected some of it in a bottle and taken it home to show her friends, it would have come out as 'a fair blue-violet cloud in the gray air of Cambridge'.

Here she spent several weeks, delighting in the brilliant scenery and the warm sun. Unable to be completely idle, she made a study of the island's trade and industries. But, more important, she met for the first time West African traders, recuperating after a bout of Coast fever, or making a call on their way home. She listened, half unbelieving, to their tales of disease and death, and she forgave them when they drank too much, putting it down to their relief at having escaped, if only for a while, from the dangers which they were so fond of describing. She realized from the first that they were mostly men of character, doing a job which brought wealth and employment to the people of England, but for which they got very little reward. Though the picture they drew of West Africa was a dark one, and though their anecdotes of friends almost invariably ended with the statement 'He's dead now', she became more and more attracted to the land and its primitive peoples.

Another motive may have driven her to go to West Africa when she was free to make her choice. It has been suggested by Stephen Gwynn, her biographer, who knew her well, that the loss of her parents may have left her with no desire to go on living; that she went to the wildest part of Africa to find a way of ending a life which had become unbearable.

The letter upon which Gwynn bases his case was written long after her first journey to Africa. It was to Matthew Nathan, and contains the following sentences:

My life has been a comic one: dead tired and feeling no one had need of me any more, when my Mother and Father died within six weeks of each other in '92, and my brother went off to the East, I went down to West Africa to die. West Africa amused me and was kind to me and was scientifically interesting—and did not want to kill me just then. I am in no hurry. I don't care one way or the other, for a year or so.

Nothing could be more explicit; yet when she wrote this, in 1899, Mary was under great strain. For months she had fought a losing battle with the Colonial Office, and seen almost all her allies desert her; within the last year she had produced a book of over five hundred pages, written numerous articles, given dozens of lectures, and found time to look after her brother. Never robust, her health had deteriorated under the strain and her letters make constant reference to headaches, neuralgia of the eyes, and frequent attacks of influenza. Finally, when for the first time in her life she became emotionally involved with a man of her own age, he made it quite clear that he was not interested in her. It is hardly surprising that she should feel that life was hardly worth living. Whether she had felt the same in 1893 is open to doubt.

On her return from the Canaries, she found that there was a lot to be done. Her brother, who had finished his studies at Christ's, wished to live in London. There was nothing to keep Mary in Cambridge, which had such painful memories for her, and she set about making arrangements for the move. With her usual efficiency she disposed of most of her parents' belongings, and superintended the removal of the rest to a little flat at the top of a wide stone staircase at 100 Addison Road, near the Uxbridge Road Station. Here she and her brother lived whenever he was in England. Her journeys had to be planned very carefully, for she could only set out when he was abroad, and she had to be back in time to meet him from his boat, and to see that everything was arranged for his comfort at Addison Road.

Charles Kingsley was a pale imitation of his father: just as selfish and irresponsible, but lacking the doctor's flamboyant, dominating personality. He must have been a tiresome man to live with. Even Mary lost patience at times with his dilatory, nerveless way of managing his affairs, and reluctantly came to the conclusion that the two thousand pounds which had been spent on his education had probably been wasted. He had literary ambitions and planned to edit his father's papers, and, after his sister's death, to write her biography. It was left to Mary to do the former, while the latter was not completed at the time of Charles' death in 1909. He meant to travel in the East as the preliminary to a study of Chinese thought, yet, even when his mind was made up, it was months before he could bring himself to take the first practical step towards leaving England.

When at last he sailed in 1893, Mary, for the first time in her life, found herself 'in possession of five or six months which were not heavily forestalled, and feeling like a boy with a new half-crown', she began to make plans how best to use them. For the study of primitive peoples three regions seemed most suitable: Malaya, South America, or West Africa. Even if she had not been biased in favour of the last by what she had learned of it in the Canaries, she would probably have decided on this region for her studies, since the journey to Malaya was too costly, and yellow fever was endemic in South East America.

Very methodically she began to find out all she could about West Africa. Most of her friends knew nothing of it though almost all advised her not to go there. Some had relatives, usually the black sheep of their families, who had been sent there, and had hated the country before dying and being forgiven for their sins.

One lady kindly remembered a case of a gentleman who had resided some few years at Fernando Po, but when he returned an aged wreck of forty he shook so violently with ague as to dislodge a chandelier, thereby destroying a valuable tea-service and flattening the silver teapot in its midst.

Her doctor friends were no more reassuring: they told her it was the deadliest spot on earth and showed her maps of the geographical distribution of disease to prove their point. From north of Sierra Leone to south of the Congo, West Africa was coloured black. When she turned to the missionaries for support, they agreed with the medical men. She did, however, learn from them something of the conditions in West Africa.

I gathered that there existed, firstly the native human beings—the raw material, as it were—and that these were led either to good or bad respectively by the missionary and the trader. There were also the government representatives, whose chief business it was to strengthen and consolidate the missionary's work, a function they carried on but indifferently well. But for those traders! well, I put them down under the dangers of West Africa at once. Subsequently I came across the good old coast yarn of how, when a trader from that region went thence, it goes without saying where, the Fallen Angel without a moment's hesitation vacated the infernal throne (Milton) in his favour.

She was offered all sorts of advice on what she should take, when her friends at last found that they could not dissuade her from going. Gifts of medical comforts to protect her against the deadly climate arrived up to the very last moment before her ship sailed. Her limited means and her practical commonsense prevented her from burdening herself with masses of baggage which would have been only a hindrance on the kind of expeditions she intended to make. In the end she simply bought a long waterproof sack, closed at the top with a bar and a handle, into which she put such things as blankets, boots, books, a pair of her brother's trousers for an emergency, and all those other miscellaneous objects which she could not squeeze into her portmanteau or her black bag. She found that it served her well throughout her travels.

She wanted to make some contribution to science. Her friends, Dr. Guillemard of Cambridge, and Dr. Gunther of the

C

British Museum, agreed that the most useful thing she could do was to bring back fish from the rivers and lakes which she visited. To do this meant she had to carry a heavy load of preserving jars, and medical spirit. A revolver, never to be used, completed her tropical equipment, and she left England for the swamps, rivers, and forests of Africa very much as though she were visiting friends on the other side of London. She bought no tropical clothes, but made all her journeys in the long black skirt, white blouse, and quaint black head-dress in which she had appeared in Cambridge.

No one would have guessed that the young woman, with humorous yet determined mouth, standing surrounded by strange bags and cases on the docks at Liverpool in August 1893, was about to set out, with no official backing or letters of introduction, for one of the most dangerous places in the world.

4

EDUCATION OF A COASTER

On her journey to the Canaries in 1892, Mary had enjoyed the luxury of a *Castle* liner; in 1893 she booked her passage on a Liverpool cargo boat trading with the West African ports. The booking clerk had caused her to think for a moment when he told her that it was not usual to issue return tickets. She was even more staggered when she saw her ship, which lay alongside the dock. The *Lagos* was a veteran of the fleet, with her cabin aft—a sure sign of age—and caked with grime. She was already heavily laden, and Mary saw with surprise that her freight was not yet all aboard, for a lighter made fast and numbers of kegs of gunpowder were transferred to the old ship's hold. Even so, the captain was apparently not content, for the whistle screamed and squeaked for more cargo. This insatiable greed, shown by the captain and his officers, was to infect the passengers with a commercial spirit, and before Mary reached the South West Coast she began her career as an African trader by selling paraffin oil in cases in the various ports. Even missionaries and government officials who boarded the ship became preoccupied, making plans for the storing of sectional churches or houses in her capacious holds.

Captain Murray, the commander of the *Lagos*, was a man after Mary's own heart, and she soon made friends with him. When he learned that she sailed for the Coast, he decided it was his duty to dispel any false ideas she might have got from her friends or from books. He had sailed there for thirty years, and from his store of first-hand knowledge he was able to warn her of the real dangers and problems that she would have to face. While he told her about West Africa, he was careful not to shock her, for he believed that newcomers were often so frightened on board the outgoing steamers that they fell a prey to the first cold they caught on landing, thinking that it was yellow fever.

Meanwhile the holds of the steamer had been crammed full and the hatches battened down, and, thrusting her way out of the Mersey and through the Irish Channel, she headed for the Bay of Biscay. Here, a fresh wind was blowing and the ship, well down to her Plimsoll line, plunged and wallowed in the great rollers. Mary found to her intense satisfaction that she was a good sailor, and could keep to the deck while most of her fellow passengers were sick below. Soon she too was ordered below, for every now and then a great wave would rake the ship from stem to stern. Even in the saloon, passengers were not entirely free from the swirling rush of the sea, and a keen lookout had to be kept to make sure that the doors were firmly bolted to keep the water out.

Mary's cabin was near the saloon, and one particularly rough night she was awakened by alarming noises coming from it. Hastily dressing, she waited for the moment when the decks were free of water, and dashed across to see what was happening. Flinging open the doors, she looked in upon a scene of the greatest confusion. The piano had broken loose from its moorings on a narrow dais at the end of the room, and was crashing from side to side of the cabin as the ship rolled. A stewardess stood helpless among the overturned tables and chairs. In spite of the bottles of beer and of sauce which rolled about the floor and occasionally hurtled through the air, Mary made a rush for the piano and, assisted by the stewardess, held it down until help arrived. She and her companion were cut and smeared with sauce but not seriously harmed.

Several days now passed before she saw anything of her fellow passengers. When the weather began to clear, some of them appeared and began to take their share in the conversation. Captain Murray tried to set an example to the other old Coasters by introducing harmless topics of conversation at meal times, speaking of his life on his father's ranch in America, or of his experiences in the China Seas, or the Indian Ocean. They were not to be turned from their favourite topic, however, and Mary once more sat and listened to tales of death and disaster. Here is a typical meal-time conversation recorded by her:

A government official who had been out before, would kindly turn to a colleague out for the first time, and say,

'Brought any dress clothes with you?'

The unfortunate newcomer, scenting an allusion to a more cheerful phase of Coast life, gladly answered in the affirmative.

'That's right,' says the interlocutor, 'you want them to wear at funerals. Do you know,' he remarks, turning to another old Coaster, 'my dress trousers did not get mouldy once during last wet season.'

'Get along,' says his friend, 'you can't hang a thing up for twenty-four hours without its being fit to graze a cow on.'

'Do you get anything else but fever down there?' asks a newcomer nervously.

'Haven't time as a general rule, but I have known some fellows get kraw kraw.'

'And the Portuguese itch, abscesses, ulcers, the Guinea worm and the small-pox,' observe the chorus calmly.

'Well,' says the first, kindly but regretfully, as if it pained him to admit this wealth of disease was denied his particular locality; 'they are mostly on the South West Coast.'

Mary was not easily scared; indeed it was the old Coasters who tired first. The gusto with which she relates their tales of disease and death suggests that she listened to them with a certain macabre glee. Soon they fell to discussing trade, which, next to fish and fetish, was her main interest. Her education as a bush trader began, and useful advice was given on the way to protect oneself against African insects. Her friends told her that it was safest to keep clear of them: if they swarmed into her house, she must abandon it to them until they went away. Under no circumstances must she try to keep them at bay or attack them, for such tactics would lead only to a great deal of trouble and to greater activity on the part of the enemy. After a few weeks ashore, during which she took a 'general, natural historical interest' in them, Mary realized how sound this advice had been.

Soon they reached Canary. Her fellow passengers, who, to do them justice, had thought she was only sailing as far as Las Palmas for a holiday, very civilly said good-bye. Great was their surprise when they saw her in her place at dinner when the *Lagos* sailed. On first seeing her, they thought she was a lady missionary, but when she showed no interest in the religious services held aboard, and, indeed, seemed very amused on one occasion when the purser and the third mate made a hopeless mess of a service in the Bay of Biscay, they realized they had guessed wrong. They were even more mystified when they noticed her listening eagerly to their stories, not in the least shocked when in moments of forgetfulness they used language which would have offended most young women.

The officers and crew, too, had been puzzled by Mary from the moment she stepped on board. They had met the wives of missionaries and government officials who sailed to West Africa from a sense of duty, but they had never seen anyone like the soberly dressed young woman who walked the decks even in the Bay of Biscay until ordered below, and showed a keen and expert interest in the running of the ship. After a week or so they realized she was not just an inquisitive tourist, but one who loved the sea and ships. They began to teach her, and to treat her as one of their fraternity. Wherever she went, Mary mixed freely and naturally with men of action.

Mary felt that she owed some explanation of her presence to the traders and government officials. The best she could do was to tell them that she was interested in natural history and was going to the Coast to continue her studies. She told them, too, that she was particularly interested in the Antarctic Drift, which some of them at first confused with a gold-mine. At last understanding her reasons for sailing, they felt that it was their duty to persuade her to turn back at Sierra Leone, and not risk her life for such frivolous studies. When they found that these arguments had no effect, they joined the captain in his self-imposed task of saving her life by educating her. They told her all they knew about West Africa, and to the knowledge that she picked up from them Mary attributed her success in avoiding all kinds of serious illness, and in coming safely through a number of complicated and dangerous adventures.

Two of the old Coasters never spoke unless they had something useful and improving to say. . . . For general social purposes these silent ones used coughs, and the one whose seat was always next to mine at table kept me in a state of much anxiety, for I used to turn round, after having been rivetted to the captain's conversation for minutes, and find him holding some dish for me to help myself from; he never took the least notice of my apologies, and I felt that he had made up his mind that, if I did it again, he would take me by the scruff of my neck some night and drop me overboard. He was an alarmingly powerfully built man, and I quite understood the local African tribe wishing to have him for a specimen. Some short time before he had left for home last trip, they had attempted to acquire his head for their local Ju Ju house, from mixed aesthetic and religious reasons. In a way it was creditable of them, I suppose, for it would have caused them grave domestic inconvenience to have removed thereby, at one fell swoop, their complete set of tradesmen; and as a fellow collector of specimens I am bound to admit the soundness of their methods of collecting! Wishing for this gentleman's head they shot him in the legs. . . . A recital of the incident did not fire me with the desire to repeat their performance; indeed, so discouraged was I by their failure that I hesitated about asking him for his skeleton when he had done with it.

Mary enjoyed every moment of the cruise from Canary to Cape Verde. The weather was delightful, the sky clear, and the air sweet, for they were in the track of the North East Trade Winds. The change when they neared the coast was all the more unpleasant: as the rounded hills rose into view, the foul air came off the land, and Mary was for the first time daunted. She began to believe all the unpleasant things which had been told her about Africa; she even asked herself if she had made a mistake in coming to such an evil-smelling place. Nor did this feeling leave her as the ship coasted south towards Sierra Leone. It needed all her determination to go on.

Violent showers fell on the ship as it steamed through the humid air, and Mary decided to give up any attempt to keep dry. She saw that the old Coasters sat calmly smoking and disregarding the fact that the new flannel suits, into which they had changed on approaching the land, were shrinking, and their colour running down on to the deck. She imitated them and paid no attention to the rain. One afternoon, however, she was alarmed by the first officer, who, with furious energy, rushed about shouting orders to the crew. He insisted that all awnings should be stowed, and every bit of loose gear should be made fast. There was no wind, and Mary could not guess the cause for this feverish activity until she saw a low arch of black cloud coming towards them from the land. Her description of this, her first experience of a tornado, is as near as Mary Kingsley ever got to poetry:

We were surrounded by a wild, strange sky. Indeed there seemed to be two skies, one upper, and one lower; for parts of it were showing evidences of terrific activity, others of a sublime, utterly indifferent calm. At one part of our horizon were great columns of black cloud, expanding and coalescing at their capitals. These were mounted on a background of most exquisite pale green. Away to leeward was a gigantic black cloud-mountain, across whose vast face were bands and wreaths of delicate white and silver clouds, and from whose grim depths every few seconds flashed palpitating, fitful, livid lightnings. Striding towards us across the sea came the tornado, lashing it into spray mist with the tremendous artillery of its rain, and shaking the air with its own thunder-growls. Away to windward leisurely boomed and grumbled a third thunder-storm, apparently not addressing the tornado but the cloud-mountain, while in between these phenomena wandered strange, wild winds, made out of lost souls frightened and wailing to be let back into hell, or taken care of somehow by someone.

Soon the tornado struck the ship. The wind screamed through the rigging and rolled the old vessel about as though it were a barrel, for its keel, designed for the shallow waters at the mouths of West African rivers, was not deep enough to keep it steady against the fury of the attack. Albert Schweitzer was to suffer from this peculiarity of the West Coast steamers just twenty years later, on his way out to Lambaréné, when he spent a fearsome night listening to his heavy trunks chasing each other in his cabin. The *Lagos*, however, suffered no damage, not even a deck-chair being snatched overboard.

Deeper still into the rain-belt steamed the ship, but Mary continued to come on deck to talk to her fellow passengers and to watch the seamen. She saw that the first officer was working hard to make his ship spick and span before she reached port. All day sailors, perched on planks slung overboard, with their feet dangling perilously near the shark-infested sea, banged away at her outer coat of grime and rust. From stem to stern, and from her Plimsoll line to the top of her funnels, she was cleaned and scraped, and then eager hands gave her a splendid new coat of paint. The first officer still had to be on the alert, however, to protect her decks from the second mate, who was in charge of cargo, and thought nothing of hauling out burst bacon barrels or leaking lime casks from the holds. The engineer was his enemy too, for he always seemed to find it necessary to shift coal aft from the forward bunkers just as the ship was being made ready for an immaculate entrance into some port. If these two were defeated, there was still the cook, whose grease tub was a constant menace to the decks in high seas. Every move in this war was watched with the keenest interest by Mary, and she regretted that she had not time to write a monograph on the natural history of sailors.

Torrential and persistent rain now deluged the ship, and lashed down so furiously on the sea that they seemed to be moving through a mist in which visibility was reduced to a few score feet. Occasionally their little world would be invaded by another ship ploughing along through the spouts of water, but this soon vanished again and left them completely isolated. For weeks during the voyage this kind of weather continued, until Mary grew accustomed to it, and found a strange, restful comfort in a state of existence in which the outer world made no demands.

Thus they steamed on southward, and reached Sierra Leone one afternoon in such thick weather that Captain Murray let go his ship's anchor rather than take the risk of running her aground on the Carpenter Rock. A dreadful night was spent, with the ship rolling and every bit of movable gear crashing with each lurch. But Mary was up early, for she was eager to see the land which she had chosen for her first adventure. With joy she saw the mist lift and reveal Free Town, Sierra Leone, and its lovely harbour. She recognized it at the first glance from the accounts she had read in the old books of the seventeenth- and eighteenth-century sea captains who had visited it in their voyages in search of gold and slaves:

I knew the place so well. Yes; there were all the bays, Kru, English and Pirate; and the mountains, whose thunder rumbling caused Pedro do Centra to call the place Sierra Leone when he discovered it in 1462. And had not my old friend, Charles Johnson, writing in 1724, given me all manner of information about it during those delicious hours rescued from school books and dedicated to a most contentious study of *A General History of Robberies and Murders of the Most Notorious Pyrates*? That those bays away now on my right hand 'were safe and convenient for cleaning and watering;' and so on, and there rose up before my eyes a vision of the society here in 1724 that lived 'very friendly with the natives—being thirty Englishmen in all; men who in some part of their lives had been either privateering, buccaneering, or pirating, and still retain and have the riots and humours common to that sort of life'.

She went ashore and wandered about Free Town, which from
the sea had appeared to be built of grey stone, but which on
closer inspection proved to be mainly of painted wood and
corrugated iron. The noise, the smell, and the heat of the town
were unlike anything that she had ever experienced. But in spite
of the strange sensations, now that she was at last in Africa her
eye missed nothing. She saw with astonishment the costumes of
the inhabitants, for though the Mohammedans in the main wore
graceful, long, white shirts under a mohair or silk gown, the rest
of the population were dressed in anything they could lay hands
on. Their motley garments were not even securely fastened, but
hung precariously on their dark bodies. A European shirt was
the favourite wear, and if a man had this he cared little for the
rest of his dress, whether it consisted of trousers, a loin-cloth, a
red flannel petticoat, or rice-bag drawers. Here and there she
saw a black man fashionably draped in a black coat surmounted
by a top hat, or more quietly in a tweed suit. The women, with
their gay dresses and cheerful faces, charmed her, and from this,
her first hour in Africa, she fell a victim to their laughing eyes.

She was delighted with the clean and tidy appearance of the
market buildings, and interested in the great variety of incon-
gruous articles offered for sale. There were fruits and vegetables
which she would not see again for many months: lettuces,
yellow oranges, tomatoes and onions, a number of spices next
door to 'little heaps of Reckitt's Blue, vivid-coloured Berlin
wools, pumpkins, pineapples, and alligator pears . . . kola nuts,
old iron, antelope horns, monkey skins, porcupine quills, and
snails'. Brooding over the market and town sat the evil-looking
jack crows, with their great wings half-spread and their generally
drunken and dishevelled appearance.

When she returned from the town she found the ship in an
uproar. The Africans of Sierra Leone were never so happy as
when they could haul an Englishman before the law courts, where
they could employ all their considerable powers of rhetoric in
laying accusations against him and generally insulting him with
impunity. An enormous African laundress had come aboard for
this purpose. On seeing the *Lagos* enter port she had hastened to
a magistrate to lay a charge against the second mate. She had
procured a warrant for his arrest, and had boarded the ship
attended by four Hausa policemen to see it executed. She accused

him of leaving on a previous occasion without paying his washing bill. Her brother, a small frightened man, was by her side to give her moral support and to help in the identification of the offender.

The second mate, after a hard morning's work shipping cargo in the stewing heat, had retired to his cabin to sleep. Mary arrived just as he had been peremptorily summoned by the Hausas:

Unfortunately for the lady, it was not the same gallant officer who held the post of second mate, but another, and our injured innocent, joining in the chorus, returned thanks for his disturbance in language of singular fluency. He is the only man I have ever met whose powers of expression are equal to his feelings, and it is a merciful providence for him it is so, for what that man feels sometimes I think would burst a rock.

The lady and her brother went crestfallen ashore, but the policemen stayed on board until we left, getting exceedingly drunk the while. Looking over the side, I saw one of them fold himself over the gunwale of the boat in which they were going ashore with his head close to the water. His companions heeded not, and I insisted on my friend the quartermaster rescuing the sufferer, and arranging him in the bottom of the boat, for not only was he in danger of drowning, but of acting as an all too tempting live-bait for the sharks, which swarm in the harbour. The quartermaster evidently thought this was foolish weakness on my part, for it 'was only a policeman, and what are policemen but a kind of a sort of a custom house officer, and what are custom house officers but the very deuce?'

She was to see Africans in greater numbers aboard before the ship reached Accra, and to hear the second officer in full spate again. Ships of the Royal African Line took on additional crew in the shape of Krumen to assist them in loading cargo as they called in at the West Coast ports. Mary was astounded when they came aboard: never had she imagined that a body of men could make such an overpowering din. After a few weeks in Africa she realized that if she was to survive she must steel herself against the perpetual uproar. She was forced to the conclusion that the uneducated African thought aloud rather as a child does. She often heard them holding animated conversations as they walked alone through the forest, and noticed that when a gang was working together, all its members issued instructions and warnings at the top of their voices, without ever for a moment thinking of listening to what was being said by anyone else. The man in charge of them had to have stentorian lungs, or to resort to physical violence to get them to do what he wanted.

Though the human voice was undoubtedly most to blame for the din in which Mary lived while in Africa, she found that the Africans had many mechanical aids. First, there was the tom-tom, effective whether made from a tree-trunk or from a paraffin oil can; next, perhaps, came the kitty-katty, which made 'the strange scratching-vibrating sound of an excruciating mouth harp'; then the impressive African horn which, to Mary's regret, she was unable to play, since to produce a note on it required 'a whole S.W. gale of wind'; lastly, and not nearly so disturbing, there were instruments of the xylophonic family, most often called marimbas, which produced dulcet sounds. At one time or another Mary made the attempt, under African teachers, to play every instrument she came across. Her tutors assured her that with practice she would become a 'decent performer on the harp and xylophone, and had the makings of a genius for the tom-tom'. Her greatest success, however, was achieved on an instrument made from an old powder keg, with both ends removed and a piece of raw hide tied tightly round it. A hole was made in the skin and through this a stick with a knob of rubber was inserted. The performer grasped this and by working it up and down through the skin made a remarkable screeching noise at the same time as the knob struck the taut drum. An occasional howl or wail completed the effect. It is not surprising that Mary met with no encouragement when she tried to show off her skill on this instrument to her white friends.

For the moment, however, Mary was safe on board ship, and had only the Krumen to disturb her. After leaving Sierra Leone, they steamed on past Liberia, the Grain Coast, and the Ivory Coast, towards Cape Coast Castle, which was the next port of call. The rain came down incessantly and everything on board became reeking wet. Moisture dripped from the cabin walls, clothes became damp and musty, and towels useless. Most of the passengers were depressed, but Mary was light-hearted and full of delight. She had enjoyed herself in Sierra Leone and felt sure she would do the same further south.

On the evening of the first day out from Free Town she was alarmed to see the captain, the first officer, and the third mate in red slippers. She had only seen the captain thus shod twice before: once during the heavy weather in the Bay of Biscay, and again when the *Lagos* approached Sierra Leone in heavy fog. It was clear that a state of emergency existed although the sky was clear for once and the wind light. She borrowed a chart from one of the officers and studied it carefully. It was not reassuring:

The thing looked like an exhibition pattern of a prize shot gun, with the quantity of rocks marked down on it.

'Look here' [said one of the group of passengers who were now looking over her shoulder at the chart]: 'why are some of these rocks named after the Company's ships?'

'Think,' said a calm old Coaster.

'Oh, I say! hang it all, you don't mean to say they've been wrecked here? Anyhow, if they have, they got off all right. How is it the *Yoruba Rock* and the *Gambia Rock*? The *Yoruba* and the *Gambia* are running now.'

'Those,' explains the old Coaster kindly, 'were the old *Yoruba* and *Gambia*. The *Bonny* that runs now isn't the old *Bonny*. It's the way with most of them, isn't it?' he says, turning to a fellow old Coaster.

'Naturally,' says his friend. 'But this is the old original, you know, and it's just about time she wrote up her name on one of these tombstones. You don't save ships,' he continues, for the instruction of the newcomers, attentive enough now; 'that go on the Kru coast, and if you get ashore you don't save the things you stand up in—the natives strip you.'

'Cannibals!' I suggest.

'Oh, of course they are cannibals; they are all cannibals are natives down here when they get the chance. But that does not matter; you see what I object to is being brought on board the next steamer that happens to call crowded with all sorts of people you know, and with a lady missionary or so among them, just with nothing on but a flyaway native cloth. You remember D——?'

'Well,' says his friend. Strengthened by this support, he goes on to instruct the young critic, saying soothingly, 'There, don't you worry; have a good dinner' (it was just being laid). 'For if you do get ashore the food is something beastly. But, after all, what with the sharks and the surf and the cannibals, you know the chances are a thousand to one against your living to miss your trousers.'

These and subsequent graveyards of the Company's ships were weathered, however, and the rain and mist cleared now and then to give Mary a glimpse of the land. She was surprised to see the magnificent green woods coming almost down to the narrow strip of yellow sand on which the traders' factories were built. At first it was a most attractive picture, but as the days passed and she saw the same unvarying line of forest standing darkly above the sand, and saw too that to seaward the white line of the surf never varied, she began to sympathize with the men whose lives were spent there. Later, she met many of them and found that while some looked haunted and tried to find relief in company, others had become so introverted that the outside world no longer mattered to them.

Tornadoes now attacked the ship with alarming frequency, but even so, they were less to be feared than the rocks among which they continued to thread their way. These were always lurking, and since most were submerged, and many inaccurately charted, they constituted a far more serious menace than the storms, which at least gave warning of their approach. They passed the 'bottomless pit' off the Ivory Coast. This presented no danger to the steamer, but Mary learnt that the deep submarine valley, running out some fifteen miles to sea near Bassam, and varying in width from about a mile near the shore to nine miles farther out, had caused the loss of many a sailing ship whose captain had dropped anchor on its edge because of fog, only to find that it had dragged, lost bottom, and failed to prevent his ship from going ashore.

In the Bight of Benin she saw some of the few Bristol sailing ships which, in 1893, still sailed from port to port collecting cargo much as their predecessors had done a hundred years earlier. Instead of slaves, however, they traded in palm oil which was taken aboard the steamers for transport to England, while the Bristol ship returned to its dreary and deadly task along the coast. From the deck of the *Lagos* she watched the exciting struggles of the Africans to ship mahogany from the Timber ports. They towed the great logs through the surf by boat and then swam around to make them fast to the ropes from the ship's donkey engine. Only the noise and splashing they made saved them from the sharks. Next, the great logs were heaved on board, and either lowered on to the deck or swung straight into the hold. That Mary missed no detail of these operations can be seen from her animated description:

The officer in charge of this particular hatch presently shouts 'Lower away!' waving his hand gracefully from the wrist as though he were practising for piano playing, but really to guide Shoo Fly, who is driving the donkey engine. The tremendous log hovers over the hatch, and then gradually, 'softly, softly', as Shoo Fly would say, disappears into the bowels of the ship, until a heterogeneous yell in English and Kru warns the trained intelligence that it is low enough, or more probably too low. 'Heave a link!' shouts the officer, and Shoo Fly and the donkey engine heaveth. Then the official hand waves, and the crane swings round with a whiddle, whiddle, and there is a moment's pause, the rope strains, and groans, and waits, and as soon as the most important people on board, such as the Captain, the Doctor and myself, are within its reach to give advice, and look down the hatch to see what is going on, that rope likes to break, and comes clawing at us a mass of bent and broken wire, and as we scatter, the great log goes with a crash into the hold. Fortunately, the particular log I remember as indulging in this catastrophe did not go through the ship's bottom, as I confidently expected it had at the time, nor was anyone killed, such a batch of miraculous escapes occurring for the benefit of the officer and men below as can only be reasonably accounted for by their having expected this sort of thing to happen.

When they dropped anchor off Cape Coast Castle, on the Gold Coast, Mary was charmed by its clean, white-washed appearance from the roadstead, and by the low heavily forested hills that rose almost from the seashore. The fine mass of the old castle and of the other three stone forts that overlooked the town seemed to her to give it an air of permanency which contrasted favourably with the ramshackle look of most West African settlements. After the exciting and distinctly frightening experience of passing through the surf, she landed and found that she had not, as at Sierra Leone, been deceived by her first, distant view of the place: the buildings really were of stone and not of painted wood.

Later, when she had seen all the West Coast ports many times, she placed them in order of attractiveness: 'First in order of beauty comes San Paul de Loanda, then Cape Coast with its satellite Elmina, then Gaboon, then Accra with its satellite Christianborg, and lastly, Sierra Leone.' None of the others in her opinion had any attraction.

After Cape Coast, she went ashore at Accra and found that although the corrugated-iron houses looked neat and quite picturesque, rather resembling an encampment of snow-white tents among the coconut palms, yet they were intolerable to live in. During the day they became far hotter than the mud huts of the Africans, and in the mornings and evenings they were cold and clammy. She attributed the frequent fevers of the white population to the draughts that constantly chilled them. But she did not stay long enough to suffer herself. The *Lagos* had no time to spare and was soon on its way again; calling at Calabar, Fernando Po, the Cameroons, a number of smaller ports and trading stations, Bonny, and finally San Paul de Loanda.

Mary made a point of landing whenever it was possible. Bonny, perhaps, made the most unfavourable impression upon her. She stood on deck as Captain Murray took his ship over the bar, and gave orders for the anchor to be dropped just off the white-painted factories. In every direction, save to seaward, she could see the apparently endless walls of mangrove, varying hardly at all in colour, form, or even height. All around her stretched the foul-smelling, dirty-coloured waters of Bonny River, with nothing to break the monotony but the black ribs of the old hulks which had formerly been used as trading stations. The peculiar smell, which came off the mud, frightened her; for she, in common with most people, believed that it carried malaria. Once again a doubt crept into her mind as to whether she could live for months in such a land.

She went ashore to see Captain Boler, one of the traders who was of particular interest to her, since he had made a serious study of African religion and law. As she took tea with him, he felt called upon to give her some good advice:

'It's not safe to go among bush tribes, but if you are such a fool as to go, you needn't go and be a bigger fool still, you have done enough.'

Mary made it clear to him that she had come to Africa for the sole purpose of getting in touch with the Africans of the interior, for these were the men whose way of life and religious beliefs were least influenced by European ideas. When he saw that nothing he could say would deter her, Captain Boler volunteered one last aphorism:

'Never be afraid of a black man.'

'What if I can't help it?' asked Mary.

'Don't show it,' said he.

The talk then turned to the last epidemic of fever in Bonny, when nine out of the eleven white residents had died. Mary returned convinced that the conversation of the men who had to live among the mangrove swamps was perfectly in keeping with their surroundings. From the deck she saw the mist creeping up from the dark face of the water and crawling on board the ship. Only the incessant beating of the rain and the depressing cry of the curlews with which the river abounded broke the unnatural silence; but Mary could not sleep. After six or seven hours, even the screeching of the ship's winch, as the crew started to ship cargo in the early hours of the morning, came as a relief.

Thus Mary travelled to the South West Coast, frequently landing, always eager to meet the traders and the Africans and to listen attentively to what they had to say. Not the Bights, nor even the Bonny River, could damp her spirits for long, and by the time the *Lagos* approached Loanda, the long, grey years in England were almost forgotten, and she thought of little save the land of which she had heard so much and which she was now to study for herself. Africa and its people had captured her imagination. From the moment when, in Sierra Leone, she had seen the hurrying carriers, with great burdens on their heads, and the stately Mandingoes, Akers, and Fulani, with their lithe bodies and elastic step, until her death, she found no deep satisfaction save on African soil.

5

'MORE AMUSING THAN INSTRUCTIVE'

M ARY left the *Lagos*, with its kindly captain, in Loanda
harbour. She had become friendly with its officers and
crew, and they seemed sorry to see her go ashore for
the last time. The second mate, who had taught her Kru English,
and had unconsciously provided her with many an amusing scene,
told her bluntly, as he said good-bye, that Africa was no place
for her, and that he hoped she would have the sense to take the
next boat home. He may have been a good judge of Kru seamen,
but he realized how wrong he had been about Mary when he saw
her, two years later, expertly climbing the swinging rope ladder to
board his new ship, the *Benguella*, in the rough water off Lagos bar.

Unfortunately Mary regarded this, her first stay in Africa, as
more amusing than instructive, and left no connected account
of her travels in any of her published works. She took voluminous
notes, and used them subsequently when she wrote of the laws
and customs of the Africans of the South West Coast, but these,
together with a number of her personal papers, were accidentally
destroyed after her death. It is thus impossible to follow her in
her wanderings from Loanda in Portuguese territory, northward
through parts of the Congo Free State to French Congo, and
eventually to the British possession of Old Calabar. We know
that she made her way to Ambriz by land, visited and stayed for
a while at Kabinda, went up the Congo by steamer as far as
Matadi, and made short journeys, unaccompanied by any other
European, among races who had rarely or never seen a white
person. She saw and learned enough to convince her that she had
chosen rightly in going to the South West Coast.

Although she left no record of these months, in her books,
articles, lectures, and letters to her friends, she made numerous
references to her experiences in 1893, so that some idea, however
vague and fragmentary, can be formed of her activities and

manner of living. Her main business was to study the religion and customs of the more primitive African communities, but she also observed carefully the way in which the ruling white men treated the subject peoples in the territories through which she passed. The Portuguese of Angola were hospitable, and she made several close friends during her stay there, although she could find little praise for them as colonial administrators.

She saw that they had not succeeded, as some European powers had, in developing their dependencies. She attributed this partly to the corruption of the Portuguese colonial officials, and partly to incompetence. When she was there in 1893, the criticisms of the other powers had led them to try to introduce improvements in Angola. They ordered street lamps, a telephone, and a water supply for Loanda. For four hundred years the city's water had been brought daily in boats from the Bengo River, and for lighting it had relied on the private enterprise of its citizens. The water had just been laid on when Mary arrived, and she watched with amusement the African women's attempts to make use of this amenity without paying for it: 'These dear ladies . . . finally arranged that one of a party visiting a stand-pipe every morning would devote her time to scratching the official (who was there to collect the money for the water drawn) while the rest filled their water pots and hers.'

The street lighting was not a great success. Gas standards had been ordered from England, but when at last they arrived they were useless since there was no gas at that time in Loanda. Oil lamps were therefore ordered to place in the standards, but even when, after another long delay, these arrived, the officials failed to supply the lamp-lighters with ladders, and by the time they had scaled each post dawn was usually breaking.

Mary never enjoyed herself so much as when she was on or near water, and at Loanda she spent glorious days in the beautiful African canoes, with their sails made of small fringed mats, sewn together, and of a warm, rich, sand colour. She tried her hand at all the local methods of fishing, from the passive one of trapping her prey in hollow logs with one end open to catch the unwary fish, to the more strenuous one of dragging the waters of the harbour with nets made of pineapple fibre. The African's favourite way of fishing, by means of which Mary got most of the specimens which she took home from the higher reaches of rivers and

creeks, was the stockade trap. Stakes were driven in close together, leaving one opening towards the up-river end so that the
downstream would wash the fish into the trap. When the
fishermen thought there were enough fish inside, the opening
was closed, the water was baled out, and the fish were collected in
baskets.

When she came to fish further north, in the region of the
mangrove swamps which stretched from the Rio del Rey River
along the coast as far as Sierra Leone, she found that the pastime
was not without its dangers:

The other day I went out for a day's fishing on an African river,
I and two black men, in a canoe, in company with a round net, three
stout fishing-lines, three paddles, Dr Gunther's *Study of Fishes*, some
bait in an old Morton's boiled-mutton tin, a little manioc, stinking
awfully (as is its wont), a broken calabash baler, a lot of dirty water to
sit in, and happy and contented minds. I catalogue these things because
they are essential to, or inseparable from, a good day's sport in West
Africa.

We paddled away, far up a mangrove creek, and then went up
against the black mud-bank, with its great network of grey-white
roots, surmounted by the closely-interlaced black-green foliage.
Absolute silence reigned, as it can only reign in Africa in a mangrove
swamp. The water-laden air wrapped round us like a warm, wet
blanket. The big mangrove flies came silently to feed on us and leave
their progeny behind them in the wounds to do likewise. The stink of
the mud, strong enough to break a window, mingled fraternally with
that of the sour manioc.

I was reading, the negroes, always quiet enough when fishing, were
silently carrying on that great African native industry—scratching
themselves—so, with our lines over side, life slid away like a dreamless
sleep, until the middle man hooked a cat-fish. It came on board with
an awful grunt, right in the middle of us; flop, swish, scurry and yell
followed; I tucked the *Study of Fishes* in general under my arm and
attended to this individual specimen, shouting, 'Lef em, lef em; hev
em for water one time, you sons of unsanctified house-lizards,' and
such like valuable advice and admonition.

The man in the more remote end of the canoe made an awful swipe
at the three foot long, grunting, flopping, yellow-grey, slimy thing,
but never reached it owing to the paddle meeting in mid-air with the
flying leg of the man in front of him, drawing blood profusely. I
really fancy about this time, that, barring the cat-fish and myself, the

occupants of the canoe were standing on their heads, with a view of removing their lower limbs from the terrible pectoral and dorsal fins, with which our prey made such lively play.

'Brevi spatio interjecto,' as Caesar says, in the middle of a bad battle, over went the canoe, while the cat-fish went off home with the line and hook. One black man went to the bank, whither, with a blind prescience of our fate, I had flung, a second before, the most valuable occupant of the canoe, *The Study of Fishes.* I went personally to investigate fluvial deposit *in situ.* When I returned to the surface—accompanied by great swirls of mud and great bubbles of the gasses of decomposition I had liberated on my visit to the bottom of the river—I observed the canoe floating bottom upwards, accompanied by Morton's tin, the calabash, and the paddles, while on the bank one black man was engaged in hauling the other one out by the legs, fortunately this one's individual god had seen to it that his toes should become entangled in the net, and this floated, and so indicated to his companion where he was, when he had dived into the mud and got fairly imbedded.

Now it's my belief that the most difficult thing in the world is to turn over a round-bottomed canoe that is wrong side up, when you are in the water with the said canoe. The next most difficult thing to do is to get into the canoe, after accomplishing triumph number one, and had it not been for my black friends that afternoon, I should not have done those things successfully, and there would be by now another haunted creek in West Africa, with a mud and blood bespattered ghost trying for ever to turn over the ghost of a little canoe. However, all ended happily. We collected all our possessions, except the result of the day's fishing—the cat-fish—but we had had as much of him as we wanted, and so, adding a thankful mind to our contented ones, went home.

Not in the least daunted by this experience, Mary went on searching for new specimens of fish wherever she might be. She seems to have taken a particular pleasure in paddling alone among the mangrove trees when the tide was high; threading her way between the trunks of trees until she had left the main stream far behind. That she learnt how dangerous this pastime could be is shown in the following passage:

For one thing you are certain to come across crocodiles. Now a crocodile drifting down in deep water, or lying asleep with its jaws open on a sand bank in the sun, is a picturesque adornment to the landscape when you are on the deck of a steamer, and you can write home about it and frighten your relations on your behalf; but when you are away among the swamps in a small dugout canoe, and that crocodile and his relations are awake—a thing he makes a point of being at flood-tide because of fish coming along—and when he has got his foot upon his native heath—that is to say, his tail within holding reach of his native mud—he is highly interesting and you may not be able to write home about him—and you get frightened on your own behalf. For crocodiles can, and often do, in such places, grab at people in small canoes. I have known of several natives losing their lives in this way; some native villages are approachable from the main river by a short cut through the mangrove swamps, and the inhabitants of such villages will now and then go across this way with small canoes instead of by the constant channel to the village, which is almost always winding.

In addition to this unpleasantness you are liable to get tide-trapped away in the swamps, the water falling around you when you are away in some deep pool or lagoon, and you find you cannot get back to the main river. For you cannot get out and drag your canoe across the stretches of mud that separate you from it, because the mud is of too unstable a nature and too deep, and sinking in it means staying in it. . . . If you are a mere ordinary person of retiring nature, like me, you stop in your lagoon until the tide rises again; [and] most of your attention is directed to dealing with an 'at home' to crocodiles and mangrove flies, and the fearful stench of the slime round you. What little time you have over you will employ in wondering why you came to West Africa, and why, after having reached this point of absurdity, you need have gone and painted the lily and adorned the rose, by being such a colossal ass as to come fooling about in mangrove swamps.

Twice this chatty little incident has happened to me, but never again if I can help it. On one occasion, the last, a mighty Silurian, as the *Daily Telegraph* would call him, chose to get his front paws over the stern of my canoe, and endeavoured to improve our acquaintance. I had to retire to the bows, to keep the balance right, and fetch him a clip on the snout with a paddle, when he withdrew, and I paddled into the very middle of the lagoon, hoping the water there was too deep for him or any of his friends to repeat the performance. Presumably it was, for no one did it again. I should think that crocodile was eight feet long; but don't go and say I measured him. . . .

(Footnote: It is no use saying because I was frightened, for this miserably understates the case.)

It is not surprising that, since she was prepared to take risks of this order, the fish she brought back at the end of her first expedition so impressed the authorities of the British Museum that they provided her with an elaborate collector's outfit for her second attempt. But fishing was, after all, only a secondary matter with her. Her main quest was for the primitive African, whose religion she wished to study. From the moment of her landing she withdrew herself from white society, and made plans to reach districts where the Africans were least affected by Christian or Mohammedan ideas.

In many ways she was an ideal person to undertake such an inquiry: she was a sympathetic and understanding listener, unlikely by her appearance or manner to intimidate those whom she met and cause them to hide their real opinions. She was used to hearing strange tales from her father, and had learnt to be attentive and critical at the same time. Believing in no revealed religion, she did not start with the preconceived idea that all African beliefs were either childish or devilish.

The weeks she spent in Portuguese territory finally convinced her that she must get away from regions where missionaries had been at work, for there the Africans carefully concealed beliefs which they feared would bring only derision or contempt from the white man. Moreover, she found that there were traditions, Christian in origin, which had been so changed in the course of years that the unwary student might make the mistake of accepting them as primitive beliefs. As an example she gives the following story which she heard when she was staying among the Kabindas:

God made at first all men black and then He went across a great river and called men to follow Him, and the wisest and the bravest plunged into the great river and crossed it; and the water washed them white, so they are the ancestors of the white men. But the others were afraid too much, and said, 'No, we are comfortable here; we have our dances, and our tom-toms, and plenty to eat—we won't risk it, we'll stay here'; and they remained in the old place, and from them came the black men. But to this day the white men come to the bank, on the other side of the river, and call to the black men, saying, 'Come, it is better over here.' I fear there is little doubt that this story is a modified version of some parable preached to the Kabindas at the time the Jesuit Fathers had such influence among them, before they were driven out of the lower Congo regions more than a hundred years ago, for political reasons, by the Portuguese. The Kabindas have quite forgotten its origin—'it is old story'—and they keep it on, in much the same way as a neighbouring tribe keeps on the ringing of the old bells, morning and evening, which were once bells in a Jesuit monastery long since forgotten.

Investigation was more worth while in the bush, far from the coastal settlements. Some have wondered how Mary learnt anything from tribes whose languages differ so widely. She claims that this presented no insuperable difficulty: interpreters were usually available, or failing these she fell back on 'trade English' which was so widely diffused that it was a rare event to find a village without one or two men who could speak it. A greater difficulty, she found, lay in ridding her mind of all pre-conceived notions, even if they were derived from such authoritative sources as Frazer's *Golden Bough*. Yet she was convinced that this was essential if she wished to succeed in getting to grips with African ways of thought.

After leaving Loanda, she lived in some discomfort, and subject to alarms and strange encounters. Few would have believed that this woman of thirty-one, who until a few weeks previously had seen nothing of Africa, could enjoy pursuing her studies in such circumstances as these:

When I was first in West Africa, I had made friends with a distinguished witch doctor, or, more correctly speaking, he had made friends with me. I was then living in a deserted house, the main charm of which was that it was the house that Mr. H. M. Stanley had lived in while he was waiting for a boat home after his first crossing Africa. This charm had not kept the house tidy, and it was a beetle-some place by day, while after nightfall, if you wanted to see some of the best insect society in Africa . . . you had only to light a lamp; but these things were advantageous to an insect collector like myself, therefore I lodge no complaint against the firm of traders to whom that house belongs.

Well, my friend the witch doctor used to call on me, and I apologetically confess I first thought his interest in me arose from material objects. I wronged that man in thought, as I have many others, for one night, about 11 p.m., I heard a pawing at the shutters—my African friends don't knock. I got up and opened the door, and there he was. I made some observations, which I regret now, about tobacco at that time of night, and he said,

'No. You be big man, suppose pusson sick?'

I acknowledged the soft impeachment.

'Pusson sick too much; pusson live for die. You fit for come?'

'Fit,' said I.

'Suppose you come, you no fit to talk?' said he.

'No fit,' said I, with a shrewd notion that it was one of my Portuguese friends who was ill and who did not want a blazing blister on, a thing that was inevitable if you called in the local white medical man, so, picking up a medicine case, I went out into the darkness with my darker friend.

After getting outside the closed ground he led the way towards the forest, and I thought it was someone sick at the Roman Catholic Mission. On we went down the path that might go there; but when we got to where you turn off for it, he took no heed, but kept on, and then away up over a low hill and down into deeper forest still, I steering by his white cloth. But Africa is an alarming place to walk about in at night, both for a witch doctor who believes in all his local forest devils, and a lady who believes in all the local material ones, so we both got a good deal chipped and frayed and frightened one way and another; but nothing worse happened than our walking up against a python, which had thoughtfully festooned himself across the path, out of the way of ground ants, to sleep off a heavy meal. My eminent friend, in the inky darkness and his hurry to reach his patient, failed to see this, and went fair up against it. I, being close behind, did ditto. Then my leader ducked under the excited festoon and went down the path at headlong speed, with me after him, alike terrified of losing sight of his guiding cloth and at the python, whom we heard going away into the bush with that peculiar-sounding crackle a big snake gives when he is badly hurried.

Finally we reached a small bush village, and on the ground before one of the huts was the patient extended, surrounded by unavailing, wailing women. He was suffering from a disease common in West Africa, but amenable to treatment by European drugs, which I gave to the medical man, who gave them to his patient with proper incantations and a few little things of his own that apparently did not hinder their action. As soon as the patient had got relief, my friend saw me home, and when we got in, I said, Why did you do this, that and the other, as is usual with me, and he sat down, looked far away, and talked for an hour, softly, wordily, and gently; and the gist of what that man talked was Goethe's *Prometheus*. I recognized it after half an hour, and when he had done said,

'You got that stuff from a white man.'

'No, sir,' he said, 'that no be white man fash, that be country fash, white man no fit to savee our fash.'

'Aren't they, my friend?' I said; and we parted for the night, I the wiser for it, he the richer.

Mary loved adventures such as this. Unfortunately, when she came to write of her travels, she deliberately left out some of her most exciting experiences. It was not her aim to make herself out to be a daring explorer: she gave detailed accounts of the way in which she collected information with the sole object of proving that her material was authentic. She meant to be taken seriously as an anthropologist, though she was much too modest to claim any distinction in this field.

Her friends had tried to persuade her not to go to Africa; the traders had advised her to turn back; and government officials made it clear that they would in no way be held responsible for her safety. She had listened to them all and decided not to heed their warnings, carrying on with her plans with the same quiet persistence and strength of will that she had shown in England. She proved to herself in this first expedition that she had been right. At last she was living the kind of life she had always wanted, and was finding it deeply satisfying.

Before she had been many weeks in Africa, she had become convinced that the white men who ruled that vast land were making mistakes which would not only bring loss and hardship to the European powers, but also untold misery to the subject races. The completion of her father's work on the religion and law of primitive peoples became of only secondary importance. Instead she became the champion of the African, and, from 1893 onwards, set out to prove that only by a painstaking and sympathetic study of his institutions could the white man hope to rule justly and well.

Things were not always what they seemed in Africa. She told the following story, on her return, to warn those who reached their conclusions too lightly. It is told in the flippant and casual way against which her friends and critics protested in vain. It was part of her nature to belittle anything she did, but, by reading between the lines, it is easy to see and appreciate the cool disregard for danger which brought her safely through so many strange adventures.

Do not think that we, who study such things as tribal organization, secret societies and Fetish religions, hold that our path is an easy one to follow, for those things are difficult to understand, and in studying them exceeding caution is necessary, for the opportunities the material affords you for making mistakes are numerous. I have made, in my time, many out there, but I have been so conscious of my duty to science that all material I was not quite sure was soundly sifted, I have kept to myself. The most terrifying mistake I ever made I made when I was pottering about Mount Njawki, beetle hunting etc.

One afternoon when walking down a bush path alone, I found myself facing on a little open space seven men all got up in the most extraordinary costumes imaginable—hoods made of beads and bits of cloth, and mantles made of strips of skin and cloth, and having beads, shells and hawksbills on them for trimming. My heart went into my mouth and my mind went into my heels, for oh! thinks I, here's one of those precious men secret societies in full session. I knew that it was death for an uninitiated man or any native woman to see such a thing; what it might be for me I did not know—I did not want to. I executed what I hoped would be a masterly retreat, full of hope that, as they all seemed sitting sound asleep, they had not seen me.

I soon heard the phit-phat of a man's running feet coming after me, and knew retreat was no good; so I turned and faced him. The moment I did so he stood in his tracks; and I said, 'My esteemed Ethiopian acquaintance, what do you want?' He said no word but respectfully beckoned in silence for me to follow him. Well, there are no policemen round there; you cannot hail a cab and drive away from things in the Okanda country; so I went back down the path with that extraordinarily dressed strange young man.

When we reached the other pack of dandies they spoke not a word but saluted respectfully, and off we all went, in an indian file procession, down the forest path ahead. My thoughts ran to the tune of 'Oh, to be in England now it's springtime there', my companions made things all the more cheerful by now and again uttering strange cries, long clucks, melancholy whines and howls, but they spoke not one word. After going thus for about a mile, we came to another little open space. Down my companions sat again and reassumed the sleeping attitude I first found them in. I stood with my back against a tree . . . and I wondered what was going to happen next.

I soon saw. We were not a secret society, we were just merely out hunting monkeys. The way the thing worked was this: monkeys are people in whose breasts rages continuous war between curiosity and caution; my black friends know it, so of course, by getting themselves up uncommon queer, they attract monkeyan curiosity, and then by pretending to be asleep, they take monkeyan caution; so after they had sat still about twenty minutes, or, as I felt, some 2,000 years, down the monkeys came, clinging to each other for better protection, intent on investigation. Then, from under the mantles of my companions came a flight of arrows; three monkeys dropped, and as the rest fled jabbering away, another flight of arrows brought down two more, and then my companions threw off their fancy dresses and explained, I am sure with no uncivil intention, that as I was quite the very queerest object they had personally ever seen, they thought I was a heaven-sent addition to a monkey hunt. Well, if I had known that earlier I might have spent a more comfortable afternoon.

After some weeks in Portuguese territory, Mary crossed into the French Congo. There she stayed with an unusual trader, R. E. Dunnett, who had lived for years among the Fjort and made a study of their customs and religion. He published two books, *Seven Years Among the Fjort*, and *Folklore of the Fjort*, for the latter of which Mary, then an authority on West African affairs, was to write an introduction. As she sat alone with him in his hut, Mary listened to his talk on fetish, African diseases, and the strange customs of the tribes near Kacongo. She was not unduly perturbed when he broke off to hold a conversation with God, for she understood how a man could be affected by years of solitude and the strain of maintaining his influence and preserving his life amongst people so different from himself. She had a great respect for his knowledge and judgement and in the years that followed frequently wrote to him for facts and opinions.

But she met and liked traders far different from Dunnett. Once she lost her way when alone in a canoe, and, finding herself at Cheloango, she remembered that her firm, Hatton and Cookson, had a trading hulk there. She determined, although it was night, to find it. First she boarded a small vessel and stumbled over an African asleep on the deck. With a shriek at the sight of this apparition from the darkness, he fled below, and Mary hurriedly dropped back into her canoe. Coming to another anchored vessel, she boarded it and found the agents. Meanwhile the calm of the African night was broken by rifle fire and beating to quarters, for the first ship she had boarded had been the Portuguese guardship. She expained to the alarmed traders the cause of the din. They did not hesitate for a moment, but took her below and made her as comfortable as they could. She spent four days with them, and during the whole of this time they treated her with the greatest kindness and consideration. Yet these men were the very dregs of the trading fraternity: one being unable to read, and the other possessing a vocabulary which consisted almost entirely of swear words. When she was again in Cheloango, she stayed with them, though they were the roughest characters she had met, rather than live ashore among Portuguese government officials whom she despised.

It was not only the traders, however, with whom she made friends. She formed a lasting attachment to two Portuguese ladies in Kacongo, and enjoyed the company of the various nuns of the Catholic missions on the South West Coast. When, finally, she reached Calabar, she met Sir Claude MacDonald, the British Commissioner for the Oil River Protectorate, who liked her so much that he not only offered to help her in any way in his power if she wished, on her return to Africa, to search for fish in the Calabar River, but arranged that his wife, who was coming out to join him, should make her first voyage to the Coast in Mary's company.

South West Africa had lived up to Mary's wildest hopes. She had lived amongst men whom she could admire, and who had accepted her as their equal. At last she counted as a real person: Africans and traders had realized that in this young woman, so determined and so careless of danger, they had met their match. She had not only found a purpose in life and a cause to champion, but she had also felt the keen delight of a forceful character in going her own way and bending others to her will.

6

BACK TO THE COAST

MARY KINGSLEY returned to England and landed quietly and unobtrusively at Liverpool. She had made many friends on the Coast, of whom the most influential were Sir Claude MacDonald, and C. G. Hudson, the Agent General of the trading company of Cookson and Hatton; she had brought back with her specimens of reptiles, insects, and fishes which pleased Gunther; she had made a beginning with her study of native religion and law, and she had realized her youthful dreams of following in the wake of the old slavers and buccaneers. But more important than any of these achievements was the fact that she had at last found a way of life which satisfied her deepest needs. She had succumbed to the charm of West Africa as soon as she left Sierra Leone, and had found just the kind of exciting and dangerous work that she loved.

She had changed profoundly during the few months that she had been away from England. In 1893 she had boarded the *Lagos* sad at heart from her recent loss, feeling that nobody needed her and that life held nothing for her. Now she had proved herself a true Kingsley. She had found people who treated her with kindness and respect once they realized her quality. Several years later she recorded her first impressions of the Coast and its peoples:

On my first voyage out I did not know the Coast and the Coast did not know me, and we mutually terrified each other. I fully expected to get killed by the local nobility and gentry; they thought I was connected with the World's Women's Temperance Association, and collecting shocking details for subsequent magic-lantern lectures on the liquor traffic; so fearful misunderstandings arose, but we gradually educated each other, and I had the best of the affair; for all I had to teach them was that I was only a beetle and fetish hunter and so forth, while they had to teach me a new world, and a very fascinating course of study I found it. And whatever the Coast may have to say against me—for my continual desire for hairpins, and other pins, my intolerable habit of getting into water and abominations full of ants, that I brought into their houses, or things emitting at unexpectedly short notice vivid and awful stenches—they cannot but say that I was a diligent pupil, who honestly tried to learn the lessons they taught me so kindly, though some of those lessons were hard to a person who had never previously been in even a tame bit of tropics, and whose life for many years had been an entirely domestic one in a University town.

One by one I took my old ideas derived from books and thoughts based on imperfect knowledge and weighed them against the real life around me, and found them either worthless or wanting. The greatest recantation I had to make I made humbly before I had been three months on the Coast in 1893. It was of my ideas of the traders. What I had expected to find them was a very different thing from what I did find them; and of their kindness to me I can never sufficiently speak, for on that voyage I was utterly out of touch with the governmental circles, and utterly dependent on the traders, and the most useful lesson of all the lessons I learnt on the West Coast in 1893 was that I could trust them. Had I not learnt this very thoroughly I could never have gone out again. . . .

Though the traders had helped her, Mary had been almost entirely dependent on her own resources. She had travelled alone, often with only a few African porters, who were in no way responsible for her safety; she had lived in the huts of the villagers whom she visited; she had even eaten their food—a hardship which no white trader would dream of enduring unless misfortune drove him to it. Always at the back of her mind was the thought that a false step or a failure of character at a critical moment would end in disaster; but she was so confident of her power and so certain of her judgement that she made light of the danger.

After almost a year at home, looking after her brother, who took her devotion for granted, and even made light of her adventurous journey, she found herself free once more to do as she pleased. She had worked on the mass of notes which she brought home with her, but did not yet feel herself well enough informed to write about Africa. The first had been merely an exploratory expedition; now she knew what conditions were like, she could really get down to work.

Charles Kingsley took a long time to prepare for his proposed journey to the Far East, and when she had at last seen him off,

Mary had to wait for Lady MacDonald, whom she had promised
to accompany as far as Calabar. By the 22nd of December, however, the two ladies were ready, and on that day they boarded the
Batanga, a ship of the Royal Africa Line. By a strange coincidence,
Captain Murray had been transferred to this ship, and Mary
immediately felt at home. On the 22nd it blew too hard for the
dock gates to be opened, but the next day the ship left the Mersey
and Mary's spirits lifted as she once more headed for Africa.

Lady MacDonald was at first a little over-awed by her scientific companion. She felt that she ought to try to show an interest
in natural history—especially in fishes—and, during the first
days of their voyage, drew Mary's attention to any form of
marine life she saw overboard. She was gently informed that
Mary was in search of freshwater fish from rivers north of the
Congo. She soon realized that her 'honorary aide-de-camp' had
other interests than science, and was a most lively and amusing
conversationalist. During the month that they spent together on
the *Batanga*, the two women came to be close and lasting friends.

The ship called at the Canaries, islands which never failed to
fascinate Mary, and reached Sierra Leone on 7th January. She
went ashore with the purser, a talkative, friendly Irishman, and
spent a very interesting time wandering about in Free Town. In
her account of her travels she wrote at some length of its people
and its industries, but the town is now so well known that her
description is of no special interest. One conclusion, which was
confirmed by her observation along the West Coast, she came to:
that the Mohammedan was in nine cases out of ten the best man
in West Africa. Stately and dignified in appearance, often finely
dressed in a long, white, loose-sleeved shirt under a dark gown,
made of mohair or silk, they contrasted sharply with the rest of
the motley population. They produced excellent work in leather
and iron, and the quaint hats that they offered for sale so attracted
Mary that she was only prevented from buying one by reminding
herself that it was not decent to go about in Africa in a hat that she
would not dare to put on in Piccadilly. It was doubtless this
principle which made her confine herself throughout her travels
to the long black skirts, white blouses, and sombre headgear
that she had been accustomed to wear in Cambridge.

As they steamed from Sierra Leone to Cape Coast Castle,
Mary made the acquaintance of Mr and Mrs Kemp, and when the

party landed she preferred to stay with them at the Wesleyan Mission rather than to join Lady MacDonald in accepting the hospitality of Government House. Her friendship for Dennis Kemp, who was the Superintendent of the Wesleyan Mission in the Gold Coast, was to act as a restraining influence when she came to write about missionaries and their work among Africans.

Government officials and missionaries must have been shocked when a niece of Charles Kingsley threw in her lot with the 'palm-oil ruffians' whom they blamed for the corruption of the African. Yet, from the very beginning of her second journey, she made it quite clear where she stood. She was a born rebel, with an instinctive distrust of all who were in authority. She disliked what she called 'the missionary party' which lorded it over the independent traders and seemed to forget that they too were Englishmen doing a job essential to England's prosperity. Mary found out how hide-bound they were when she stated her intention of nursing a trader who was desperately ill with fever. A lady, for whom she had up to then had the greatest regard, protested that she could not possibly spend a night in the sick man's house—it was not 'respectable'. Needless to say, Mary went. She had come to Africa to get away from just such conventional humbug.

While the *Batanga* lay at anchor off Accra, a visit was paid to the old Danish fort of Christianborg, now the residence of the British Governor, Sir Brandford Griffiths. This vast and solid edifice, built more than a hundred years before, was far better fitted to protect its occupants from the climate than more modern buildings, though it stood so exposed to the spray from the surf that its walls were mouldy, and no furniture could long survive the damp. The Governor received his visitors warmly, but Mary found the conversation of the government officials whom she met extraordinarily boring, being confined to horse-racing, in which she was not at all interested, their new cathedral, for which she cared even less, or Ashanti affairs of which she as yet knew little or nothing. She was confirmed in the opinion that the Gold Coast was not the place for her.

The outward voyage really ended at Calabar, where Lady MacDonald was met on the quay by Sir Claude, and the whole settlement, black and white, turned out to do her honour. Sir Claude, however, had business in Fernando Po, and he and his

E

wife, accompanied by Mary, left immediately, still on the *Batanga*, for that island. Here they made the acquaintance of the Spanish Governor, whom Mary found charming. She listened with sympathetic amusement to his account of his early days on the island. He had been assured by his friends that his appointment was equivalent to a sentence of death; and within a month of his arrival, as he lay sick with fever in the bed in which his predecessor had died, he became convinced that their dreadful prophecies had been true.

Much to his surprise he recovered, and decided that he would not spend a day more than he could help in the deadly port of Clarence. The seat of government was at once moved to Basile, high up in the mountains near the last native village on the island, and there he offered hospitality to the three British visitors. The climate of Basile, in Mary's opinion, with its heavy rainfall and its rapid changes of temperature, was just as unhealthy as that of Clarence; and she could only attribute the Governor's robust health and jovial spirits to the fact that he had escaped from the contaminated water supply of the port, and, in quenching his thirst, had relied entirely upon an excellent form of light sherry.

Mary was delighted by the grandeur of the scenery and intrigued by the inhabitants of Fernando Po. On the second day of her visit she set out to explore. She soon grew tired of Clarence, where she found that the main attraction was a massive dump of coal—left by the British when they abandoned their naval station and returned the island to the Spaniards in 1858—and the main topic of conversation the establishment of a café which, it was feared, would win for this sedate town a reputation comparable to that of Paris or Monte Carlo. Since the morals of the fifty-two white laymen on the island were well guarded by fifty-four priests, there seemed little ground for apprehension.

Leaving the town behind, Mary set out along the southern shore: on her left the grand, densely forested mountains, and on her right the sparkling Atlantic. Now and then she had to climb over rocks or to scramble and wade across the bars of small rivers which came creeping out from among the trees 'smelling certainly unpleasant, but a joy to the eye'. She wandered on and on, visiting farms where cocoa was being tended, and where the friendly natives talked to her on all manner of subjects, until at last she turned back, well satisfied with her afternoon. Just as she passed the first farm she had paused at, she found that what she had regarded as a dry-land shrub-belt was nothing of the kind:

The tide had come in and taken full possession of it, running up to the forest wall. The forest was far too thick to get through, so there was nothing for it but a hurried waist-high wade. I went in for this remembering that I had been informed that there were very nasty crocodiles on the island, and that I had got to get past the mouth of that largest river—as crocodiley-looking a spot as you could wish for, if you had a gun. I saw none however, and so presume there were none there, for it is the habit of these animals, when they are handy to the sea, to lounge down and meet the in-coming tide. The worst part of the affair was getting round the projecting bits of rocky cliff where the sea was breaking; not roughly, or I should not be writing this.

During her short stay on the island, she spent most of her time studying the customs and fetish of the Bubis, the original inhabitants. Little was known about them at this time and Mary's account, detailed, racy, and written with evident pleasure, was of interest to anthropologists as well as to the ordinary reader. The Bubis were not attracted by civilization: their villages were carefully hidden, they showed no interest in trade, and they had a positive aversion to clothes. It was with the greatest difficulty that the Spanish authorities induced them to wear even the most meagre covering when they were visiting the towns on the island, and Mary was amused to see them hastily removing these rags as soon as they were out of sight of the settlements. Yet they were very particular about their personal appearance, covering their bodies with a plaster of pomatum and showing great taste and love of variety in their hats, without which they would never dream of taking even the shortest walk. Ear-rings of wood, bracelets and leglets of beads or twisted grass, and belts made from shells completed the adornment of a 'dandy'.

When she did find her way into one of their villages, Mary saw huts, made of logs stuck in edgeways, with acute-angled roofs of thatch; she handled their crude wooden weapons, with which they hunted pythons, crocodiles, and gazelles, and listened to the awe-inspiring noises made by their musical instruments which they played at unreasonable hours. They were an orderly people, yielding ready obedience to their tribal chiefs, who, in their turn, were subservient to one great chief whom no white man had ever seen. Rum they liked and drank in moderation, but their drinking was reserved for special occasions, and they were by no means habitual drunkards, neither were they prepared to work in order to earn money with which to buy more spirits.

Quite happy to hunt and fish, and cultivate yams, kako (another edible root), and plantains, the Bubis had successfully resisted all the efforts of the Spaniards to make them work. When they needed a little money to buy rum or other European luxuries they sold some of their excellent yams. At the time of Mary's visit, the government was trying to reduce them to a dependent state by discouraging this export trade, for their labour was needed on the coffee and cocoa plantations. She hoped that this attempt would fail, being convinced that it would lead to the extinction of the Bubis, who were profoundly unhappy away from their own villages and way of life.

Though she would willingly have spent longer on Fernando Po, Mary accompanied her friends when they returned to Calabar. Almost immediately they arrived, Sir Claude was called away to take command of a force which had been mobilized to quell a rising of the people of Brass. Mary, of course, remained at Calabar with Lady MacDonald, and was a great help to her in a number of ways. Her medical experience—combined with her knowledge of the habits of Coasters—came in useful on one occasion. An assistant at the government office was reported to be very ill, and, since all the doctors were away with the expedition, it was feared he would die. He was brought to Government House and put to bed. Mary had no difficulty in diagnosing his complaint as an attack of *delirium tremens*, and she and Lady MacDonald nursed him safely through it.

She remained in Calabar River from January 1895 until May collecting fish and insects and studying the fetish of the Eboes. Most of her time was spent in 'puddling about the river and the forest round Duke Town and Creek Town'. Here she had more adventures with crocodiles, but could not resist the temptation to steer her canoe in among mangrove trees at high water, even though she knew from experience how dangerous it could be if she were tide-trapped. She found out a great deal about the customs and religion of the Africans—sometimes under rather trying conditions, as is shown by the following extract from her diary:

They are at it down in Duke Town tonight, not only rubbing the drum, but singing one of the big tunes. I'll just go down and see to it, though it's inky dark, and Calabar has not risen to the cultural level of oil streetlamps; still there's a lot of sheet lightning.—Two and a half hours later.—It's a perfect scandal they do not keep those Duke Town paths in a better state. They are nothing in the world but drains, and precious bad at that. There ought to be one fixed light at Mr Fynn's ditch, or by the bridge, and *then* you would know which was which before you were waist-high in water.

Secret societies have always played an important part in African life and Mary never missed an opportunity of finding out more about them. This was an extremely dangerous occupation, since an uninitiated person—especially a woman—caught observing any one of the rites of these societies ran the risk of sudden death. On one occasion she was fortunate enough to witness the way in which Africans trap the spirits upon whose advice and by whose authority the hierarchy of a secret society controls its members:

Egbo (the secret society of the Africans of Calabar) has the most grades of initiation, except Poorah (a society of Sierra Leone), and it exercises jurisdiction over all classes of crime except witchcraft. Any Effik man who wishes to become an influential person in the tribe must buy himself into as high a grade of Egbo as he can afford, and these grades are expensive, £1500 or £1000 English being required for the higher grades, I am informed. But it is worth it to a great trader, as an influential Effik necessarily is, for he can call out his own class of Egbo and send it against those of his debtors who may be of lower grades, and as the Egbo methods of delivering its orders to pay up consist in placing Egbo at a man's doorway, and until it removes itself from that doorway the man dare not venture outside his house, it is most successful.

Of course the higher a man is in Egbo rank, the greater his power and security, for lower grades cannot proceed against higher ones. Indeed when a man meets the paraphernalia of a higher grade of Egbo than that to which he belongs, he has to act as if he were lame, and limp along past it humbly, as if the sight of it had taken all the strength out of him, and, needless to remark, higher grade debtors flip their fingers at lower grade creditors.

After talking so much about the secret society spirits, it may be as well to know what they are. They are, one and all, a kind of a sort of a something that usually lives in the bush. Last February I was making my way back from Duke Town—late, as usual; I was just by a town on the Qua River. As I was hurrying onward I heard a terrific uproar accompanied by drums in the thick bush into which, after a brief interval of open ground, the path turned. I became cautious and alarmed, and hid in some dense bush as the men making the noise approached. I saw it was some ju-ju affair. They had a sort of box which they carried on poles, and their dresses were peculiar, and abnormally ample over the upper part of their bodies. They were prancing about in an ecstatic way round the box, which had one end open, beating their drums and shouting. They were fairly close to me, but fortunately turned their attention to another bit of undergrowth, or that evening they would have landed another kind of thing from what they were after. . . . The bushes they selected they surrounded, and evidently did their best to induce something to come out of them and to go into their box arrangement. I was every bit as anxious as they were that they should succeed, and succeed rapidly, for you know there are a nasty lot of snakes and things in general, not to mention driver ants, about that Calabar bush, that do not make it at all pleasant to go sitting about in.

However, presently they got this something into their box and rejoiced exceedingly, and departed staggering under the weight. I gave them a good start, and then made the best of my way home; and all that night Duke Town howled, and sang, and thumped its tom-toms unceasingly; for I was told Egbo had come into the town. Egbo is very coy, even for a secret society spirit, and seems to loathe publicity; but when he is ensconced in his ark he utters sententious observations on the subject of current politics, and his word is law. The voice that comes out of the ark is very strange, and unlike a human voice. I heard it shortly after Egbo had been secured. I expect, from what I saw, that there was some person in that ark all the time, but I do not know. It is more than I can do to understand my ju-ju details at present, let alone explain them on rational lines.

Most white men had not troubled to study Egbo, as they considered the whole business a mass of pagan foolery. But the fact remains that secret societies, for good or ill, have exerted, and still do exert, a tremendous influence in Africa. Mary was convinced that those who ruled these areas must know something of the basic ideas of African law and morality; otherwise injustice, confusion, and bitterness were inevitable. On the whole she approved of the major secret societies, for she found that they helped to preserve law and order amongst a people to whom killing was of far less consequence than among Europeans.

But there were some secret societies which were wholly evil. They existed solely for the organization of murders—sometimes for the purpose of sacrificial cannibalism. There was one of these 'Leopard' societies in the Calabar district, in which the last member to enter had to provide, for the benefit of the other members, the body of a relative of his own. So great was the fear inspired by these murdering bands, who dressed themselves in leopard skins, that the tribesmen in the regions where they operated dare not attack actual leopards lest they should make a mistake and bring down the fury of the society upon themselves. Thus they allowed leopards to prey on their dogs, sheep, and goats, only rousing themselves to self-defence when a human being was attacked. Mary actually experienced this when on one of her lonely journeys up the Calabar River. In one village where she spent the night, leopards had killed fourteen goats and five slaves during the previous eight days. The only precaution the villagers had taken was to make their goat-houses stronger. Tales are still told of murders committed by members of these societies, which no administration has succeeded in utterly destroying.

Leopards were treated with reverence all along the Coast, and when an African was forced reluctantly to kill one, its body was taken to his village and a very formal gathering of relations and fellow tribesmen witnessed the removal and burning of its gall-bladder—which was believed to be a deadly poison—and the dismembering of its body. Only the more reckless young hunters dared to place the leopard's whiskers in their hair, for these were believed to be a very potent ju-ju, and those who wore them ran the risk of being taken for witches. The skin, however, was either sold—without the whiskers—or used as a dress.

Mary had several encounters with leopards, and although it is impossible to discover exactly where they occurred, the probability is that she was wandering in the hinterland of Calabar, which is notorious for these animals, on at least one of the occasions which she subsequently described:

I must say the African leopard is an audacious animal, although it is ungrateful of me to say a word against him, after the way he has let me off personally, and I will speak of his extreme beauty as compensation for my ingratitude. I really think, taken as a whole, he is the most lovely animal I have ever seen; only seeing him, in the one way you can gain a full idea of his beauty, namely in his native forest, is not an unmixed joy to a person, like myself, of a nervous disposition. I may remark that my nervousness regarding the big game of Africa is of a rather peculiar kind. I can confidently say that I am not afraid of any wild animal—until I see it—and then—well I will yield to nobody in terror; fortunately as I say my terror is a special variety; fortunately because no one can manage their own terror. You can suppress alarm, excitement, fear, fright, and all those small-fry emotions, but the real terror is as dependent on the inner make of you as the colour of your eyes, or the shape of your nose; and when terror ascends its throne in my mind I become preternaturally artful, and intelligent to an extent utterly foreign to my true nature, and save, in the case of close quarters with bad big animals, a feeling of rage against some unknown person that such things as leopards, elephants, crocodiles, etc., should be allowed out loose in that disgracefully dangerous way, I do not think much about it at the time. Whenever I have come across an awful animal in the forest and know it has seen me I take Jerome's advice, and instead of relying on the power of the human eye, rely upon that of the human leg, and effect a masterly retreat in the face of the enemy. If I know it has not seen me I sink in my tracks and keep an eye on it, hoping that it will go away soon.

Once I thus came upon a leopard. I had got caught in a tornado in a dense forest. The massive, mighty trees were swaying like a wheatfield in an autumn gale in England, and I dare say that a field-mouse in a wheatfield in a gale would have heard much the same uproar. The tornado shrieked like ten thousand vengeful demons. The great trees creaked and groaned and strained against it and their bush-rope cables groaned and smacked like whips, and ever and anon a thundering crash with snaps like pistol shots told that they and their mighty tree had struggled in vain. The fierce rain came in a roar, tearing to shreds the leaves and blossoms and deluging everything. I was making bad weather of it, and climbing up over a lot of rocks out of a gully bottom where I had been half drowned in a stream, and on getting my head to the level of a block of rock I observed right in front of my eyes, broadside on, maybe a yard off, certainly not more, a big leopard.

He was crouching on the ground, with his magnificent head thrown back and his eyes shut. His fore-paws were spread out in front of him and he lashed the ground with his tail, and I grieve to say, in face of that awful danger—I don't mean me, but the tornado—that depraved creature swore, softly, but repeatedly and profoundly. I did not get all these facts up in one glance, for no sooner did I see him than I ducked under the rocks, and remembered thankfully that leopards are said to have no power of smell. But I heard his observation on the weather, and the flip-flap of his tail on the ground.

Every now and then I cautiously took a look at him with one eye round a rock edge, and he remained in the same position. My feelings tell me he remained there twelve months, but my calmer judgment puts the time down at twenty minutes; and at last, on taking another cautious peep, I saw he was gone. At the time I wished I knew exactly where, but I do not care about that detail now, for I saw no more of him. He had moved off in one of those weird lulls which you get in a tornado, when for a few seconds the wild herd of hurrying winds seem to have lost themselves, and wander round crying and wailing like lost souls, until their common rage seizes them again and they rush back to their work of destruction.

It was an immense pleasure to have seen the great creature like that; he was so evidently enraged and baffled by the uproar and dazzled by the floods of lightning that swept down into the deepest recesses of the forest, showing at one second every detail of twig, leaf, branch and stone round you, and then leaving you in a sort of swirling dark until the next flash came; this, and the great conglomerate roar of the wind, rain and thunder, was enough to bewilder any living thing.

I have never hurt a leopard intentionally; I am habitually kind to animals, and besides I do not think it ladylike to go shooting things with a gun. Twice, however, I have been in collision with them. On one occasion a big leopard had attacked a dog, who, with her family, was occupying a broken-down hut next to mine. The dog was a half-breed boarhound, and a savage brute on her own account. I, being roused by the uproar, rushed into the feeble moonlight, thinking she was having one of her habitual turn-ups with other dogs, and I saw a whirling mass of animal matter within a yard of me. I fired two mushroom-shaped native stools in rapid succession into the brown of it, and the meeting broke up into a leopard and a dog. The leopard crouched, I think to spring on me. I can see its great, beautiful, lambent eyes still, and I seized an earthen water-cooler and flung it straight at them. It was a noble shot; it burst on the leopard's head like a shell and the leopard went for the bush one time.

Twenty minutes after, people began to drop in cautiously and inquire if anything was the matter, and I civilly asked them to go and ask the leopard in the bush, but they firmly refused. We found the dog had got her shoulder slit open as though by a blow from a cutlass, and the leopard had evidently seized the dog by the scruff of her neck, but owing to the folds of skin no bones were broken and she got round all right after much ointment from me, which she paid me for with several bites. Do not mistake this for a sporting adventure. I no more thought it was a leopard than that it was a lotus when I joined the fight.

The other encounter was some months later, when Mary was in the French Congo. One day she entered a Fan village where she found a magnificent leopard tethered to a number of stakes by bush ropes. It was the custom of the Fans, when they had captured one of these ferocious creatures, to leave it a prisoner in the ropes which formed the trap, until it either starved to death or grew so feeble that they could kill it without danger and without damaging unduly its valuable skin. Mary and her carriers went to bed for the night in a hut near the leopard. The cries of the captive were pitiful. At last Mary could endure them no longer. Rising from her hard pallet of wood, she hurried out into the night without pausing even to put on her boots. When she came near the tethered beast, she began to pull up the stakes. Meanwhile the leopard made furious, frenzied rushes at her. Once it came near enough to rip her dress from top to bottom, but she went steadily on with her task until she considered that she had pulled up enough stakes to enable the beast to free itself eventually. She had judged correctly, for as she retreated it made a mighty effort and uprooted the remaining stakes.

To her horror, instead of making for the bush, it advanced on her and walked, snarling, around her. Even in this fearful predicament Mary's 'preternatural intelligence' did not desert her. She stood her ground and said sharply, 'Go home, you fool!' The leopard turned and vanished into the bush. A moment later she heard a thud. One of the bolder Fans from her band had heard the noise and come out to see what was happening. Seeing what her intention was, he had hastily climbed a tree. He had seen the leopard released from the trap, heard her sharp command, and watched the retreat of the animal. Now he knelt at the feet of this very superior spirit to show his respect and awe. It is not surprising that the fierce huntsmen in whose company she travelled sometimes treated her with a deference which was almost idolatrous.

Mary took the opportunity while she was staying with Lady MacDonald to go upstream to pay a visit to Miss Mary Slessor. This remarkable woman had originally been a mill-hand in

Dundee, but for the past eighteen years she had been working as a Presbyterian missionary among the unruly tribesmen of the Okyon district. She lived far from any white people, but such was the force of her personality that she had established a complete ascendency over the neighbouring Africans.

On the very afternoon of Mary's arrival she had an opportunity of seeing Miss Slessor deal with a very difficult situation. Twins were regarded with horror throughout the lands of the Niger delta, and both they and their mother were customarily killed in the more remote regions, where there was little chance of interference by government officials. On this occasion twins had been born to an Ebo slave girl in a village near Miss Slessor's house. Only fear of the missionary's anger had saved mother and children from death. As it was, the twins had been thrust into a gin case together with the rest of the slave's belongings, and the whole village had joined in driving out the unfortunate girl. Miss Slessor learnt of these happenings and hurried to meet her. Weak and terrified, the mother was making her way towards the only sanctuary of which she knew. The missionary relieved the girl of her load and led her towards her house. Mary had an illustration of Mary Slessor's understanding and tolerance of harmless African superstitions. If the mother and her twins had continued down the main track through the forest it would have become contaminated and no African would have dared to use it again. Miss Slessor waited, in the broiling heat of the sun, while the villagers slashed a new path for her to her house. They worked very hard, knowing that it saved the pollution of a long track of market road. When it was completed, they went to the house by it and there she comforted the girl and attended to the two babies. One she found to be dead, but the other survived.

Here was a woman after Mary's own heart, and the two soon became friends, sitting up talking far into the night. Mary nursed and petted the numerous children who lived in the enclosure around the house—all of whom had been rescued from death. She and her new friend sat and listened to the gossip of the friendly talkative black men and women who were always paying visits. They showed no fear of the rescued twin while Mary or Miss Slessor was nursing it, but if by chance it was handed to another of Miss Slessor's flock to hold, there was an immediate stampede of men and women off the verandah, out of the yard, and over the fence into the bush. Yet so great was Miss Slessor's influence that, in spite of her defiance of some of their most powerful superstitions, the Africans of this district, who, until her settling among them, had been regarded with fear by the people of Duke Town and Creek Town, were prepared to listen to her advice and in most things to obey her orders.

Mary stayed with her for some days and from her learnt many things about the customs, diseases, and religion of the Africans. Realizing that she was in the presence of greatness, Mary never ceased to marvel at the effect of this isolated white woman on all whom she met. She was convinced that if only the ruling classes could produce a few government officials of comparable force and ability, the problem of administering England's African territories would be near solution.

Soon after her return down river from the Okyon district, Mary decided that she had stayed long enough in Calabar, and when the *Batanga* came into the river, she said good-bye to Sir Claude and Lady MacDonald and set out again for her beloved South West Coast.

7

TO THE OGOWE

MARY had met Sir George Taubman Goldie while she was in England, and he had invited her to continue her search for fish in the upper reaches of the Niger when she returned to Africa. In 1895 the whole of this region was controlled by Sir George, who was the head of the Royal Niger Company, and Mary could have collected fish and studied fetish under the most favourable conditions if she had accepted his offer. Relations between the Royal Niger Protectorate, where she had been so warmly entertained by Sir Claude MacDonald, and the Royal Niger Company, however, were so strained that she decided not to become a possible cause for dissension by moving from one to the other. She set out instead for French Congo where she could expect only very limited protection from the French authorities, and where she would once more be almost entirely dependent on the traders whom she had learned to trust during her journey in 1893.

The passage from Calabar to Gaboon, in French territory, was by no means straightforward. In 1893 vessels bound for the South West Coast from Liverpool had called at Calabar, but by 1895 this practice had been discontinued, and Mary had first to take a homeward-bound boat to Lagos, and there board another which sailed to the south. Moreover, she found that even the passage to Lagos was not without its tiresome features. Since ships could not load cargo off this town on account of the heavy swell, captains were accustomed to lie in Forçados River to wait for the cargo.

When the *Batanga* anchored there, Mary found this river the most desolate spot that she had so far seen. She had to concentrate on the lively, vociferous passengers on the ship, and on the excited African traders who brought their goods to Forçados, to prevent the stark horror of the dreary mudflats and the stench of

rotting vegetation from making her lose heart. Later, she visited
this difficult anchorage so many times that she knew all the
dangers of the bar across the narrow entrance to the river.
One captain at least, she claimed, was so confident of her knowledge and judgement that he allowed her to pilot his ship, a
2000-tonner, into the river.

On this first occasion she met an old African woman who
made a good living by buying chickens at Lagos, transporting
them to Opobo, and there selling them at a very much higher
price. She then returned to Lagos with her empty crates, upon
which she was determined not to pay freight charges. Her tactics,
air of injured innocence, and skill in dealing with any first mate
who was foolhardy enough to try to make her pay for her crates,
afforded Mary great delight, helping to pass the long days that
the ship lay in the river.

Wise and experienced chief officers never see Mrs S.'s crates, but
young and truculent ones do, and determine, in their hearts, she shall
pay for them, advertising this resolve of theirs openly all the way from
Opobo, which is foolish. When it comes to sending heavy goods
overside into the branch boat at Forçados, the wise chief officer lets
those crates go, but the truculent one says:

'Here, Mrs S., now you have got to pay for those crates.'

'Lor, mussy me, sar,' says Mrs S., 'those crates no 'long to me,
sar.'

'Then,' says the truculent one, 'heave 'em over side! We don't
want that stuff lumbering up our deck.'

Mrs S. then expostulates and explains they are the property of
a lone, lorn lady in Lagos to whom Mrs S. is taking them from the
highest motives; motives 'such a nice gentleman' as the first officer
must understand, and which it will be a pleasure to him to share in,
and she cites instances of other chief officers who according to her have
felt, as it were, a ray of sunlight come into their lives when they saw
those chicken crates and felt it was in their power to share in the noble
work of returning them to Lagos freight free. The truculent one then
loses his head and some of his temper and avows himself a heartless
villain, totally indifferent to the sex, and says all sorts of things, but my
faith in the ultimate victory of Mrs. S. never wavers. My money is on
her all the time, and she has never disappointed me, and when I am
quite rich some day, I will give Mrs S. purses of gold in the eastern
manner for the many delicious scenes she had played before me with
those crates in dreary Forçados.

The *Batanga* at last reached Lagos, where those passengers bound for the South West Coast were to be trans-shipped to the *Benguella*. Careful and detailed instructions were issued on the method of getting from the steamship to the small branch boat which would pick these passengers up. The need for care was emphasized by the story of the gentleman 'who came to the Coast for pleasure and lost a leg to a shark while so engaged'. When Mary saw the branch boat, the *Eko*, thrusting its way through the terrifying breakers of the bar, she felt for a moment that she had made a mistake in deciding to go to the South West Coast, and she had to call to mind all the attractions of that region to prevent herself from staying on the *Batanga* and returning quietly to England.

She had made up her mind, however, by the time the *Eko* had anchored near them, and permitted herself to be lowered over the side in a chair by the ship's winch. The passage in the small boat was rough and she was not reassured when she had climbed on board the *Eko*. All the gear was in a state of the greatest confusion as a result of the fury of the bar; the African passengers on the lower deck were drenched, and, for once, silent, while the captain's cabin, which that chivalrous gentleman at once placed at her disposal, was in a chaotic state. Everything on board was covered with a layer of wet coal-dust. When she emerged from the cabin, Mary learned to her dismay that they were to await the *Benguella* anchored outside the bar.

Anxiously the horizon was scanned for signs of her approach. The ship rolled, the gear crashed, the passengers moaned, but there was nothing to raise their hopes until the late afternoon— Mary had been put on board in the morning—when a steamer was seen heading towards the bar. She proved to be not the *Benguella* but a German trading vessel, the *Janette Woermann*, and as soon as the anchor was down, her captain, a gigantic Dane, came aboard the *Eko* to inquire about the prospects of cargo. When he learned of the predicament of Mary and of a government official who had come out on the branch boat to see at first hand the difficulties of crossing the bar, he offered them hospitality on his ship, and Mary was soon 'playing bob cherry again with Lagos sharks going down into his boat by the *Eko*'s rope ladder'.

Captain Heldt, the Danish skipper, entertained them lavishly, giving up his own comfortable cabin to her, providing her and

her companion with an excellent dinner, and, not satisfied with
this, trying to raise their spirits by playing on his auto-harp. This
stroke of good fortune saved Mary from a foodless and sleepless
night on the branch boat, for the *Benguella* did not steam into the
roadstead until two o'clock on the following afternoon. Then
Mary was escorted to her new ship by her two friends. As she
got her head over the bulwarks after climbing the rope ladder
in a truly nautical way, the first person she saw was her old
acquaintance, the second mate of the *Lagos*. He was the man whose
last words to her when she had left the ship at Loanda in 1893
had been an assurance that she would take the first boat home.
His surprise at seeing her still in African waters can well be
imagined.

Mary claimed that she was fortunate to find sympathetic,
well-informed people on board the *Benguella*. Since she felt the
same about every ship on which she sailed, she must have been
the kind of person who brought out the best in the rough traders
and sailors with whom she spent so much of her time. No one
could shock her; curses and oaths merely amused her; her sense
of humour was always in evidence, and, above all, she was a ready
and sympathetic listener. On the *Benguella* she made friends with
the ship's purser, Mr Fothergill, and since he had spent a long
time on shore in the French Congo, and was only too ready to
recount his experiences, she soon knew a great deal about the
land she was about to visit.

He had, I should say, overdone his experiences with the natives,
as far as personal comfort and pleasure at the time went, having been
nearly killed and considerably chivvied by them. Now I do not wish
a man, however much I may deplore his total lack of local knowledge,
to go so far as this. Mr Fothergill gave his accounts of these incidents
calmly, and in an undecorated way that gave them a power and
convincingness verging on being unpleasant, although useful, to a
person who was going into the region where they had occurred, for
one felt there was no mortal reason why one should not personally get
involved in similar affairs. And I must here acknowledge the great
subsequent service Mr Fothergill's wonderfully accurate descriptions
of the peculiar characteristics of the Ogowe forests were to me when I
subsequently came to deal with these forests on my own account, as
every district of forest has peculiar characteristics of its own which you
require to know.

Mary was neither reckless of the dangers of the West Coast nor did she doubt their existence. On her first voyage out she had found it difficult to believe the stories of fever told to her by the old Coasters, for she had not understood that these men lived so close to death that they thought nothing of joking about it. But a short experience of Coast life had soon convinced her of the underlying horror of this sickness—a horror which so gripped weaker men that they fell a prey to the very thing they dreaded most. Those who survived developed the same stoical, cynical attitude towards it that a soldier on active service does towards wounds and death. She believed, too, in the dangers inseparable from life amongst savage, uncontrolled tribesmen and fierce animals, but, having taken every precaution which her limited means permitted, she faced them all with a calm disregard for danger.

Mary was one of the small band who never know fear. Often she wrote of her 'terror', but this was merely a literary trick of exaggerating her emotions in order to give a humorous twist to her narrative. After her death, an acquaintance wrote to the *Spectator* describing how he once asked her, 'Have you ever known what it is to be frightened, or at least flustered, when you saw death not only staring into your face, but also shouting into your ear?' Mary replied: 'I have never felt that. I don't know what it is; I have an idea that if once I *did* feel so, I should collapse entirely. But whenever I have been in real instant danger, which simply needed every effort of every bit of me, I had a strong salt taste in my mouth. Whenever I feel *that*, I know I've got to take myself as seriously as I know how.'

Her ostensible object in going to French Equatorial Africa was to get above the tide line of the Ogowe, the greatest African river between the Niger and the Congo, where she hoped to find new and interesting species of fish. Doubtless, the knowledge that this was the wildest and most dangerous part of West Africa was an added attraction, for it was only where Africans were living in primitive communities, almost entirely outside the control of white men, that she could play the game with death that so stirred her imagination and gave such zest to her life. Her description of the Fan race, written after months spent amongst them, illustrates more fully her attitude to danger:

F

I have been considerably chaffed both by whites and blacks about my partiality for this tribe, but as I like Africans in my way—not *à la Sierra Leone*—and these Africans have more of the qualities I like than any other tribe I have met, it is but natural that I should prefer them. They are brave and so you can respect them, which is an essential element in a friendly feeling. They are on the whole a fine race, particularly those in the mountain districts of the Sierra del Cristal, where one continually sees magnificent specimens of human beings, both male and female. Their colour is light bronze, many of the men have beards, and albinoes are rare among them. The average height in the mountain districts is five feet six to five feet eight, the difference in stature between men and women not being great. Their countenances are very bright and expressive, and if once you have been among them, you can never mistake a Fan.

But it is in their mental characteristics that their difference from the lethargic, dying-out Coast tribes is most marked. The Fan is full of fire, temper, intelligence and go; very teachable, rather difficult to manage, quick to take offence, and utterly indifferent to human life. I ought to say that other people, who should know him better than I, say he is a treacherous, thievish, murderous cannibal. I never found him treacherous; but then I never trusted him. . . .

My favourite form of literature, I may remark, is accounts of mountaineering exploits, though I have never seen a glacier or a permanent snow mountain in my life. I do not care a row of pins how badly they may be written, and what sort of bumble-puppy grammar and composition is employed, as long as the writer will walk along the edge of a precipice with a sheer fall of thousands of feet on one side and a sheer wall on the other; or better still crawl up an *arête* with a precipice on either. Nothing on earth would persuade me to do either of these things myself, but they remind me of bits of country I have been through where you walk along a narrow line of security with gulfs of murder looming on each side, and where in exactly the same way you are as safe as if you were in your easy chair at home, as long as you get sufficient holding ground: not on rock in the bush village inhabited by murderous cannibals, but on ideas in those men's and women's minds; and these ideas which I think I may say you will always find, give you safety. It is not advisable to play with them, or to attempt to eradicate them, because you regard them as superstitious; and never, never shoot too soon. I have never had to shoot, and hope never to have to; because in such a situation, one white alone with no troops to back him means a clean finish. But this would not discourage me if I had to start, only it makes me more inclined to walk round the obstacle than to become a mere blood splotch against it, if this can be done without losing your self-respect, which is the mainspring of your power in West Africa.

Mary, then, was excited rather than frightened by the stories which Mr Fothergill told her as they steamed towards Gaboon. When she became famous, she met Rudyard Kipling and his wife Caroline and they became close friends. Both had been captivated by her account of her travels in West Africa. Kipling spoke of her as the bravest woman he knew, and when writing of her in the *Journal of the African Society*, after her death, he said, 'Being human, she must have been afraid of something, but one never found out what it was.'

Hudson, the chief agent of Messrs Hatton and Cookson, was away when Mary landed at Gaboon on May 20th, but she found his deputy, Fildes, awaiting her. After receiving her in a most friendly way and making her feel at home, he sent her, under the escort of a French agent of the firm, to report to the Customs House:

[it] is far more remarkable for quaintness than beauty; it is two stories high, the ground floor being the local lock-up. The officer in charge lives on the topmost floor and has a long skeleton wooden staircase whereby to communicate with the lower world. The staircase is a veritable 'hen-roost' one. It is evidently made to kill people, but why? Individuals desirous of defrauding customs would not be likely to haunt this Custom House staircase, and good people, like me, who want to pay dues, should be encouraged and not killed.

The officer is having his siesta; but when aroused is courteous and kindly, but he incarcerates my revolver, giving me a feeling of iniquity for having had the thing. I am informed if I pay fifteen shillings for a licence I may have it—if I fire French ammunition out of it. This seems a heavy sum, so I ask M. Pichault, our mentor, what I may be allowed to shoot if I pay this? Will it make me free, as it were, of all the local shooting? May I daily shoot governors, heads of departments, and *sous officiers*? M. Pichault says 'Decidedly not'; I may shoot 'hippo, or elephants, or crocodiles'. Now I have never tried shooting big game in Africa with a revolver, and as I don't intend to I leave the thing in pawn. My collecting-cases and spirit, the things which I had expected to reduce me to a financial wreck by customs dues, are passed entirely free, because they are for science. *Vive la France!*

Mary was indeed lucky, for eighteen years later Dr. Schweitzer, entering the same territory in order to establish a hospital attached to the Presbyterian Mission on the Ogowe, found that he had to pay a duty of two francs on every litre of pure alcohol which he imported for medical purposes.

On the day after her arrival she was delighted to meet Dr. Nassau, the head of the American Presbyterian Mission in Gaboon and Batanga. He had come down to Hatton and Cookson's factory on learning that a lady had landed, thinking that it was a missionary he was expecting from Batanga. He was one of the greatest living authorities on the religion and customs of the Africans of this region, and Mary was soon deep in conversation with him. She visited him frequently during her stay in French territory and found him always friendly and sympathetic and willing to place his knowledge at her disposal.

From May 21st to June 5th was spent at Hatton and Cookson's factory at Glass. After a day's rest, when her only activity was a walk along the seashore in search of specimens, she was taken to Libreville, two or three miles away, to register and to apply for permission from the police to stay in the colony. As she walked along the road from Glass, Mary realized that it was just the place in which one would expect Englishmen to build their factories, for the land around it was very low-lying, and 'the English love, above all things, settling in, or as near as possible to a good reeking, stinking swamp'. When Libreville was reached, the Chief of Police proved to be an amiable old gentleman dressed in 'a white shirt and white pantaloons cut *à la Turque*'. Unfortunately the band which should have kept these garments in position was out of repair, and Mary was highly amused by his efforts to preserve his dignity and to keep his trousers up at the same time. The interview ended without disaster, however, and she was granted permission to stay.

Her most strenuous day was Sunday, the 26th, when she had expected to rest. Fildes, however, taking his duties as host very seriously, had other ideas. First, he insisted on showing her something of the river and they set out upstream with an African crew. After about half an hour's paddling, to Mary's horror she saw her host leap overboard into the yielding, stinking mud. He began to engage in a furious crab hunt, being convinced that these crustaceans would be a valuable addition to Mary's collection. He soon had all the crew hunting them, too, and together they caught a great number for Mary—who had mentioned no desire

for crabs, but had merely been noting where they were so that
she could come back alone the next day and get them without
inconveniencing her friends. They returned home for a twelve
o'clock breakfast, and then the indefatigable young man took
her for a very long walk, past the neatly made bamboo huts of the
M'pangwe, through a forest where grew acacias, and some of the
most lovely ferns she had ever seen; through Fan villages, with
their huts made of sheets of bark tied on to sticks, and with their
impressive standing drums painted in white and black patterns;
over pretty streams bridged by single planks; and finally to an
abandoned coffee plantation. Then her guide at last turned back,
with Mary following him 'going like clockwork' because she was
afraid that if she stopped she would be unable to start again.

In a day or two Hudson returned, and Mary persuaded him,
rather against his better judgement, to give her all the help he
could to further her plans to explore the upper Ogowe. When the
Mové, a small steamer which plied between Glass and the furthest
navigable point—Njole—on the Ogowe, arrived, Mary was ready
and at 9.30 a.m. on June 5th she set out on what was to be the
most exciting expedition she had yet undertaken. Hudson, a
missionary, and two traders accompanied her, while the lower deck
was crowded with African passengers. She enjoyed immensely
every moment of the sea and river trip, and when the Ogowe was
reached she felt quite sure that she had made the right decision in
choosing this river rather than the Niger.

By 10.25 we had got all our wood on board, and run up river full
speed. The river seems broader above *Fallabar* (the predecessor of the
Mové, now used as a trading hulk by Messrs. Hatton and Cookson),
but this is mainly on account of its being temporarily unencumbered
with islands. A good deal of the bank we have passed by since leaving
Nazareth bay on the south side has been island shore, with a channel
between the islands and the true south bank.

The day soon grew dull, and looked threatening, after the delusive
manner of the dry season. The climbing plants are finer here than I have
ever before seen them. They form great veils and curtains between and
over the trees, often hanging so straight and flat, in stretches of twenty
to forty feet wide, and thirty to sixty or seventy feet high, that it seems
incredible that no human hand has trained or clipped them into their
perfect forms. Sometimes these curtains are decorated with large bell-
shaped, bright-coloured flowers, sometimes with delicate sprays of

white blossoms. This forest is beyond all my expectations of tropical luxuriance and beauty, and it is a thing of another world to the forest of the Upper Calabar, which, beautiful as it is, is a sad dowdy to this. There you certainly get a great sense of grimness and vastness; here you have an equal grimness and vastness with the addition of superb colour. This forest is a Cleopatra to which Calabar is but a Quaker. Not only does this forest depend on flowers for its illumination, for there are many kinds of trees having their long shoots, crimson, brown-pink, and creamy yellow: added to this there is also the relieving aspect of the prevailing fashion among West African trees, of wearing the trunk white with here and there upon it splashes of pale pink lichen, and vermilion-red fungus, which alone is sufficient to prevent the great mass of vegetation from being a monotony in green.

All day long we steam past ever-varying scenes of loveliness whose component parts are ever the same, yet the effect ever different. Doubtless it is wrong to call it a symphony, yet I know no other word to describe the scenery of the Ogowe. It is as full of life and beauty and passion as any symphony Beethoven ever wrote; the parts changing, interweaving and returning. There are leitmotivs here in it, too. See the papyrus ahead; and you know when you get abreast of it you will find the great forest sweeping away in a bay-like curve behind it against the dull grey sky, the splendid columns of its cotton and red woods looking like a façade of some limitless inchoate temple. Then again there is that stretch of sword-grass, looking as if it grew firmly on to the bottom so steady does it stand; but as the *Mové* goes by her wash sets it undulating in waves across its broad acres of extent, showing it is only riding at anchor; and you know after a grass patch you will soon see a red dwarf clay cliff, with a village perched on its top, and the inhabitants thereof in their blue and red cloths standing by to wave and shout to the *Mové*, or legging it like lamp-lighters from the back streets and the plantations to the river frontage, to be in time to do so, and through all these changing phases there is always the strain of the vast wild forest, and the swift, deep, silent river.

At almost every village that we pass—and they are frequent after the *Fallabar*—there is an ostentatious display of firewood deposited either on the bank, or on piles driven into the mud in front of it, mutely saying in their uncivilized way, 'Try our noted chunks: best value for money'—(that is to say tobacco etc.) to the *Mové* or any other little steamer that may happen to come along hungry for fuel.

It is interesting to compare the first impressions of Dr. Schweitzer, who, in 1913, made exactly the same journey up the Ogowe. He, too, was impressed by the brilliant forest, the great

slow-moving river, the wide fields of papyrus, and the lively
Africans whose villages perched on its banks, but he felt none of
the joy that Mary experienced. He found the river and its en-
croaching vegetation monotonous; to shut one's eyes for an hour
and to open them again was only to see the same yellow water and
the same forest. In his eyes the Africans were negroes eager to
sell what logs they had, and pathetic in their excuses to a bullying
captain who abused them for not having more. He was saddened
by the sight of ruined huts where formerly there had been
thriving villages, and seems to have accepted the explanation of
the trader who stood by his side, that the desolation was entirely
due to the evil effects of alcohol. On his first evening on the
Ogowe, a realization of the pain and misery of Africa saddened
his spirits and confirmed him in his opinion that the land was
sorely in need of help and guidance.

When the steamer reached Lambaréné, Mary spent the afternoon at Hatton and Cookson's factory, where she found the
mosquitoes and sand-flies almost intolerable. She retreated into
the shadiest corner of the verandah and tried in vain to keep them
off. At dinner she bore their attacks with a fortitude which she
considered to be worthy of a Christian martyr, for she did not
wish to embarrass her hosts by making a fuss about something
which they appeared to dismiss as of no consequence. At last
Hudson turned to the sub agent in charge of the factory, and said
in a voice full of reproach:

'You have got mosquitoes here, Mr Cockshut.'

Poor Mr Cockshut didn't deny it; he had got four on his
forehead and his hands were sprinkled with them, but he
replied, 'There are none at Njole.'

Mary and Hudson thought this was a very feeble point to
make, since Njole was ninety miles upstream. The latter crushed
Cockshut by saying so in a few terse words, then he turned to
Mary:

'You don't seem to feel these things, Miss Kingsley,' he said
savagely.

For once Mary was too indignant to reply.

She spent the night on the *Mové*, and in the morning made
arrangements to stay at the Presbyterian Mission at Kangwe, a
few miles upstream from Lambaréné, with M. and Mme Jacot.
The former was in charge of the Mission and both he and his

wife treated their paying guest with the greatest kindness and
consideration. For some days she paddled about collecting fish;
met and studied Igalwa and Fan tribesmen; made a start on learning basic words in these dialects, and went for long, solitary
walks in the surrounding country. She was most conscientious
in recording all that she found out about the customs of the
Africans; only on two days did she make no notes, and there were
good reasons for this.

It happened this way. Down on the river bank, some one and a half
miles below Kangwe, lies Fula, a large Fan village. Through Fula
I passed that day with all the *éclat* of Wombwell's menagerie. Having
been escorted by half the population for a half a mile or so beyond the
town, and being then nervous about Fans, from information received,
I decided to return to Kangwe by another road, if I could find it. I had
not gone far on my quest before I saw another village, and having had
enough village work for one day, I made my way up quietly into the
forest on the steep hillside overhanging the said village. There was no
sort of path up there, and going through a clump of shenja, I slipped,
slid, and finally fell plump through the roof of an unprotected hut.
What the unfortunate inhabitants were doing, I don't know, but I am
pretty sure they were not expecting me to drop in, and a scene of great
confusion ensued. My knowledge of Fan dialect then consisted of
Kor-Kor, so I said that in as fascinating a tone as I could, and explained
the rest with three pocket handkerchiefs, a head of tobacco, and a knife
that providentially I had stowed in what my nautical friends would call
my after-hold—my pockets. I also said I'd pay for the damage, and
although this important communication had to be made in trade
English, they seemed to understand, for when I pointed to the roof
and indicated writing out a book for it, the master of the house said,
'Um,' and then laid hold of an old lady and pointed to her and then to
the roof, meaning clearly I had equally damaged both, and that she
was equally valuable. I squared the family all right, and I returned to
Kangwe via Fula, without delay and without the skin on my elbow.

On the Ogowe, as elsewhere, Mary was to find trade English
extremely useful, for even in remote villages she usually met at
least one African who knew the *lingua franca* of the bush traders.
Her published works and her letters are full of words and phrases
taken from this universal language of the Coast, and, since their
meaning is not usually clear, it will be necessary to translate them
as they occur. A 'book' was a written agreement to pay for services

or goods received; it was usually made out on a particular firm (in Mary's case, on Hatton and Cookson's) who made payment in goods from any store at which the 'book' might be presented. A 'head of tobacco', which was the nearest approach to currency in the more primitive regions, consisted of seven leaves of tobacco. When she travelled alone on the Upper Ogowe or in the Great Forest, Mary took these 'heads' with which to pay her men, buy food, or make presents. She found Africans everywhere much addicted to smoking, and on a journey her porters would pass the pipe from hand to hand as they paddled their canoes or walked through the forest.

The mosquitoes, the intolerable heat, and the close, confined life at Lambaréné, shut in as it is by the forest and sheltered by the great trees from any breath of moving air, soon began to affect Mary, and she made plans to move up the Ogowe to new fields. Towards the end of June the *Éclaireur* arrived. This was the rival of the *Mové*: both carried goods and passengers between Gaboon and Njole. Mary was delighted with its spick-and-span appearance. Her black bag, portmanteau, and traveller's sack were soon packed, and the trade goods which she had either brought with her or bought from the traders at Lambaréné, safely locked in a wooden chest, and she boarded the little stern-wheel steamer. She loved all kinds of craft, and this river steamboat, with its comfortable deckhouse, running almost the whole length of the ship, and its snug cabins, appealed to her immensely. She took her place on the upper deck—the lower, as usual, was reserved for African passengers—and saw Lambaréné fall astern.

She was to make several cruises on this steamer and to get to know its captain, Verdier, and his engineer very well indeed, for in spite of her admirable cabins, the *Éclaireur* had only one saloon, and life on board was very much *en famille*. Nor was the captain the man to hold himself aloof. He was full of vitality and ready at any moment to begin a violent argument with anyone on board, especially if he thought that France or his ship was being treated with insufficient respect. The engineer was more subdued, appearing quite satisfied to support his superior with a dutiful and formal, '*Oui, oui, certainement*,' whenever the captain appealed to him. These two comprised the white staff, but on this first occasion there were three other white passengers: Cockshut, on one of his tours of inspection of sub-factories, a lively French government official who was on his way to Franceville, and the engineer's brother, a quiet, gentlemanly man. Mary regretted that her knowledge of French was so limited that most of the animated discourse of the official was lost on her, and a promising row that the captain had begun with her, on the iniquity of the English merchants of Calabar in using only English ships to carry their cargoes, dried up for lack of words.

The *Éclaireur* was no pleasure steamer in spite of her trim appearance, and after she had thrust her way some miles above Lambaréné she ran up alongside a big street of a village to discharge cargo and to disembark African passengers:

Inhabitants in scores rush out and form an excited row along the vertical bank edge, several of the more excited individuals falling over it into the water. Yells from our passengers on the lower deck. Yells from inhabitants on shore. Yells of *vite, vite* from the captain. Dogs bark, horns bray, some exhilarated individual thumps the village drum, canoes fly out from the bank towards us. Fearful scrimmage heard going on all the time on the deck below. As soon as the canoes are alongside, our passengers from the lower deck, with their bundles and their dogs, pour over the side into them. Canoes rock wildly and wobble off rapidly towards the bank, frightening the passengers because they have their best clothes on, and fear that the *Éclaireur* will start and upset them altogether with her wash.

After this noisy interlude, the steamer swung out into the current again and resumed her way upstream, but not before the villagers had fired a salute in her honour, and the captain had returned the compliment from his cabin, almost deafening his lady passenger who had been watching the fun quietly with her back against his door. Apologies having been made and accepted, peace was restored.

This was typical of the calls made at the numerous villages along the bank of the river. In each village there was a sub-factory, usually in the charge of an African agent, and to these isolated spots oil, ivory, and rubber filtered down from the hinterland and awaited collection by the *Éclaireur* or the *Mové*. Between Lambaréné and Njole, some ninety miles, there was only one white factor, a Frenchman who looked no more than a boy, but who, Mary found, was twenty. Sometimes two months would go by without his seeing another white face. When the steamer drew up alongside his village, he came on board to celebrate, and Mary was kept awake until very late by the singing and dancing in the saloon, which was next to her cabin. She recognized the tunes they were singing as hymns she had heard at Jacot's services, and at first she very much regretted that she could not translate the words. On reflection, however, she came to the conclusion that the violent dancing and the shouts of laughter which accompanied these songs made them, perhaps, an unsuitable subject of study for her.

As they approached Talagouga, the banks grew higher and the river narrower, and the current became so strong that the little steamer had hard work stemming it. On arrival, Mary learned that there was no accommodation for her beyond this village, so she once more arranged with the missionaries to take her in. (She was never the guest of those with whom she stayed: at Talagouga she paid Forget ten guineas for her board, and, on her return to England, continued to contribute to the funds of the Mission.) Before she settled down at Talagouga, however, she went upstream as far as Njole, spending a day or so more on the steamer. There she went for one of her solitary walks, and finding to her astonishment a real road, she set off down it. It was hedged on each side with pineapples; behind them, carefully tended, were acres of coffee bushes planted in long rows. Before her stretched the country like a beautiful valley surrounded by purple-blue mountains. She passed neatly built Igalwa huts, with people sitting on the bright clean ground outside them making mats and baskets. They were friendly and shouted to her, pausing from their work to stare at such an unusual sight.

Suddenly she was alarmed by an awful hiss. For a moment she thought she was about to be attacked by a snake. She was mistaken: the attack came from a number of geese, and she had reason to bless her long, sturdy skirts before she had driven them off. After a further attack, this time from a turkey cock, she realized she was in a farmyard. Soon she heard shouts coming from a banana clump, and saw the owner of the farm striding towards her. He was extraordinarily polite, and invited her into his house, but since he knew no English they could only sit in embarrassed silence. They were saved by the appearance of the engineer's brother who soon explained who she was to the planter, and then the two Frenchmen insisted on showing her round the plantation. She found it to be the most well-ordered, well-cultivated one she had ever seen, and her admiration for the French, who could subdue even the African forest, knew no bounds.

At Njole, Mary met the deputy Commissioner of the Ogowe, Dr. Pélessier. Then, having spent another night on the *Éclaireur*, she returned to Talagouga, said good-bye to her friend the captain, and made for the shore in a canoe under the care of Forget.

8

THE RAPIDS OF THE OGOWE

THE Mission, where Mary was to stay for the next week or
two, was perched on a rocky hillside which rose abruptly
from the river. Forget's house was only a few feet from the
precipitous bank, and there seemed a very real danger of falling
off the verandah straight into the dark, deep Ogowe which
flowed swiftly past. A delightful room was given to the traveller,
though she was rather disconcerted by its neat and tidy appearance until she discovered a bathroom built out from the main
building. There she could make what she called her 'awful
messes' with fishes, insects, and reptiles, without compromising
the reputation of the English for cleanliness.

The white people of this remote station consisted of the
missionary, his wife, and their baby daughter, together with
another Frenchman, M. Gacon, and his wife. Mary found the
two young Frenchwomen altogether charming, and their husbands most helpful; she and Oranie, the baby, were soon great
friends, for all babies and children seem to have taken to her on
sight. The rest of the people living there were Africans, several
of whom were lay Bible-readers, whose task it was to visit the
surrounding villages to teach Christianity. All made it a custom
to meet very early in the morning for a service in the pretty
little wooden church. After her first night, Mary was awakened
by a noise which she thought resembled the braying of an
epileptic donkey. Though she learnt that it was caused by the
Africans singing hymns, the din continued to awaken her with a
shock every day she stayed at Talagouga.

On the first day she set about her task of collecting specimens,
and M. Forget spread the news among the surrounding villages
that his visitor was prepared to buy all sorts of fishes. She offered
a good price, and was soon visited by so many Fans, eager to
sell, that there was a serious danger of her running out of bottles

and preserving spirit. Her kind host rescued her from this
predicament by providing pure alcohol from his dispensary. The
bartering with the tribesmen gave her a good deal of fun, and
her meeting the Fans in the way of trade made things easier
for her later, when she came across them during her solitary walks
through the dense forests with which the hillside was clothed.
All Africans, she discovered, were interested in trade and were
eager to buy and sell, no matter how strange the visiting merchant
might be. As soon as she showed them her goods they understood
why she was there, and so were not shocked to see her; while
she grew used to their savage appearance.

Sometimes she needed all her resolution when she was alone
searching for insects, beetles, and snakes. Her way was often
barred by great fallen trees, uprooted by furious tornadoes;
snakes and scorpions made their homes beneath them, and a
careless step meant death. Deeper in the forest, a trail of flattened
undergrowth and a horrid, musky stench would warn her that
she was in the track of a boa-constrictor. On two occasions she
found that she was being stalked by Fan huntsmen, 'Big, lithe
men with their toilet concentrated on their hair.' Luckily these
hunters had so little faith in their ancient guns that they always
got as near as possible to their prey before shooting, and so discovered their error in time. Then they stood and stared at the
strange creature, grunted, uttered a few unintelligible words,
and stalked off.

Fighting her way to the tops of the hills above the mission,
a task more difficult than a twenty-mile journey in the forests
of Old Calabar, she was rewarded by magnificent views of the
Sierra del Cristal range of mountains with the grim forests
stretching away below her. She learnt to catch snakes with a
forked stick, concentrating on catching their heads between the
prongs and disregarding the whisking tails which wound round
her wrist. One snake, indeed, had to be avoided, for in the dim
light of the forest there was no certainty of telling its head from
its tail, and it was very poisonous. Once or twice she took a rest
from collecting specimens, and, in company with Forget, crossed
the Ogowe by canoe and visited the Fans who lived on Talagouga
island. The missionary showed her the site of a village which
until a short time before had been the home of pygmies.

On the afternoon following one of her encounters with

hunters on the hillside, when she needed a change from the menacing forest, she determined to learn how to control an African canoe. To glide about at will on the dark, rushing river, as the Igalwas and the Fans did, would be most exciting. So, first making sure the Forgets and the Gacons were out of the way, for she knew that they would try to stop her, she moved furtively to the bank where the canoes were drawn up, and, choosing the smallest one, launched it. Two promontories ran out into the river from the mission beach, and between them was an expanse of slack water where she thought she could safely practise steering. She knelt in the bows of the unstable dugout and found this a fairly simple art. Her craft, however, moved forward at only a snail's pace, and she was working so hard to increase its speed that she failed to notice she was approaching the main current. Looking up at the last moment, she realized her danger, and paddled furiously to turn her canoe. But it was fifteen feet long, and as the stern swung round, the current got hold of it, dragging the canoe round and round and finally sweeping it downstream.

Fortunately a big tree, which had got lodged against a projecting rock, caught her craft as it moved swiftly along, and Mary was able to haul it to safety. Undeterred by this frightening experience, she determined to try again, from a position in the stern this time. Cries from the bank attracted her attention as she began cautiously to move into her new position. Mme Forget, Mme Gacon, M. Gacon, and a crowd of mission children yelled frantically to her to hold on until help came. Disregarding their advice, she thrust the canoe from the rock where it was wedged and drove it towards the nearest point of the bank. She reached it safely, made the boat fast, and confronted her friends.

'You'll be drowned,' they said.

'Gracious goodness!' said she, 'I thought that half an hour ago, but it's all right now I can steer.'

She persuaded them to let her go on with her new sport, and, kneeling in the stern, which they told her was the only place for a single paddler, she pushed off once more. She could soon steer, and moved forward quite quickly. Suddenly the current seized her a second time, but by some 'very showy, high-class steering' she got back into the slack water, and finally paddled her canoe to the place from which she had originally taken it. Later on, when she had time to spare at Lambaréné, she went on with her canoeing studies

in pursuit of the attainment of pace. Success crowned my efforts, and I can honestly and truly say that there are only two things that I am proud of—one is that Dr. Gunther has approved of my fishes, and the other is that I can paddle an Ogowe canoe, pace, style, steering and all, as if I were an Ogowe African.

Her hosts were kind, there were strange Africans to study, and new specimens to collect; yet Mary was not content. Perhaps the grim forest and the dark, swift river oppressed her spirits. Certainly the mission station, deep in the gorge of the Ogowe, never sweetened by the feeblest breeze, became for her a melancholy place of imprisonment and she began to make plans to leave. She intended to ascend the Ogowe, into the regions where the French had little or no control, and where she would be far from missionary influences. The two Frenchmen advised her not to go: apart from the danger of the rapids, there was the likelihood that she would fall into the hands of the up-river Fans, who were treacherous, untamed cannibals. If she came to any harm, the French authorities might avenge her, but they would be powerless to help her. Mary was prepared to take this risk and at last persuaded Forget to write a letter to the French officials at Njole on her behalf. Then she offered a hundred francs to anyone who would provide a canoe and a crew, for whose wages and food she would be responsible.

Gacon offered her a strong, heavily built canoe, with a crew of two Igalwas. Eight men at least, however, were necessary to paddle and pole such a craft through the rapids, so the Frenchman tried hard to find six Fans who were prepared to make the journey. Mary, delighted, packed her small portmanteau, bought some trade goods, borrowed hairpins from Mme Forget and prepared to set out. Then came disappointment: no Fans could be found who dared to go above Njole; all were certain that they would be killed and eaten by the Fans of the upper river. Not deterred, Mary at last found six Igalwas whom she persuaded to start on the hazardous journey, and without losing a moment she set out for Njole.

Seating herself on her portmanteau, with her back against

the box in which her trade goods were packed, she said good-bye to her friends, who were sad at parting, and obviously afraid that she might never return. Though their gloom, and the threat of a rain-storm, did not make her change her mind, Mary was very depressed as M'bo, the head man, standing in the bows of the canoe, gave orders to his crew to push off into the stream of the Ogowe. She sat just behind him, while behind her six Igalwas paddled, and Pierre, the second in command, stood in the stern and steered. The craft in which she sat was roomy and looked as though it would stand a lot of knocking about in the rapids before it sank. Stem and stern were exactly the same, a fact which puzzled Mary until she reached the rough water, when she soon saw the advantages of its unusual shape, for then the Ogowe, in its fiercer moments, pounced on her craft and took control, and its crew were liable to find, without a moment's warning, that they were going rapidly backwards. They thereupon turned about and, steering and paddling vigorously, usually managed to avoid the rocks with which the bed of the river was studded.

The rain came, soaking them to the skin. Her men, after paddling on for some miles, tied up to a bank to rob a plantation of a supply of stout poles, which would be needed higher up when paddles became ineffective. When they set off again it was clear that the crew had 'the grumbles'. Mary asked what was troubling them, very much afraid that their courage was deserting them at the prospect of facing the rapids and the cannibal Fans. It was a relief to learn that their only complaint was that they had nothing tasty to eat; they had brought plenty of plantain, but no fish or meat to eat with it. When she promised that on reaching Njole she would buy as much meat as they could wish for, their eyes sparkled, and they sang as they drove the canoe upstream.

Unfortunately, Pélessier, who Mary felt understood her, was away when she went ashore, and she had to try to persuade two minor officials, neither of whom knew English, to give her permission to proceed. Pierre knew enough English to act as interpreter, and Forget's letter had some effect, but they were still very unwilling to take responsibility for her safety beyond Njole. Mary declared that no one but herself need be held responsible, and reminded them that a lady, Mme Quinée, had ascended the rapids before her. To this the senior official replied

G

that that lady had been accompanied by her husband and many
Adoomas, a race familiar with the rapids.

'True, O King!' she retorted through her interpreter, 'but
Madame Quinée went right up to Lestourville, whereas I only
want to go sufficiently high up the rapids to get typical fish.
And these Igalwas are great men at canoe work, and can go in a
canoe anywhere that any mortal man can go.' The last part of
this speech was put in to cheer up her interpreter; then she
went on to make the main point: 'As for [having] a husband,
neither the Royal Geographical Society's list, in their *Hints to
travellers*, nor Messrs. Silver, in their elaborate list of articles
necessary for a traveller in tropical climates, make mention of
husbands.'

Realizing that they had met more than their match in this
strange Englishwoman, the officials gave way gracefully, but
they parted with her in a sad manner as 'with one bent on self-
destruction'.

Mary now tried in vain to keep her promise to buy meat or
fish for her crew, for neither Hatton and Cookson's nor the other
English firm, John Holt's, had any in stock. When as a last
resort she tried the French store, a very amiable trader let her
have as much meat as she wanted, and gave her some delightful
bread biscuits into the bargain. M'bo and his men beamed with
satisfaction, and carried off their 'chop' to the canoe. Mary,
however, was disconcerted when she found that the trader
would not let her pay for it. It is typical of her that as soon as he
was engaged with another customer, she hastily bought some
trade goods and paid for them over the counter.

Njole was the last white station for five hundred miles, but
the little party set off in cheerful spirits. They were drying
fast from their late soaking; she was now looking forward to new
experiences, and the Igalwas to a tasty meal. A few miles above
Njole the river began to narrow, the current to flow more swiftly,
and the mountains to close in. They faced their first rapid at
the end of two hours' paddling. Rising from the river bed ahead
were great, grey-black masses of rock, washed smooth by the
swirling water. They crept along close to the right-hand bank,
codging out of the way of the swiftest current. When they were
unable to force their way round projecting parts of the bank, the
crew paddled and poled as far as possible, yelling and shouting at

the top of their voices, then M'bo bellowed, 'Jump for bank, sar!' and Mary stood up and jumped, followed by half the crew.

In her journal she describes how they rounded one great rock:

One appalling corner I shall never forget, for I had to jump at a rock wall, and hang on to it in a manner more befitting an insect than an insect-hunter, and then scramble up into a close-set forest, heavily burdened with boulders of all sizes. . . . While I was engaged in climbing across these promontories, the crew would be busy shouting and hauling the canoe round the point by means of the stout chain provided for such emergencies fixed to the bow. When this was done, in we got again and paddled away until we met our next affliction.

In this way Mary's Igalwas made progress through the lower rapids, but she knew that ahead of them the Ogowe swirled and foamed with a fury compared with which the present rush of waters was a mere English mill stream. She was wet through again, tired from her frequent scrambles over difficult ground, and a little scared, for this was a new game that she played and a slip might well be fatal. Yet the contest was exhilarating, and when they reached the first Fan village, where they had been assured of a friendly reception and had planned to spend the night, she decided that as there were still some hours of daylight left, she would go on to a village higher up.

They tied up to the bank, however, to ask about the Fans who lived upstream. From the low, bark huts of the village along the river front, the excited inhabitants, who had been watching their approach, charged down to greet these unusual visitors. All shouted and gesticulated at the same time, and Mary was beginning to give up hope of learning anything from the yelling mob, when a chief pushed his way to the front, and, silencing his people with his vehement 'Azuna! Azuna!', gave a frightening and probably scandalous account of the villages farther upstream. He did, however, show the position of these villages by means of an ingenious diagram, consisting of pieces of plantain leaves placed on the gunwale of the canoe to represent the size and distance apart of the next five settlements. In his opinion, only the fourth village was safe to land at, all the others were wicked, and neither Mary nor her property would be safe there.

Nowhere in her travels did Mary find Fans with a good word to say for their neighbours.

When the chief had been rewarded with a head of tobacco, and a hymn tune from M'bo and Pierre, the Igalwas pushed off and paddled swiftly upstream to impress the Fans. They were not to get out of sight of the village in this dignified way, however. They had paddled no more than two hundred yards when a current, swirling round the end of a reef of rocks, proved too strong for them. Mary's account of the incident shows the delight she took in making fun of her adventures:

On to the bank I was ordered and went; it was a low slip of rugged, confused boulders and fragments of rocks, carelessly arranged and evidently under water in the wet season; I scrambled along, the men yelled and shouted and hauled the canoe, and the inhabitants of the village, seeing we were becoming amusing again, came, legging it like lamp-lighters, after us, young and old, male and female, to say nothing of the dogs. Some good souls helped the men haul, while I did my best to amuse the others by diving headlong from a large rock on to which I had elaborately climbed, into a thick clump of willow-leaved shrubs. They applauded my performance vociferously, and then assisted my efforts to extricate myself, and during the rest of my scramble they kept close to me, with keen competition for the front row, in hopes that I would do something like it again. But I refused the *encore*, because, bashful as I am, I could not but feel that my last performance was carried out with all the superb, reckless *abandon* of a Sarah Bernhardt, and a display of art of this order should satisfy any African village for a year at least. At last I got across the rocks to a lovely little beach of white sand, and stood there talking, surrounded by my audience, until the canoe got over its difficulties and arrived almost as scratched as I; and then we again said farewell and paddled away, to the great grief of the natives, for they don't get a circus up above Njole every week, poor dears.

It was a long time before they saw the first village of the chief's chart; it took even longer to reach village number two, and by the time they saw number three perched high on a hillside, it was getting dark and the water was more turbulent than ever. Anxiously they looked for the fourth village, but in vain, for suddenly the darkness came. Now only the light of the stars showed the flying foam of the rapids around them. Great trees that had fallen into the water, thrust out at them; rocks materialized out of the blackness ahead a mere second before the canoe struck them. Paddling and poling strenuously, they moved slowly forward.

By nine-thirty they had seen no fires to guide them to a village. Suddenly, on rounding a bend, they found themselves in a savage rapid. They fought hard; the canoe jammed itself on some sunken rocks; they shoved it over them; whereupon the boat tilted over and threw them out. They righted their canoe and drove on again, until suddenly a pole and a paddle snapped at the same moment. The current instantly took control:

We had to go down for shelter somewhere, anywhere, and down at a terrific pace in the white water we went. While hitched among the rocks the arrangement of our crew had been altered, Pierre joining M'bo in the bows; this piece of precaution was frustrated by our getting turned round; so our position was what you might call precarious, until we got into another whirlpool, when we persuaded nature to start us right end on. This was only a matter of minutes, whirlpools being plentiful, and then M'bo and Pierre, provided with our surviving poles, stood in the bows to fend us off rocks, as we shot towards them; while we midship paddlers sat, helping to steer, and, when occasion arose, which occasion did with lightning rapidity, to whack the whirlpools with the flat of our paddles, to break their force. Cook crouched in the stern concentrating his mind on steering only. A most excellent arrangement in theory and the safest practical one no doubt, but it did not work out what you might call brilliantly well; though each department did its best. We dashed full tilt towards high rocks, things twenty to fifty feet above the water. Midship backed and flapped like fury; M'bo and Pierre received the shock on their poles; sometimes we glanced successfully aside and flew on; sometimes we didn't. The shock being too much for M'bo and Pierre they were driven back on me, who got flattened on to the cargo of bundles which, being now firmly tied in, couldn't spread the confusion further aft; but the shock of the canoe's nose against the rock did so in style, and the rest of the crew fell forward on to the bundles, me, and themselves. So shaken up together were we several times that night, that it's a wonder to me, considering the hurry, that we sorted ourselves out correctly with our own particular arms and legs. And though we in the middle of the canoe did some very spirited flapping, our whirlpool breaking was no more successful than M'bo and Pierre's fending-off, and many a wild waltz we danced that night with the waters of the river Ogowe.

For more than an hour the river swept them downstream in this terrifying way, until at last a stray current landed them hard on a black reef of rock. Since all their efforts failed to get the canoe afloat again, they decided to try to reach a dark mass of land looming up near at hand out of the river. Scrambling and climbing over boulders, wading waist-deep in the rushing water, and paddling across sandy beaches, they at last got ashore. M'bo decided there must be a village nearby, and led his party up a steep hillside, encumbered with rocks and thick forest. When they reached the top they saw fires, heard the sound of a drum, and, as they descended, saw almost-naked, vermilion-painted Africans dancing enthusiastically to the rhythm thumped out on the drum. Two head men, dressed in old French military coats, made the party welcome and put Mary in possession of what she thought must have been the remains of the village club-house.

The whole village sadly needed repairs, for its low huts, built of palms and brush, were very squalid. Mary learnt that its people were Adoomas, a tribe whose territory lies in the Congo region south-west of Franceville, and that a few months previously they had been attacked by their Fan neighbours. Several of the Adoomas had been killed and eaten, and the rest had fled to the settlement at Njole for protection. In due course the French had sent a punitive column against the Fans, whose village had been burnt. Now the Adoomas had established themselves once more on Kembe Island, but they had not yet had time to rebuild their huts.

When she had eaten the meal prepared by Isaaco, the cook, Mary, tired as she was, walked down to the shore to look again at the majestic scene. The moon was rising and the peaks of the Sierra del Cristal, surrounded by wreaths and clouds of silver-grey mist, were silhouetted against the sky. Thousands of fire-flies flitted around her, the white foam of the rapids danced before her eyes, and their thunder filled her ears. As she stood entranced, she seemed to 'lose all sense of human individuality, all memory of human life, with its grief and worry and doubt, and become part of the atmosphere'. Africa had this power over her, and once she had felt its sway she could never escape.

She was roused sharply from her reverie by an agonized scream which pierced the roar of the rapids. Fearing that one of her men had been speared, she hurried in the direction from which the shriek had come. But the Adoomas, who had resumed their dancing, were not responsible; one of the Igalwas, worn out by his labours in the rapids, had fallen asleep too near the fire, and a flame had run along the log on which he sat and burnt him. She left him cooling himself in a pool of water, entered her hut, which consisted of little more than a few upright poles supporting a roof, and, creeping under her mosquito net on to a hard wood bench, read herself to sleep with her old, damp *Horace*, which accompanied her throughout her travels. Once during the night she awoke, to find that she had rolled off the bench right outside the hut. Fortunately there were no mosquitoes, and she returned to sleep soundly until six o'clock.

Her men were up early, cutting new poles to replace those they had lost on the previous day. Soon they had refloated the canoe, and set off with an Adooma as pilot. As they paddled, the Igalwas sang M'pangwe songs, in which each singer takes up a verse, boasting of his wives and his possessions, and poking fun at his less fortunate friends. Since the tune never varied, the best singer was the man who made up the most humorous or the most exciting verses. This pleasant way of passing the time was interrupted by a current, 'a quiet devil of a thing', which caught the nose of their canoe as they rounded a corner, swept them right across the river, and upset them among rocks over which the water surged and boiled. Up to their knees in water, hardly able to keep their footing in the torrent, they at last managed to shove their craft off again and returned to 'have it out with that current'. They won, and poled and paddled upstream until they reached a stretch of comparatively still water, with the main current hurrying past close to the opposite bank. As they passed a little bay they saw Fan women breaking up a stockaded fish-trap, and the paddlers rested while Mary talked to the women and bought some of their fish.

In this way she and her hard-working crew forced their way slowly up the Ogowe, with a current or a rapid doing its best to hurl them back every mile or so. Up the rapids of Boko Boko, past the entrance of the Okana River, through whirlpools and slooping, black sheets of water they pushed and paddled until they reached the island of Kondo Kondo, where Mary decided to stay for a while. There she saw the superb Alemba rapid thundering down past the northern shore of the island, and there she was so successful in her fishing that Gunther was delighted with the specimens which she sent to him on her return.

It was while she was in these upper reaches of the Ogowe that the dangers of living with the up-river Fans were brought home to her forcefully. She had made friends with three daring ivory hunters of the Ajumba tribe, and persuaded them to take her with them on one of their business trips. They agreed to convey her and her few trade goods in their canoe to a village, to give her an excellent character to the chiefs of that village, and to leave her there until their return. She paid them well to make sure that their testimonial would be entirely satisfactory. She described this excursion in a lecture:

They duly took me, gave the village the idea that I was *just* the sort of thing to improve the local society tone, and left me. I was horribly nervous when they did, for on our way up to it we had come across a gentleman who danced and howled on the bank, and wanted to sell something badly as we were a trading company. We went for him like an arrow, thinking it might be a tooth—an elephant's I mean, not his own. It wasn't—it was a leg—not his own either, but the leg of a gentleman of some kind. This upset my companions and made them sick, and it and their conversation on those Fans which followed, made me nervous.

The first night, however, that I was there, something happened. It was just before what we call out there *the second making-up of the fire*, say 3.30 a.m. The moon had been shining, but had set, and so it was inky dark, when there came a tremendous bellow and a crash. The whole line of huts, in one of which I was, was shaken and wrenched off the ground, which quivered in rapid pulsations; then came another crash, quicker than one can say, and another bellow, and a something went tearing away into the dense, high, dark forest that surrounded the village. I need hardly say the Fans were by this time in the street with lights, to see what had happened.

What had happened was plain enough. That something had torn its way right through the village at the further end, smashing down the frail huts and scattering the people in them, and their possessions. What had done it of course the Fans knew, but I did not for a time, because they were too busy yelling and using bad language against the thing to tell me. The families whose homes had been broken up were taken in by their neighbours for the night, and the row was just commencing to subside, and I was making my mind up to go indoors, when again came the bellow and the crash and the earth quiver, and right through the south end of the village an immense hippopotamus tore full tilt, and went splash into the river. The animal was about twelve feet long, and bulky as a small elephant, and weighed a ton or two.

Of course this quite took up the rest of the night, and was not done by breakfast time. Meantime I learnt that it is the habit of these great river beasts to come out of the river at night and go and feed on the natives' farms, if there were any handy; and as each hippopotamus's stomach holds between five and six bushels, they cause an acute form of agricultural depression. They are also very nervous creatures and prone to get flurried when on land, and now and again, when the moon has gone down on them while away destroying crops, one of them gets separated from the others; it loses its head and its way, and dashes to and fro until the daylight comes. If you can picture to yourself a furniture van in hysterics, you will realize the sort of thing that went through that unfortunate village in the middle of the night.

The next morning the Fans turned their attention to me, and started selling to me their store of elephant tusks and india-rubber. I did not want those things then, but still felt too nervous of the Fans to point this out firmly, and so had to buy. I made it as long an affair as I could, and was very frightened all the time I was doing it, because I had given my word to the black and white traders not to spoil prices, namely, not to raise prices by giving more than the customary value, and I gradually found myself the proud owner of balls of rubber and a tooth or so, and alas! my little stock of cloth and tobacco all going fast. Now, to be short of money anywhere is bad, but to be short of money in a Fan village is extremely bad, because these Fans, when a trader has no more goods to sell them, are liable to start trade all over again by killing him, and taking back their ivory and rubber and keeping it until another trader comes along. So I kept my eye up-river most anxiously on the look-out for my black-trader friends' canoe, and for days in vain. All my trade stuff was by now exhausted, and I had to start selling my own belongings, and for the first time in my life I felt the want of a big outfit.

My own clothes I certainly did insist on having more for, pointing out that they were rare and curious. A dozen white ladies' blouses sold well, I cannot say they looked well when worn by a brawny warrior in conjunction with *nothing* else but red paint and a bunch of leopard tails, particularly when the warrior failed to tie the strings at the back. But I did not hint at this, and I *quite* realize that a pair of stockings can be made to go further than we make them by using one at a time and putting the top part over the head and letting the rest of the garment float in the breeze. But I had too few, and they were all gone before that canoe came; indeed, everything but what I stood up in was. The last thing I parted with was my tooth-brush, and the afternoon that it had gone, down came the canoe, just as I was making up my mind to set up in business as a witch-doctor. The black traders said they were very pleased to see me again, but I should have a very hard time if I came down with them, because *they* also had sold right out, and therefore dare not call at any village before reaching the main river. I said 'Oh, don't mention that, *pray*, I'll come with you,' and to the grief of those Fans I left them.

They did indeed have a hard time on the return journey to the Ogowe; they could only travel at night for fear of being seen, and had to lie hidden in great beds of water reeds during the day. Here they were profoundly uncomfortable, for the reed-beds were infested with flies, the traders' ivory stank, and the moist heat was almost intolerable. At night they glided ghost-like with the current, hardly daring to paddle lest they should attract the attention of any wakeful villager. Thus they made their way down the deep, narrow river, between the heavily forested mountain walls of the Sierra del Cristal, drifting in darkness past villages where Africans danced by the light of fires and to the thumping of drums, until at last they reached the main stream and safety.

9

THE LOWER OGOWE

THE fight with the rapids of the Ogowe, which had been such an exciting experience for Mary, was followed by one of those 'odd jobs' which were always coming her way. On returning to Talagouga, she found both her friends sick with fever—Forget very ill indeed—and she immediately undertook the task of nursing them and of keeping things going at the mission. Fortunately relief came quickly. Pélessier arrived on the *Éclaireur* and prescribed for the missionaries, and within a few days Mme Forget had recovered, and her husband's health was sufficiently restored for Mary to leave Talagouga, which held no further attractions for her.

On board the *Éclaireur*, Verdier and his engineer were in excellent spirits. The captain's English was improving so fast that he was able to enjoy several fierce arguments with his passenger. Their craft, with the current under it, swept along swiftly and without effort, with just enough power from her motors to give her steerage way. But the cruise was not to be entirely without incident. Mary was seated in her cabin engaged in sewing her skirt, which had been badly torn in her adventures in the rapids, when she was startled by an 'inchoate howl of agony' which rent the heavy, hot, afternoon air. Dropping her needlework, she hurried on deck—only to find that the noise came from the cabin of the engineer, who was practising on his clarionet.

A few minutes later, the captain roused the ship with the shout, 'Hippopotame!' Mary had become used to this yell on her way upstream and she expected the two white men to rush for their rifles and to open fire. Nothing of the sort happened, however; nor was there any sign of a hippopotamus in the water. As she leaned over the rail, the captain hurriedly sent off a crew of Africans in the canoe which the *Éclaireur* was towing alongside. Unable to restrain her curiosity she asked him where the beast was. He pointed to four stumps showing above the water some distance away, and told her that these were doubtless the legs of a hippopotamus which the engineer had fired at on the way up.

After a great struggle, they hauled the carcass of this beast aboard. Mary subsequently described the scene which followed:

My esteemed friends, the captain and the engineer, who of course had been below during this hauling, now rush on to the upper deck, each coatless and carrying an enormous butcher's knife. They dash into the saloon, where a terrific sharpening of these instruments takes place on the steel belonging to the saloon carving-knife, and down-stairs again. By looking down the ladder, I can see the pink, pig-like hippo, whose colour has been soaked out by the water lying on the lower deck and the captain and engineer slitting down the skin intent on gralloching operations. Providentially my prophetic soul induces me to leave the top of the ladder and go forward—'run to win'ard' as Captain Murray would say,—for within two minutes the captain and engineer were up the ladder as if they had been blown up by the boilers bursting, and go as one man for the brandy bottle; and they wanted it if ever man did; for remember that hippo had been dead in the warm river-water for more than a week. The captain had had enough of it, he said, but the engineer stuck to the job with a courage I profoundly admire, and he saw it through and then retired to his cabin; sand-and-canvassed himself first, and then soaked and saturated himself in Florida water. The flesh gladdened the hearts of the crew and lower-deck passengers and also of the inhabitants of Lambaréné who got dashes of it on our arrival there.

This arrival was made in darkness, and Mary was unable to rejoin the Jacots at Kangwe. Another night on the comfortable little steamer was no hardship, though once she was awakened by the sound of dismal wails coming from the large Igalwa village off which the *Éclaireur* was anchored. She feared that murder was being done. No one else on board seemed to have been awakened, or, at any rate, no one showed any interest, and when the disturbing noise died down Mary fell asleep again.

In the morning a canoe took her across to the mission settle-ment where Jacot gave her a warm welcome. Looking out of the window of her room, she was surprised to see a great, grace-ful palm-frond sticking out of the water opposite the mission beach. After a few days she realized that it marked the position of a delightful sand-bank, which gradually made its appearance as the water of the river fell. At last, acres of it were bare, and canoe-loads of African boys and girls made their way there to use it as a playground. They spent their time fishing, washing, singing, and just lounging on the golden sand during the day, and at night, dancing in the moonlight with bush-torches in their hands.

Mme Jacot, who was normally so busy that she had no time to sit down during the day, now found time to take her sewing on to the verandah. Frequently Mary caught her gaze stealing towards the new island. The missionary's wife disapproved of the singing and dancing—for the *Mission Évangelique* was a Presbyterian body and held the firm belief that light-hearted happiness and idleness afforded opportunities to the devil—yet she seemed fascinated by what she saw. Mary asked her why she was so interested in the sand-bank and the children.

'It is such a relief,' replied Mme Jacot.

'A relief?' asked Mary.

The missionary's wife replied with an unusual display of feeling: 'Yes, do you not see that until it shows, there is nothing but forest, forest, forest, and that still stretch of river. That bank is the only piece of clear ground I see in the year, and that only lasts a few weeks until the wet season comes, and then it goes, and there is nothing but forest, forest, forest, for another year. It is two years now since I came to this place; it may be I know not how many more before we go home again.'

Although Mary thought that all missions to Africa on balance did more harm than good, she became deeply attached to many of the missionaries whom she met, and even when she subsequently spoke her mind frankly about their work, she showed only admiration for the men and women who, however misguidedly, risked their lives for the cause they believed in. Dennis Kemp of the Gold Coast became a very close friend; for Nassau of Gaboon and Forget of Talagouga she had great respect, and Jacot in her opinion had a greater influence over the Africans than any other missionary she had met. She was impressed by the amount of work done by members of the *Mission Évangelique* at Lambaréné, and her description of their activities is of particular interest since it was to this outpost that Dr. Schweitzer came, eighteen years later, to devote his life to looking after the bodily welfare of the tribes of the Ogowe.

Not content with running a school and holding services in their own chapel, the missionaries travelled over vast areas, making converts amongst some of the most predatory and uncivilized tribes in Africa. They frequently spent weeks away from home on the rivers of this wild, dangerous country. The missionary in charge trained African Christians, who in their turn went out amongst the neighbouring tribesmen. The protection of these preachers was a heavy strain on the white staff, for they were more likely to be attacked and killed than was a Frenchman, who would be promptly avenged by the government.

Running a store was an essential part of the Mission, for since there was no native currency on the Ogowe, all the African evangelists, black Bible-readers, and labourers on the station had to be paid in kind. Storekeeping involved a great deal of hard, tedious, and unrewarding work. The Africans who came to be paid for their goods or services found it very difficult to make up their minds what goods to accept, yet they demanded immediate attention. While the storekeeper was attending to one man, another was liable to help himself to anything that could be secreted on his person. In addition, the goods in the store had to be constantly protected from mildew and white ants.

The mission schools, in Mary's opinion, were a failure. They did not, with few exceptions, teach the boys and girls technical subjects: all the instruction the boys got was religious and scholastic, and the missionary's wife wasted her time teaching sewing, ironing, and good-housekeeping to girls who, on their return to their families or their husbands, would live in a one-roomed hut, and own at most one dress which had to serve a number of purposes. Africa needed planters and farmers, not clerks, and it was the last that most of the schools produced. Perhaps the saddest aspect of all this education was commented on by Dr. Schweitzer; the African who was educated along European lines became, in effect, a stateless person; he could find neither wife nor friend amongst his uneducated tribesmen— for their habits and their ways of thought were now distasteful to him—nor was he accepted as a fellow citizen by the whites among whom he lived and worked.

Mary was not content to stay for long at the mission station, and was soon to be seen, in a little canoe which she had procured, setting out on short exploratory voyages on the Ogowe. She ventured out into the main current of the river to reach Lambaréné Island, and before she had become fully mistress of her craft she had several misadventures. On one occasion she was swept right past the island and was in imminent danger of drowning; on another she had to threaten with her paddle an elderly Fan, who had found her drifting downstream and considered that he had a perfect right to tow her to his village for the entertainment of his friends. He saw by her determined manner that he had made a mistake, and landed her on the island.

Meanwhile she had not forgotten the main object of her journey to Africa. She began to make a careful study of the Igalwas who lived on Lambaréné Island. She admired their neat houses, built of bamboo, and fitted with windows and shutters to close at night; their clean, sandy streets—so different from the filthy, malodorous paths of a Fan village—where the men sat and talked while the women and slaves worked; and, above all, the beauty of the African women she saw there. She declared she was prepared 'to back them against any of those South Sea Island young ladies we nowadays hear so much about, thanks to Mr Stevenson, yea, even though these may be wreathed with fragrant flowers'.

She learned a lot about the customs of this tribe. Marriage, she found, was not by direct purchase, but necessitated from the suitor a certain fixed present to the bride's mother and uncle, a present which had to be returned if the pair were divorced. This was a frequent occurrence, for Igalwa women were determined 'naggers', and their exasperated husbands sometimes went too far in attempting to curb their tongues. They could by custom thrash their wives, but if they chanced to draw blood, the wife had the right to return to her own people. Mary discovered that the screams that had so disturbed her sleep when she lay off the island in the *Éclaireur*, had been made by one of these Igalwa wives receiving punishment. Recently infant marriage had been introduced among the Igalwas. Mary, in her common-sense way, was not in the least shocked: she merely attributed the popularity of the new arrangement to the inherent laziness of the African male. He no longer had to dress himself in his best, or to run the risk of having to fight a rival, or even to expose himself to the dangers of the night to serenade his mistress; he simply chose some little girl of four or five, came to an agreement with her parents, married her, and waited patiently for her to reach mature years.

The laws and beliefs of the Ogowe Africans were studied by Mary. Secret societies have always played an important part in African life, and she had a chance to experience how one of them functioned while she was at Lambaréné. Jacot had fallen ill and was confined to his bed, when word came from a village on the River Orimbo Vungo—a branch of the Ogowe, which at Lambaréné is a system of rivers rather than a single stream—that two Africans had been condemned to death by the tribal secret society, the Ukukar. In his feverish state, the missionary was so distressed at learning this that his wife feared for his life. Without hesitation, Mary offered to do what she could to save the lives of the two condemned people, and immediately set out for the village in a canoe manned by mission Africans. Though he lived and worked in one of the most dangerous parts of French Congo, Jacot had never called in the help of the French authorities, nor had he ever caused a gun to be fired at another man. Force, then, was out of the question. Moreover, Mary learned that the French gun-boat was far away, a fact which was known to all the surrounding tribesmen. She had to rely on her own resources entirely.

When she reached the village she demanded to see the head man of the tribal society. She thereupon had 'twenty-four hours of the very hottest [argument]' with this man who was the local representative of the Ukukar, which ruled the Igalwa. At the end of this fight, she left with the two condemned Africans in her canoe, and made the best speed she could to her friends at Kangwe. In a lecture to an English audience, years later, she gave the following modest reasons for her success:

As to how I did it, well, I did not take the missionary's name in vain, or the French government's. I worked it on my own responsibility through the head man of the tribal secret society, by talking over points of his law and by adding to my bill with the local traders. I got criticism, very sharp criticism, from the missionary, for associating with pagan practices, but I got none from his wife. . . .

Mary Kingsley was essentially a woman who did things on her own responsibility.

Meanwhile, the lower reaches of the Ogowe, of which she had caught such a delightful glimpse as she came upstream on the *Mové*, were calling irresistibly. Numbers of smaller rivers poured their waters into the main stream, and opened the way for a bold explorer into a country whose people had rarely or never seen a white face. The most dangerous, and so the most compelling, district lay on the northern bank of the great river. It was here, in Ouronogou, that Mary decided to ask questions about primitive customs and laws, and almost as soon as she arrived she found herself involved in an African law-case.

She had reached Ouronogou country by canoe, with a crew which was frightened and unreliable. They had just paddled into a narrow river when an African appeared on the bank, and, after some dismal howls, fired point-blank at them. Fortunately his weapon was one of the thoroughly inaccurate, useless ones with which most of the delta tribesmen seemed to be armed, and no one was hurt. Mary's crew were badly scared, and started to turn the canoe in order to make a hasty retreat. This was dangerous, for the stranger would have a chance to reload and fire again. Mary made them paddle for the bank as hard as they could, and, on reaching it, she scrambled ashore and made straight for their assailant. He turned and fled, but she caught him, and grabbing hold of his powder bag, brought him to a halt. She demanded to know why he had made his murderous attack on harmless travellers. Her crew, who saw that the danger was past, surrounded him, and one of them acting as interpreter she heard the following explanation:

I found out that the gentleman was suffering from severe domestic affliction and merely wanted to interest our sympathy and help in the affair. You see, one of his wives had run away with a gentleman from another village, and that village was too powerful for his village to tackle on the point right away. Therefore it was necessary for them to get allies, and so according to the custom of the country he lay in wait for any canoe from yet another village to come by and then fired at it. If he killed a member of the canoe crew, the rest of them and the village they belonged to would have to come and help him attack the village of the gentleman who had stolen his wife, and by so doing driven him into shooting one of them—an affair, you see, that was no

H

fault of *his* at all, but entirely *that other man's*. This was so sweetly reasonable that I was charmed with it and moreover I found that it was local law, that if, after being called on to an affair, you refused to act, you became the enemy of both parties concerned in the matter. Therefore I and my crew joined this gentleman's party.

When they reached the injured man's village, Mary found that the elders were strongly in favour of settling the dispute by force of arms now that they had got such valuable reinforcements. Though she was offered the command of the expedition, she was not convinced by their arguments, and came down strongly in favour of arbitration. Every man in her crew, it is true, was armed with a gun, but most of these antiquated weapons were a greater danger to the men who fired than to an enemy; moreover, it became clear during the debate that the tribesmen who were to be attacked had new, effective guns. Through her interpreter, Mary made it quite clear that she had no intention of leading a punitive expedition, and in the end it was decided to open negotiations with the enemy.

There followed a long palaver with the elders of the erring village, at which Mary, as a completely impartial outsider, acted as chief judge. She had to decide on the compensation to be paid, and, although it was an extremely difficult task, for the complainants put a very high price on the eloping wife, extolling her as 'the most precious woman of modern times', and the defendants expressed a very different opinion of her worth, Mary managed to give a judgement which both sides agreed to accept.

She felt that her introduction to the delta tribes was promising: she had learnt that it was impossible to understand or judge the African unless one saw and studied him in his own forest and got below the surface appearance of his actions. Research here would be rewarding, and she made plans to find a village far from the beaten track where she could stay for a while. She gave orders to her canoe-men and they paddled out of the creek, into the main stream of the Ogowe. This time they did not turn into a tributary, but headed into a bay. They appeared to be driving straight for the tall trees which stood like a wall on either side. On they went, however, forcing their way through papyrus reed for an hour or so, until at last they were fairly among the

trees, and Mary saw that there was no bank—the water stretched
on into the gloom and splendour of the forest.

The canoe moved now beneath a dense canopy, a hundred
and fifty feet above their heads. In the dim light, they entered an
enchanted land:

around you on all sides in the green gloom are countless thousands of
grey bare tree-columns, as straight as ships' masts, and between them
a twisted medley of great bare black bush-ropes, looking as if they
were some Homeric battle of serpents that at its height had been fixed
for ever by some magic spell, while beneath you and away into the
shadowed vastness lay the stagnant currentless dark waters, making
a floor for the forest, a floor whose face is like that of a mirror seen in
gloom—dimly showing you the forms outside it, seeming to have in it
images of unknown things.

In this inundated forest Mary found a village, built above
water level on a clay mound, but even so with its huts perched
upon crazy, fragile-looking poles to keep them above the flood-
waters during the rainy season. Fishermen and their wives came
to live there at certain times of the year, leaving their permanent
settlements on the slopes of the mountains some miles away.
No children, chickens, or dogs were to be found there, for at
night crocodiles visited the mud-banks between the poles. On
her first night Mary heard the swish of their tails as she lay down
to sleep, and was afraid they might bring down the huts and their
occupants. Yet, in spite of her fears, and the stink of fish offal,
and the swarms of mosquitoes, Mary was fascinated by these
villages deep in the forest swamp.

The one she had chosen stood amongst the trees which
surrounded a wide lake, and in the morning, while she was still
in darkness, she could look up and see the summit of the mountain in the distance

taking on to itself flushes of amethyst, daffodil and rose, the light of the
dawn, for it comes among us and makes everything glorious with
colour, warmth and beauty, while the night, accompanied by crocodiles, slides away down into the dark waters. . . . It is like a vision of
heaven. It does not last long; the white mists soon curl up out of the
swamp waters around you, and wrap you up in their chill embrace for
hours, and then they fade away and leave you with the grey sky over-
head again, a heavy grey sky that seems to rest on the hilltops during

the dry season, and of course if you are not on a lake you cannot see your vision at all, because you are too shut in, and you only know when the dawn is come by the chill of it and the mist creeping up in the swamp forest round you—coiling and twisting among the tree-tops like vast serpents, playing with the wind as only West African mists can.

She spent some days on the shores of this lake, living with the Africans who had come down for the fishing. In a lecture to the girls of Cheltenham Ladies' College, she gave a lively account of how she spent her time, and it is easy to see why she was such a welcome guest:

While in this country I inadvertently had several collisons with crocodiles. Once an hippopotamus and I were on an island together, and I wanted one of us to leave. I preferred it should be myself, but the hippo was close to my canoe, and looked like staying, so I made cautious and timorous advances to him and finally scratched him behind the ear with my umbrella and we parted on good terms. But with the crocodile it was different.

At one of those Ouronogou villages there was a man named Nohumba who had had three separate wives bitten by one crocodile at different times, when they had been fetching water from the bank-side. I was in touch at the time of catastrophe No. 3, and as I was coming down the hen-roosty ladder from her house after bandaging her up, I saw her husband Nohumba, and I asked him *why* he did not catch the crocodile. He said respectfully there were reasons—his gun.

'Don't so much as mention that gun,' I said, 'after yesterday's performance'—yesterday's performance having been the accidental discharging of that hoary weapon through the bottom of a canoe, whereby I and some more friends of Nohumba's, and that worthy himself, had been near being drowned. 'Catch the crocodile with a hook!'

He grinned and said you could not.

'You're wrong, my friend,' I said, 'it's been done.'

Nohumba became interested. He was getting used to me, and he gleefully suggested *I* should catch that crocodile with a hook.

'Very well,' said I, 'you and half a dozen other men come with me to the pool before sundown.'

I spent the rest of the day cutting wood-hooks, and securing the interior arrangements of a goat that had been killed, and requisitioning the village for its best bush-rope, and a billet of bar-wood to serve as a float, fixing the hooks and the bait on carefully; and sundown found us with our paraphernalia at the pool, making no end of a fuss. Three of us, I being one, got into a canoe with the hook and tackle, leaving the shore end of the bush-rope in charge of the rest of the party on the bank, and having fixed on our bar-wood float, we commenced a wordy discussion as to the best place to sink the bait, so that the crocodile *could not miss* coming across it. We finally hit off the correct spot to a nicety. Before the hooks had touched the thick brown water, the crocodile's jaws rose then and there out of it, and closed over the bait with a snap. We, being severely frightened, automatically hung on to the line; the crocodile gave the swing of the head they always do when seizing things. Over went the canoe, and there we were, crocodile and all, in the water together. Needless to say, before proceeding further with this undertaking, we made for the bank.

On reaching the bank, I said to my companions, 'There, *you* have made a pretty mess of it. Why in the name of common sense didn't you fellows at the shore end of the rope hold on when you saw us upsetting?'

We let the crowd on the bank know, within a little, what we thought of people who just howled and danced when they saw devoted members of society, trying to catch a man-eating crocodile, upset and pretty well killed *through their foolishness*. This being done, I smoothed things over by congratulating everyone on the fact that the principle and practicality of catching crocodiles with hooks were demonstrated; all that was now required was a *little* more caution in the application of the method, and something to kill the crocodile with when it had been caught things we had forgotten before, although we knew what he had swallowed would not even give him indigestion.

The next day I was sent for early to a village to see a man who was ill, and I was away with him all day, not returning to my village until about 11 p.m. When paddling myself along in a tiny one-man canoe up the creek towards home, I heard a sound of revelry by night which astonished me, for my village usually returned to bed about nine o'clock. On arrival I found high festival; they, all alone and by themselves, had caught that crocodile with a hook, and were having some for supper. I was besieged by accounts of the triumph. One gentleman who had a nasty wound from a blow from the crocodile's tail was *the* hero of the evening, and receiving much attention from the ladies, who had done him up with suitable leaves. Nohumba, however, claimed *the* credit of the performance, loudly, in consequence of having shot the crocodile with his gun, the only one in the village. Like *all* great men in Africa, he had his detractors. Particularly critical of his performance was a gentleman who said, 'If Nohumba had emptied his weapon *entirely* into the crocodile instead of partially into it and partially in another gentleman's legs it would have been better.' And considering the trouble it gave me, tired as I was, to extract some of Nohumba's charge from those legs, I quite agreed with him. But on the whole it was a triumph and we rejoiced exceedingly.

This was Mary Kingsley's idea of 'studying and skylarking' in West Africa.

10

THROUGH THE GREAT FOREST

It requires indeed someone who has personally sampled Africa to form a just estimate of the value of certain bits of work from what I may call an artistic standpoint. The 'armchair explorer' may be impressed by the greatness of length of the red line route of an explorer; but the person locally acquainted with the region may know that some of those long red lines are very easily made in Africa—thanks to the exertions of travellers who have gone before or to what one of my German friends once poetically called the lamb-like-calfheadedness of the natives, or to the country itself being of a reasonably traversable nature. In other regions a small red line means four hundred times the work and danger, and requires four thousand times the pluck, perseverance and tact. These regions we may call choice spots.

Needless to say, Mary Kingsley was not directly referring to her own exploration when she wrote these words. She was describing the travels of one of her heroes, De Brazza, whom she considered to be the greatest of all West African explorers. His journeys up the Ogowe and across to the Congo valley combined the 'long line' and the 'choice spots'. Du Chaillu, too, who had preceded him, though he failed to find the Ogowe, spent most of his time in extremely dangerous places. On his return to England in 1861, the latter wrote of his experiences amongst cannibals and gorillas. So many people refused to believe his stories that when Mary followed in his trail she was very careful to omit any mention of her more dangerous adventures lest her book should be read with the same scepticism, and her work as an anthropologist suffer as a result. Yet she claimed that she had never come across anything while in the region through which he travelled which led her to think that he had lied about his experiences.

It was with the object of following in Chaillu's footsteps, and those of De Brazza, that she left her friends at Lambaréné on

July 22nd and, with four Ajumbas as crew, set out to make her way from the Ogowe to the Rembwe River through the Great Forest. Mme Jacot came down to the beach to see them off when they left at two o'clock. As was so often the case when she set out on a journey which she knew to be dangerous, Mary's nerves were stretched to breaking point. She had a headache, and feared that she was in for a bout of fever. There was no turning back, however, and once she was under way, her headache disappeared and the fever never developed.

The Ajumbas were very different men from those with whom she had explored the lower Ogowe. They were traders, who had travelled often among the Fans and who claimed to have friends in the most remote spots. She studied them as she sat in the roomy Aduma canoe in which the first stage of her journey was to be made. They were frightening to look at, but they turned out to be dependable and friendly companions. Mary named them according to her fancy: one, 'a gentlemanly looking man', who wore a grey shirt became 'Grey Shirt'; the second, who was lively and dressed in a singlet, she called 'Singlet'; the third, a thin elderly man who rarely spoke, 'Silence', and the last, 'a strapping big fellow, as black as a wolf's mouth, of gigantic muscular development, and wearing quantities of fetish charms hung about him', she called 'Pagan'. At the last moment she had taken on board Ngouta, an Igalwa, who claimed to be an interpreter, though he proved of little use in that capacity, and a great nuisance on account of his timid and apprehensive nature.

The Ajumbas lived on the western side of Lake Ayzingo, and after some hours' paddling the party waded ashore at one of their towns, Arevooma. Grey Shirt placed his house at Mary's disposal. It was clean and neat, and he and his pretty young wife soon made their guest at home. When she had inspected her room, which contained a chair and a table, she went out again to attend an open-air service. The few Christians of the town howled hymns at the tops of their voices, while the pagans stood round and enjoyed the show. Mary was glad to get back to her lodgings and to climb into the fresh, gaily coloured bed; it was the last she was to sleep in for many days.

In the morning Mary was approached by an African who wished to get work in John Holt's factory on the Rembwe. For weeks he had waited at Arevooma, afraid to take the road between Ayzingo and the Rembwe because of the dreaded Fan villages on the way. Mary allowed him to join her party; but, now that she was meeting people who lived near the Great Forest and had first-hand experience of the Fans, she realized fully the dangers she was braving, and wondered whether she had been foolhardy in disregarding her friends' advice. Grey Shirt assured her that they would avoid the notorious villages, but when she questioned him further, she found that he was staking all on finding some trade friends of his in a village on Lake Ncovi, who he hoped would be able to lead the party by unfrequented routes to the Rembwe. She decided not to turn back, and took her place in the canoe.

Each of her crew had brought with him his best gun, loaded to the muzzle, and tied on to the baggage against which their employer was leaning. She thus sat with muzzles sticking out on each side of her head. With her keen eye for detail, she was quick to observe that these guns were not the crude weapons which she had become accustomed to see; they had been fine rifles, but now the rifling had been filed away, the locks replaced by flint locks, and they were loaded through the muzzle. The locks were covered with sheaths made from the skins of gorillas, leopards, or bush-cow, to protect them from the damp. Thus, fully armed, they paddled into the O'Rembo Vongo, the northerly branch of the Ogowe. This stream soon divided into three channels, of which they entered the one running north and south, named the Karkola, and there, after several hours' journey, they drew their canoe up on to a sand-bank.

When they resumed their voyage, they soon left the Karkola and entered a broad river which ran N.N.E. Seeing a Fan town on the eastern bank, Singlet stated, in anything but a satisfied tone of voice, 'All Fan now.' It was a strange, wild, lonely river, broad, with many islands and sand-banks, and alive with hippopotamuses and crocodiles. One immense hippopotamus heard them approach and stood up in the grass gazing calmly towards them. Then it 'yawned a yard wide and grunted its news to its companions, some of which got up and strolled towards us'. Naturally alarmed, the Ajumbas left that bank hurriedly and, paddling hard, shot down a narrow channel on the other side of the river. They found that this was studded with sand-banks, where sprawled one of the most impressive collections of crocodiles that Mary had ever seen. Poles and paddles were now plied furiously, and in a few moments the new danger was left behind. An enquiry from Mary as to whether gorillas, elephants, and bush-cow also abounded in this country, elicited the disquieting reply, 'Plenty too much!' from Pagan.

The Ajumbas were expert canoe-men and, with the current helping them, drove along at a fine pace, paddling tirelessly hour after hour. By late afternoon they had passed through a lake and into a channel which led north. Suddenly, to Mary's delight, they saw a superb white crane standing on the sandy edge of the stream. Grey Shirt seized his gun, but the bird spread its broad wings and swept away before he could get a shot at it. He put his gun down with its muzzle near Mary's left ear. A moment later the canoe struck a sand-bank. With a roar, the gun emptied its charge within an inch of her head, singeing her hair and deafening her with the blast. Grey Shirt had forgotten to uncock it! Happily the shock of the canoe striking the bank had hurled the rest of the crew down on their faces, and no one received the miscellaneous collection of old iron with which the gun was loaded.

After another hour Mary was beginning to wonder where Grey Shirt intended to spend the night. They had passed out of the channel into a lovely yet melancholy-looking lake. As they glided across the still water, their craft leaving a long trail of frosted silver bubbles behind, Mary was repelled by its sinister charm. Even her men were uneasy, and when Singlet made the observation that he 'smelt blood'—the African equivalent to feeling somebody walk over one's grave—all relieved their feelings by calling him an utter fool. This stretch of water she learned was Lake Ncovi, and on one of its heavily wooded islands stood the town of M'fetta, where Pagan claimed to have a trade friend. They headed for this island, and as they drew nearer, a large village became visible among the trees:

There was evidently some kind of a row going on in that village, that took a lot of shouting too. We made straight for the beach, and drove our canoe among its outlying rocks, and then each of my men stowed his paddle quickly, slung on his ammunition bag, and picked up his ready loaded gun, sliding the skin sheath off the lock. Pagan got out on to the stones alongside the canoe just as the inhabitants became aware of our arrival, and, abandoning what I hope was a mass meeting to remonstrate with the local authorities on the insanitary state of the town, came—a brown mass of naked humanity—down the steep cliff path to attend to us, whom they evidently regarded as an imperial interest. Things did not look restful, nor these Fans personally pleasant. Every man among them—no women showed—was armed with a gun, and they loosened their shovel-shaped knives in their sheathes as they came, evidently regarding a fight as imminent as we did. They drew up about twenty paces from us in silence. Pagan and Grey Shirt, who had joined him, held out their unembarrassed hands, and shouted out the name of the Fan man they had said they were friendly with: 'Kiva—Kiva.'

The Fans stood still and talked angrily among themselves for some minutes, and then, Silence said to me, 'It would be bad palaver if Kiva no live for this place,' in a tone which conveyed to me the idea he thought this unpleasant contingency almost a certainty. The Passenger exhibited unmistakable symptoms of wishing he had come by another boat.

I got up from my seat in the bottom of the canoe and leisurely strolled ashore, saying to the line of angry faces 'M'boloani' in an unconcerned way, although I well knew it was etiquette for them to salute first. They grunted, but did not commit themselves further. A minute after, they parted to allow a fine-looking, middle-aged man, naked save for a twist of dirty cloth round his loins and a bunch of leopard and wild-cat tails hung from his shoulder by a strip of leopard skin, to come forward. Pagan went for him with a rush, as if he were going to clasp him to his ample bosom, but holding his hands just off from touching the Fan's shoulder in the usual way, while he said in Fan, 'Don't you know me, my beloved Kiva? Surely you have not forgotten your old friend?' Kiva grunted feelingly, and raised up his hands and held them just off touching Pagan, and we breathed again. Then Grey Shirt made a rush at the crowd and went through great demonstrations of affection with another gentleman whom he recognized as being a Fan friend of his own, and whom he had not expected to meet here. I looked round to see if there was not any Fan from the Upper Ogowe whom I knew to go for, but could not see one that I could on the strength of a previous acquaintance, and on their individual merits I did not feel inclined to do even this fashionable imitation embrace. Indeed I must say that never—even in a picture book— have I seen such a set of wild, wicked-looking savages as those we faced this night, and with whom it was touch-and-go for twenty of the longest minutes I have ever lived, whether we fought—for our lives, I was going to say, but it would not have been for that, but merely for the price of them.

The Fans decided to receive this strange traveller and her
band peacefully, and after Pagan's and Grey Shirt's friends had
been formally introduced to her, the whole party headed for the
village. Though she was surrounded by scores of inquisitive
Africans, not a hand touched Mary as she made her awe-inspiring
entry into the main street. Children screamed with fright and
fled into the nearest hut, while their mothers, torn between
fright and curiosity, now pressed forward, now drew back
from danger. When they reached the palaver house, Mary made
it known that she wanted hospitality for the night and three
carriers to show her the way to the Rembwe.

The lively, excitable, and quick-tempered Fans entered into
the negotiation with tremendous zest. For an hour and three-
quarters Mary stood in the suffocating, smoky atmosphere
listening to, but only vaguely understanding, the war of words
and gesture that raged around her. At last she was escorted to the
hut of Grey Shirt's friend: a poor place, its roof no higher than
her head and its entire accommodation consisting of one room,
fourteen feet square, unlit by any window. The floor was sand,
the smoke from the fire found its way out through the roof,
while her bed consisted of a rough bench of wood, with a
few filthy cloths and a wooden pillow on it. Grey Shirt explained
that this was the best hut in the village and that her host, Kiva,
was the most renowned elephant hunter in the district.

The goods were brought up from the canoe, and, while
Ngouta made her tea, the bargaining for carriers continued.
When Pagan told her that the last palaver he had talked with
Fans had lasted for three weeks, she issued an ultimatum: the
price offered was for a start in the morning; if no carriers had
been engaged by then, she would set out without them. This
contribution to the debate brought matters to a head, and after
another hour's fierce argument outside the hut, three of the
richest men in M'fetta volunteered for the task: Kiva, the renowned elephant hunter, Fika, a fine, athletic young man, and
Wiki, another noted hunter.

These three Fans, the Ajumbas and the Igalwa, Ngouta, I think
will be enough. Moreover, I think it safer not to have an overpowering
percentage of Fans in the party, as I know we shall have considerable
stretches of uninhabited forest to traverse, and the Ajumbas say that

the Fans will kill people, i.e. the black traders who venture into their country, and cut them up into neat pieces, eat what they want at the time, and smoke the rest of the bodies for future use. Now I do not want to arrive at the Rembwe in a smoked condition, even should my fragments be neat, and I am going in a different direction from that in which I said I was going when I left Kangwe, and there are so many ways of accounting for death about here—leopard, canoe-capsize, elephants, etc.—that even if I were traced—well, nothing could be done then, anyhow—so will only take three Fans. One must diminish dead certainties to the level of sporting chances along here, or one can never get on.

No one knew exactly the way they were going, but one of the Fans said he could lead them to a big Fan town named Efoua, which lay in the right direction. No white man or black trader had ever been there, but since these people's trade goods found their way down to the Rembwe, there must be a path beyond. The three new carriers were prepared to go the whole way with her if she guaranteed to protect them. Without a moment's hesitation she assured them she would do this and agreed to pay them their wages at Hatton and Cookson's sub-factory on the Rembwe. The loads were made up by the light of bush torches, ready for an early start in the morning, and by half past eleven Mary was alone.

Mosquitoes and lice made sleep impossible, so, pushing open her bark door, she stepped quietly over Pagan, sleeping soundly across the doorway, and made her way to where the canoes had been pulled up on the stony beach. She selected a small Fan canoe and after launching it silently, paddled out on to the dark lake. She headed straight for the far side of the sheet of placid water, and drove her craft on to the bank among some long grass where she had seen some glow-worms crawling. A moment later a soft soughing noise warned her that some great beast was near at hand. As she stood motionless, with beating heart, she saw to her dismay that she had landed right in the midst of a family of hippopotamuses. She stole back to her canoe, eased it off the bank, and, paddling under water, glided out of danger.

Fearful lest, in the darkness, she should make another dangerous landing, she returned to the island, taking great care that she was alone before she beached her craft in a cove

surrounded by rocks. She was a long way from the village, and
decided she could safely have a bath to rid herself of the lice
which had made her uncomfortable since her first entry into
Kiva's hut. When this was finished, and she had dried herself
on her cummerbund, she returned, and crept into her hut without
disturbing anyone. For an hour or so she dozed, with her back
against her luggage, until Ngouta brought her tea at five-thirty.
By six o'clock the whole party was afloat.

The Fans, in their own canoe, led the way across the lake
—finally leaving it by a narrow channel. The scenery here was
savage: dark trees clothed the sides of the hills and came right
down to the banks of the stream, and Mary felt the same disquiet
that she had experienced when she first entered Lake Ncovi.
Soon their way appeared to be blocked by a fence of stakes
driven into the river bed, but as the canoes approached, a narrow
passage became apparent. Above this a spear, with a bush-rope
attached and a weight at the top of the haft, threatened any
who might pass. Approaching cautiously, they found that
under the water, holding the spear in place, was another bush-
rope which any unwary hippopotamus or other big creature
would be bound to drag out of position, thus springing the
deadly trap. With great care the Fans steered their canoe between
the posts, and Mary and her Ajumbas followed without mishap.
Then for an hour or so they paddled on, until they came to a
small, gloomy lake, on the far shore of which the party dis-
embarked, up to their knees in the stinking, yielding mud, and
pulled their canoes up after them.

There now followed a very long day's march through the
dark forest. No path was apparent to Mary, but the Fans strode
ahead at a great pace, soon leaving her behind, and even taxing
the endurance of the Ajumbas, who, although great canoe-men,
were no match for the Fans on land. Only the latters' insatiable
hunger saved the rest of the party from losing touch with them:
for every two hours they sat down and had a snack of a 'pound
or so of meat and aguma apiece, followed by a pipe of tobacco'.
The stragglers caught up with them during this rest; the Ajumbas
would sit down near them while Mary, after a minute or so spent
in conversation, would ask which way to go and set out by
herself to get a good start.

It was on one of these occasions that she came upon a herd of five elephants wading and rolling in the mud at the bottom of a ravine. Fortunately, she was down-wind, and hastily taking cover behind a tree, she lay down to watch. Soon, emboldened by their unawareness of her presence, she crept forward from tree to tree until she was within twenty yards of them. For a time they rolled in the mud, squirted water at one another, and scratched themselves on the trees, then growing tired of this game they moved off up wind. As Mary turned to rejoin her men, she put her foot in the middle of Kiva's back, and, losing her balance, slipped down the hillside. It appeared that he, being an elephant hunter, had been so fascinated by the sight of the great beasts that he had not been aware of Mary's approach, and had been almost as startled as she by their sudden meeting.

When she had picked herself up, Mary suggested that they should pile the baggage and have an elephant hunt. Her sudden fancy is difficult to explain, for she was at all other times strongly opposed to big-game hunting. Perhaps she wanted to see her own renowned Fan huntsmen in action. Kiva reluctantly declined: there were not enough men for such an exploit, he said, for he did not count the Ajumbas whom he despised, nor could they afford the ammunition, for they might need it to defend their lives before they reached the Rembwe.

The rest of the party now came up, and they had to pass through the swamp in which the elephants had wallowed. Their foot-marks, and the places where they had rolled, were by now filled up with water, while the mud underneath was hard and slippery. In spite of her determination to 'preserve an awesome and unmoved calm while among these dangerous savages', Mary had to give way and laugh explosively when she saw 'the portly, powerful Pagan suddenly convert himself into a quadruped, while Grey Shirt poised himself on one heel and waved his other leg in the air to advertise to the assembled nations that he was about to sit down'. She too, lost her balance and went down into the filthy water, but this she had expected, and regaining her feet she squelched her way to the bank, quite unmoved by the thick layer of mud which covered her from head to foot.

The Ajumbas went on up the hillside, but the Fans stopped, and Mary saw them searching themselves. Not knowing what they were at she followed the Ajumbas, but before she caught up with them she felt an extremely painful, pricking sensation.

She soon found the cause: several enormous ticks had embedded themselves in her flesh. She dug them out with some difficulty and then turned towards the Africans ahead. They too had learnt about elephant ticks, and were dancing about as they tried to pull them out. With a smile at their antics, Mary strode past, determined to seize the opportunity to gain a good lead.

Shortly after noon they struck into a mountainous and rocky country. For the first time Mary could see a track ahead through the forest. As she walked beneath the great ebony and hardwood trees, a hundred and fifty feet above her head, she came to know and like the Fans:

a certain sort of friendship soon arose between the Fans and me. We each recognized that we belonged to that same section of the human race with whom it is better to drink than to fight. We knew we each would have killed the other, if sufficient inducement were offered, and so we took a certain amount of care that the inducement should not arise. Grey Shirt and Pagan also, their trade friends, the Fans treated with an independent sort of courtesy; but Silence, Singlet, the Passenger, and above all Ngouta, they openly did not care a row of pins for, and I have small doubt that had it not been for us other three, they would have killed and eaten these very amiable gentlemen with as much compunction as an English sportsman would kill as many rabbits. They on their part hated the Fans, and never lost an opportunity of telling me 'these Fan be bad man too much'.

I must not forget to mention the other member of our party, a Fan gentleman with the manners of a duke and the habits of a dustbin. He came with us, quite uninvited by me, and never asked for any pay; I think he only wanted to see the fun, and drop in for a fight if there was one going on, and to pick up the pieces generally. He was evidently a man of some importance, from the way the others treated him; and moreover he had a splendid gun, with a gorilla skin sheath for its lock, and ornamented all over its stock with brass nails. His costume consisted of a small piece of dirty rag round his loins, and whenever we were going through dense undergrowth, or wading a swamp, he wore that filament tucked up scandalously short. Whenever we were sitting down in the forest having one of our nondescript meals, he always sat next to me, and appropriated the tin of tobacco. Then he would fill his pipe, and turning to me with the easy grace of aristocracy, would say what may be translated as:

'My dear Princess, could you favour me with a lucifer?'

I used to say, 'My dear Duke, charmed, I'm sure,' and give him one ready lit.

I dared not trust him with the box whole, having a personal conviction that he would have kept it. I asked him what he would do supposing I were not there with a box of lucifers; and he produced a bush-cow's horn with a neat wood lid tied on with *tie tie* (thin bush ropes), and from out of it he produced a flint and steel and demonstrated. Unfortunately all his grace's minor possessions, owing to the scantiness of his attire, were in one-and-the same pineapple-fibre bag which he wore slung across his shoulder; and these possessions, though not great, were as dangerous to the body as a million sterling is said to be to the soul, for they consisted largely of gunpowder and snuff, and their separate receptacles leaked and their contents commingled, so that demonstration of fire-making methods among the Fan ended in an awful bang and blow-up in a small way, and the Professor and his pupil sneezed like fury for ten minutes, and a cruel world laughed till it nearly died, for twenty.

Once Ngouta, who chanced to be ahead, fell back hurriedly on the rest of the party. He had been frightened by a viper that hung from a tree above the path. The Duke strode forward, killed it with one blow from the butt of his gun, and stuffed it carelessly into his bag. Mary and the Fans ate it for supper. Mile after mile they tramped on through the forest, until she was so tired that she suggested that they should spend the night in the bush rather than hurry on to reach Efoua before night. To strengthen her argument, she reminded them that they were by no means certain of a friendly reception in that town. They might, she suggested, finish up in the cooking-pots. In reply, the Fans pointed to trees with deep scratches on them—obviously the work of leopards. Convinced, Mary plodded on, for she no longer dared to rest in case her limbs should stiffen and prevent her from starting again. Towards evening she was wearily stumbling along a very indistinct path when suddenly the ground beneath her gave way. She fell some fifteen feet on to a lot of spikes.

It is at these times you realize the blessing of a good thick skirt. Had I paid heed to the advice of many people in England, who ought to have known better, and did not do it themselves, and adopted masculine garments, I should have been spiked to the bone and done for, whereas, save for a good many bruises, here I was with the fulness of my skirt tucked under me, sitting on nine ebony spikes some twelve inches long, in comparative comfort, howling lustily to be hauled out.

I

The Duke came along first and looked down at her.

'Get a bush-rope and haul me out,' said Mary.

He merely grunted and sat down on a log.

Next came the Passenger who looked down and asked if she were dying.

'Not much,' she replied. 'Get a bush-rope and haul me out.'

'No fit,' he answered and sat down beside the Duke.

Presently, however, Kiva and Wiki came up, and the latter, who was an expert on bush-ropes, went to select the one and only suitable rope for such a purpose. He took so long that Mary began to think she was abandoned to her fate, and to make plans to climb out without help. She soon gave up, however, for the walls were concave and smooth. At last, to her great relief, Wiki reappeared with the carefully selected rope and pulled her out, humbled, but very little hurt. A few minutes later Silence, who was leading, disappeared through the path with a despairing yell. They hauled him out, but as he was nearly naked and heavily laden, he had been badly hurt by the sharp stakes on to which he had fallen. They were obviously near Efoua, for the approaches to Fan towns were usually protected by such pits. Each man took the cover from his gun, the little party closed up, and in this warlike manner they made their entrance into the town.

The Fans of Efoua looked at them with amazement, and while the women and children ran for shelter into the huts, the men closed threateningly round the travellers. Kiva shouted the names of his friends, but no one came forward to greet him, and for a few minutes Mary felt as she had done at M'fetta when the menacing ring closed around her. Once more, however, they were lucky. Kiva's friends thrust their way through the crowd, and after a noisy, animated dispute, one of the chiefs had his hut cleared for Mary. When she had seen that all her baggage was safe, she at last sat down on a stool placed for her outside her hut. As she looked around, she was pleasantly surprised by the appearance of the town and its people: the huts were larger than those of any Fan town she had seen, its streets were clean, and its inhabitants not nearly so villainous-looking as those of M'fetta. While her tea was being prepared she talked to the two chiefs. They took her for a trader and she felt herself obliged to buy a quantity of rubber and ivory. Meanwhile the first panic of the women and children had been overcome by curiosity, and she found herself the target of scores of eyes. In vain the chiefs tried to drive their people away. Mary was desperately tired after the long journey through the forest and went inside the hut to drink her tea. Even there she was aware of eyes peering at her through every hole in the walls, and heard the sound of new holes being bored on all sides. Ngouta, as usual in a state of panic, whispered, 'P'raps them M'fetta Fan done sell we.'

Mary felt no alarm, only discomfort and an overwhelming weariness. Her feet were swollen and painful, and she wondered whether she ought to take her sodden boots off. In the end she decided not to because she was afraid she might not be able to get them on again in the morning. So, curling herself up in a corner of the hut, with her head against the tobacco box, she fell into a doze.

Suddenly she was awakened by an uproar in the town. The Duke's voice could be recognized above the cries of a mob of angry men. Hurriedly she joined him in the street, where she found him defending himself vigorously from a charge of murder. His accusers could not prove their case because some of the chief witnesses were absent on an elephant hunt, and for the time being the Duke's alibi held. Mary returned to her hut and once more tried to sleep. Soon, however, she became aware that her room was pervaded by a nauseating, putrid smell. Sleep was impossible until she had found the cause of the stench and removed it. It could only come from some bags which hung from the wall. She took down the biggest one, untied it carefully and shook its contents into her hat. They consisted of 'a human hand, three big toes, four eyes, two ears, and other portions of the human frame. The hand was fresh, the others only so so and shrivelled'. Wiki subsequently told her that though his people would eat their fellow tribesmen, yet they liked to keep a little something belonging to them as a memento. Carefully she replaced these relics, and, opening the hut door for a breath of fresh air, once more composed herself for sleep.

Her men were afoot at dawn, tying up the baggage with fresh bush-ropes, putting away their finery—for she had been amused to see that when they approached a town the Fans were not content with the meagre loin-cloths which served very well in the forest, but decked themselves out resplendently—and eager to be off. Mary made handsome presents to the two chiefs, who escorted them as far as the first plantation outside the village.

Though the first day's journey had been long, that from Efoua to Egaja proved even more tiring on account of the numerous swamps through which they had to wade. These were of two kinds: large, deep swamps on which the sun baked a crust and over which the traveller could pass if he moved lightly and without hesitation, and deep, narrow swamps, with no crust on if they happened to be shaded by the forest. Through the latter a ford had to be found. Pagan and Passenger came to grief in one of the broad swamps, through being too cautious and slow. The rest of the party rescued them before they finally sank, by hastily slashing off boughs of trees and throwing them within reach of the trapped men. In this way an impromptu raft was built around them and, assisted by bush-ropes, they were eventually dragged to firm land. The narrow swamps were even more dangerous. Sometimes the leader of the party would make three or four attempts before he found a place shallow enough to cross, going on until the black, batter-like ooze came up round his neck, and then turning back and trying in another place.

If Mary happened to be in front, the duty of finding a ford fell on her, for she insisted on sharing hardship and danger with her men. She had only contempt for those white men on the West Coast who required 'to be carried in a hammock, or wheeled in a go-cart or a Bath-chair about the streets of their coast towns, depending for the defence of their settlement on a body of black soldiers'. She took as her model the French officials and the traders, who were hardier and more daring than any African. So into the swamps she went, wading about up to her neck in filth, until she found a passage.

Swamps were not the only obstacles. When they reached the more open hills and mountain slopes of the Sierra del Cristal, they had to pass over fearful timber falls. Often great trees barred their way and as they scrambled from one rotten trunk to another sometimes one of them fell through. The Duke had a bad fall, going down twenty feet or so before he landed on the heap of decaying vegetation which lay below the roofing of dead trees. On another occasion it took the party twenty minutes to haul up Fika who had fallen with a heavy load on his back. When they at last succeeded in grasping him, Wiki, who had been in charge of the operation, fell backwards through the false floor, and they had to rescue him. On the second day of the march, Mary was fortunate, but she had her fall on the third day.

By the time the party, tired out by their exertions, were approaching Egaja, Mary was suffering badly from thirst, for on no account would she drink unboiled water, and during the greater part of this day's journey they had been exposed to the sun. Egaja, like all Fan towns, had an evil reputation, and the ten Africans and their leader grew apprehensive as they approached it in the evening. Not even the Fans had a friend there, and when they reached its outermost plantation, all looked to the priming of their guns and advanced with the greatest caution. Suddenly they were startled by an agonized howl from Silence who had put his foot on to a sharp, ebony spike planted in the middle of the path. Then, turning a corner, they came upon four young men, rubber collectors, who were camping in the plantation. When these had recovered from their astonishment at seeing Mary, one of them was induced to act as guide, and, with the injured man's pack on his back, he set off along the intricate and hazardous tracks towards the town. After a mile or so, however, he fell into a pit that was half full of thorns. He handed back Silence's load and, after receiving a present of tobacco from Mary, limped off in the direction of his camp to attend to the thorns.

After fording a swift stream that crossed their path, Mary was so exhausted that she was convinced that she had not the strength to surmount another serious obstacle. A few minutes later they were descending a hill, and she was praying that no swamp lay at the foot of it, when to her horror she saw below a deep, swift-flowing river, bridged by an enormous tree. The rest of her party, with the exception of Pagan, took one look at the tree, high above the river, and went down to the water, half wading and half swimming across. Pagan took three paces along the tree, slipped, and lost his balance. By the greatest good fortune, his hands caught hold of the tree as he fell and he managed to haul himself back to safety. Then he, too, went through the water below. Mary's legs trembled under her. She knew she could not stem the fierce current below: she had to go across the bridge. She made straight for it, crossed its bare and slippery surface as though she were a tight-rope walker, and rejoined her admiring men.

Soon after this they entered the town. There was the customary hubbub, before an evil-looking chief, smeared in soot as a sign of mourning, agreed to their staying, and put his hut at Mary's disposal. She had taken possession, with her baggage and her Ajumbas, and was waiting impatiently while Ngouta made tea, when a second chief called on her. Mary knew as soon as she saw him that he, and not the brutal, sensual-looking Fan whom she had already met, was the real master of Egaja. Powerfully built, with a strong, intelligent face, he was very superior to any African she had met since she left the Ogowe. He was extremely courteous, and, ordering two stools to be brought, offered one to Mary before he sat down on the other. Then he began to talk to his unusual visitor—with Pagan acting as interpreter:

After compliments had passed, ' "Tell the chief," I said, "that I hear this town of his is thief town."

"Better not, sir," says Pagan.

"Go on," said I, "or I'll tell him myself."

So Pagan did. It was a sad blow to the chief.

Thief town! This highly respectably town of Egaja! A town whose moral character in all matters (and a great list followed) was an example to other towns, called a thief town! Oh, what a wicked world!'

Mary said quite plainly that she would wait and see how she was treated before she gave her opinion. The chief seemed to bear her no grudge for her outspoken remarks, but on the contrary treated her with even greater respect. Soon she had worked round to her favourite subject and sat listening while the lively Fan talked about tribal customs and fetish. She was delighted to find such an intelligent African in a district which was completely free from the influence of white culture.

When the brief African evening was coming to a close, and Mary was looking forward to drinking the tea which had been waiting so long, the chief brought to her his mother who, two days before, had been bitten by 'a fish like a snake'. Her hand and arm were in a shocking condition. Mary almost vomited at the sight of them: 'the whole hand was a mass of yellow pus, streaked with zanies (a thin discharge from wounds or sores), large ulcers were burrowing into the fore-arm, while in the armpit was a big abscess'.

Before she could treat these dreadful sores, she must drink her tea, for she was almost fainting with fatigue. She ordered the Africans who stood around to fill one of their tubs with hot water and into this she poured a stiff dose of Condy's fluid. Then she made the old woman sit down and lay her whole arm in it. While the chief sat by his mother, Mary went into the hut, hastily drank her tea, and returned with lancet, antiseptics, and medicine.

It was almost dark now and she had to work by the light of torches. First, she opened the abscess. Without a sound, the chief's mother collapsed upon the ground, and for one frightening moment Mary thought that she was dying. To her great relief she found that her patient had only fallen into a deep sleep and she was able to clean the abscess and place the arm in a poultice made from cooked plantains, boiling water, and Condy's fluid. The old woman slept on—even when the poultice had grown cold, and her arm had been cleaned a second time and carefully dressed. In the end she was carried, still sleeping, to her hut, where Mary roused her for long enough to give her a dose of *pil crotonis cum hydrargi*, a very violent aperient, no longer used. Then she sank again into a peaceful sleep.

There was no chance of rest for Mary now. The news of her medicine had spread throughout the town and all the afflicted of Egaja came to her hut to be treated. She did what she could for men and women with the yaws, or with ulcers, she treated one man who had a broken spear-head in an abscess in his thigh, another suffering from filaria, and a great number who had lesser ailments. It was past eleven by the time she had finished, her men had long since been asleep, and only the chief remained beside her. To show how grateful he was, he went to his hut and returned with some rolls of bark cloth which he arranged on the plank that was to serve her as a bed. Then at last, after she had given him presents, she wished him good night, stepped carefully over her sleeping Ajumbas, and went into an inner compartment to sleep.

Her rest was soon disturbed:

At 1.45 the whole town was roused by the frantic yells of a woman.
I judged there was one of my beauties of Fans mixed up in it, and there
was, and after paying damages, I got back again by 2.30 a.m., and off
to sleep instantly. At four sharp, whole town of Egaja plunged into
emotion, and worse shindy. I suggested to the Ajumbas that they
should go out; but no, they didn't care a row of pins if one of our Fans
did get killed, so I went, recognizing Kiva's voice in high expostula-
tion. Kiva, it seems, a long time ago had a transaction *in re* a tooth of
ivory with a man who, unfortunately, happened to be in this town
tonight, and Kiva owed the said man a coat.

The creditor claimed to have called frequently at M'fetta to
receive payment for the bundle of merchandise, known as a 'coat',
but he had got no satisfaction. Now he proposed to exercise his
legal rights and seize the debtor's person and eat it. When
Mary joined the excited throng, Kiva was tied up and his creditor
was preparing to kill him as a preliminary to cooking him.

I dare say I ought to have rushed at him and cut his bonds and
killed people in a general way with a revolver, and then flown with my
band to the bush; only my band evidently had no flying in them, being
tucked up in the hut pretending to be asleep, and uninterested in the
affair; and although I could have abandoned the band without a pang
just then, I could not so light-heartedly fly with Kiva to the bush and
leave my fishes; so I shouted Azuna (listen) to the Bankruptcy Court,
and got a Fan who spoke trade English to come and interpret for me;
and from him I learnt the above stated outline of the proceedings up
to the time.

Fortunately for the reader it is impossible for me to give in full
detail the proceedings of the court. I do not think if the whole of
Mr Pitman's school of short-hand had been there to take them down
the thing could possibly have been done in word-writing. . . . I got my
friend the chief on my side; but he explained he had no jurisdiction, as
neither of the men belonged to his town; and I explained to him, that
as the proceedings were taking place in his town he had a right of
jurisdiction *ipso facto*. The Fan could not translate this phrase, so we
gave it the chief raw, and he seemed to relish it, and he and I then cut
into the affair together, I looking at him with admiration and approval
when he was saying his say, and after his 'Azuna' had produced a patch
of silence he could move his tongue in, and he similarly regarding me
during my speech for the defence. We neither, I expect, understood
each other, and we had trouble with our client, who would keep
pleading 'Not guilty', which was absurd. Anyhow we produced our

effect, my success arising from my concluding my speech with the announcement that I would give the creditor a book on Hatton and Cookson's for the coat, and I would deduct it from Kiva's pay.

In the end, since the town did not trade with Hatton and Cookson's Rembwe sub-factory because there was 'blood war on the path', she paid the fine out of her own trade goods. Then she slept in snatches until tea was brought at seven. Her main object now was to get her band out of Egaja without further trouble, for she was afraid that more cases might be brought up against Kiva, who was clearly a criminal character, or against the Duke, who might at any moment have to stand trial for murder should the elephant hunters of Efoua return home and decide to follow him. Wiki was also in danger, for he had only barely escaped from a bad 'wife palaver' in Egaja by pleading an alibi and the wickedness of a twin brother who had carried off the woman in dispute. The Fans, however, were reluctant to leave. They felt safe under her protection and meant to take advantage of this happy state of affairs to enjoy themselves. They suggested that they should make up a hunting party for her, and use Egaja as their base for a few days. The chief joined them in begging Mary to stay, at least until she had rested after her strenuous journey through the forest.

Mary resisted all their attempts. By ten o'clock she had overcome all opposition, and, accompanied by the two chiefs, she led her grumbling men out of the town. The evil-looking chief ordered his son to guide her through the dangerous paths which surrounded the settlement, while the other asked her for her opinion of his town now that she had stayed there. To his delight she declared emphatically that it was not a 'thief town', for not a finger had been placed on any of her goods during her visit. Then she gave presents to the chiefs and set out for Esoon. The young man who was her guide explained that the numerous and deadly traps which he avoided with so much skill were necessary because of the wickedness of the neighbouring Fans. Mary was not alarmed: she had heard the same story so many times, and moreover she was now thoroughly convinced that her own Fans were as murderous and lecherous as any she was likely to meet.

II

AMONG THE GORILLAS

SOON after their guide had left them, the travellers put down their loads and stretched themselves out on the ground to rest and eat. Mary sat with them that day, and talked to the Fans, teaching them English names for things while they taught her their language. She could not refrain from adding a few colloquial phrases such as 'Dear me, now!', 'Stuff, my dear sir!', which sounded peculiarly threatening when the Fan huntsmen rolled each phrase into one formidable word. Presently Wiki, who had been engaged in his favourite pastime of collecting fine, fresh bush-ropes, returned from the forest and asked Mary to go with him, very quietly, to see something. When she had joined him, they crept down into a rocky ravine on the other side of which lay the last of the Egaja plantations. As soon as he reached this open ground, Wiki lay down flat and began to worm his way forward with extreme caution. Mary followed him:

I saw before me, some thirty yards off, busily employed in pulling down plantains, and other depredations, five gorillas: one old male, one young male, and three females. One of these had clinging to her a young fellow, with beautiful wavy black hair with just a kink in it. The big male was crouching on his haunches, with his long arms hanging down on either side, with the backs of his hands on the ground, the palms upwards. The elder lady was tearing to pieces and eating a pineapple, while the others were at the plantains destroying more than they ate.

They kept up a sort of whinnying, chattering noise, quite different from the sound I had heard gorillas give when enraged, or from the one you can hear them giving when they are what the natives call 'dancing' at night. I noticed that their reach of arm was immense and that when they went from one tree to another, they squattered across the open ground in a most inelegant style, dragging their long arms with the palms upwards. I should think the big male and female were over six feet each. The others would be from four to five. I put out my hand and laid it on Wiki's gun to prevent him from firing, and he, thinking I was going to fire, gripped my wrist.

I watched the gorillas with interest for a few seconds, until I heard Wiki make a peculiar small sound, and looking at him saw his face was working in an awful way as he clutched his throat with his hand violently.

Heavens! think I, this gentleman's going to have a fit; it's lost we are entirely this time. He rolled his head to and fro, and then buried his face into a heap of dried rubbish at the foot of a plantain stem, clasped his hands over it, and gave an explosive sneeze. The gorillas let go all, raised themselves up for a second, gave a quaint sound between a bark and a howl, and then the ladies and the young gentleman started home. The old male rose to his full height (it struck me at the time that this was ten feet at least, but for scientific purposes allowance must be made for a lady's emotions) and looked straight towards us, or rather towards where that sound came from. Wiki went off into a paroxysm of falsetto sneezes the like of which I have never heard; nor evidently had the gorilla, who doubtless thinking, as one of his black co-relatives would have thought, that the phenomenon savoured of the supernatural, went off after his family with a celerity that was amazing the moment that he touched the forest, and disappeared as they had, swinging himself along through it from bough to bough, in a way that convinced me that, given the necessity of getting about in tropical forests, man had made a mistake in getting his arms shortened. I have seen many wild animals in their native wilds but never have I seen anything to equal gorillas going through bush; it is graceful, powerful, superbly perfect hand-trapeze performance.

After this sporting adventure, we returned, as I usually return from a sporting adventure, without measurements or the body.

Mary had seen most of the big game of central Africa at close quarters, and though elephants, leopards, and pythons gave her a feeling of alarm, none of them gave her the feeling of horrible disgust which she experienced on being face to face with this hideous old gorilla. Yet it seems probable that it was on this journey, somewhere between Egaja and Esoon, that she stood her ground fearlessly when one of these brutes advanced upon her, roaring with fury.

Unfortunately the adventure can only be reconstructed by referring to her chapters on fetish, to her lectures, and to casual remarks recorded by her friends; for she always remembered that it had been Du Chaillu's gorilla stories which had discredited him, and for this reason refrained from telling any herself. Certain it is that she was wandering ahead of her carriers on her way to the Rembwe when she came upon this Fan town:

I found myself facing a village clearing, a village which I did not know, but one which I saw from certain signs, was at war with the village I had left. Not that this was any definite geographical help, because for a matter of that pretty near all the villages in the country were—on account, my village said, of their iniquity. However, this particular enemy-village I had arrived at, had, guarding its gate two warriors, splendid creatures, good six-footers, painted, armed with four spears apiece, and having their hair magnificently plaited into horns—quite the Lords of Creation. I deployed and took bearings, to combine military and marine phraseology, but deciding that there was nothing else for it, came at last cautiously out of the bush, and gave those guardians greeting. They stared at me. 'Ndege wa ma yi some,' I said again. They turned as one man and fled into the village, I after them through the gateway, intent on reaching a little spot inside where I knew I was safe until I had had my say; and I just caught a back view of those gentlemen going through the door-hole of a house at the far end of the street. Now going through the door-hole of a Fan hut when hurried is not easy as a solo, but as a duet it presents far greater difficulties; and yet they managed it, and in a few moments out of that same door-hole came, not warriors armed with guns and thirsting for blood—gore, I believe, is the fashionable word to use for West Africa —but a quiet old lady.

It was evident that these warriors had just been to 'tell mother'. Of course, had I been a dozen men, or an elephant or anything reasonable, they would have laid down their lives in attempting to kill me before disturbing her; but, as I was queer, something they were not accustomed to, they most wisely went to consult her first. There was no cowardice in this, for those men were incapable of cowardice, as I learnt by subsequent experience of them. Indeed, they were the two men whom, when I was once alone with them, I saw do the bravest thing even I have ever seen men do, and the while I wished myself in Dixie they never turned a hair. Still, on my first arrival they referred me to their mother to explain my intentions, and we succeeded in getting things satisfactorily settled. We subsequently got things satisfactorily settled between the two villages, which was better for both of them and for trade, and this and many similar incidents confirmed me in the belief that women have power and position in Africa.

In any case this meeting must have occurred during her travels among the Fans who lived in the Great Forest, and it seems not improbable that these two warriors whom she saw 'do the bravest thing even I had seen' were the men who stood beside her in an encounter with an enraged gorilla. If so, they must have been leading her towards Esoon, when they came upon a family of gorillas. Again the male stood his ground while the rest of the family swung away in the trees. Then the savage beast advanced, roaring, upon the three. They stood firm. When it was no more than a score of yards away, Mary asked the Fan by her side why he did not fire.

'I must wait,' he said, 'the other man's powder is wet.'

And he waited until the muzzle of his gun almost touched the gorilla's chest; then he fired and blew its chest in.

When they reached the next village and told them that they had killed a gorilla, the people were delighted, and gave them a warm welcome, for they had just had a man killed by one of these beasts. Mary asked in a spirit of scientific enquiry how a gorilla killed. The Fans almost dragged her out of the stockade into the bush, where they proceeded to dig up the man who had been killed. She saw that the gorilla had just 'caught him round the breast and torn the shoulder-blades clean out'.

Here she must have had the dead gorilla skinned and the frame dismembered and made up into a bundle, for on the next day, when crossing a particularly treacherous swamp, one of her carriers sank into the ooze, and although they dragged him out, he left behind a good load of bottled fish and a gorilla specimen.

In Esoon Mary kept a strict watch on her men, making it clear to them that any more illicit love affairs would be punished by their having their pay reduced. She had seen quite enough court cases for the time being. As the Fans were nearly at the end of their journey, and soon to be paid, her warning had its effect and she was not called upon to rescue any of them from the usual 'wife palaver'. She had another cause for worry, however. As was almost always the case among the Fans, Esoon was at war with its neighbouring villages. The feud with the next town on the route to the Rembwe was so bitter that their enemies shot at sight anyone even coming from the direction of Esoon. The Duke suggested Mary should go up the road alone, a mile ahead of the party, and, since her appearance was so unusual, the hostile townsmen might refrain from shooting. A word of explanation would make it safe for the rest of her men to join her. She had no intention of exposing herself to the bits of old iron that would probably greet her if she adopted this plan, but her reputation for fearlessness had to be maintained.

'There's nothing like dash and courage, my dear Duke,' I said, 'even if one displays it by deputy, so this plan does you great credit; but as my knowledge of this charming language of yours is but small, I fear I might create a wrong impression in that town, and it might think I had kindly brought them a present of eight edible heathens [two only of her party were Christians]—you, and the remainder of my followers, you understand.'

The men saw the point of this argument and it was agreed to make a detour round the danger spot. Accordingly, on the next day, they set out westwards, leaving Fika behind, however, for he had heard rumours that at N'dorko, the town they hoped to reach, there was a man whom he did not wish to meet. They now crossed ridges, and waded through little rivers that flowed towards the Rembwe. Timber falls and bogs alternated, and progress was slow. It was not until the afternoon that Mary, having climbed a hill, saw a sight that made her heart stand still: 'stretching away to the west and north, winding in and out among the feet of the now-isolated mound-like mountains, was that never-to-be-mistaken, black-green, forest swamp of mangrove: doubtless the fringe of the Rembwe. . . .' But though these mangroves heralded the river she sought, there were many obstacles between her hill-top and the end of her journey.

Tired as she was, she could still enjoy the beauty of the forest through which they passed.

Lovely wine palms and raffia palms, looking as if they were grown under glass, so deliciously green and profuse was their feather-like foliage, intermingled with giant red woods, and lovely glossy green lianes, blooming in wreaths and festoons of white and mauve flowers, which gave a glorious wealth of beauty and colour to the scene. Even the monotony of the mangrove-belt alongside gave an additional charm to it, like the frame around a picture.

On they went among the ferns and flowers, until they came to a different kind of swamp from those they were accustomed to. It was beautiful but extensive. Fortunately they saw an African woman passing through ahead of them, and though she fled, alarmed by their approach, they were able to note her course and make their way safely across. Here, Mary was unfortunate. A great tree spanned the last fifty feet, and as she cautiously moved along it, she slipped and fell into a deep stream which flowed beneath. Her men pulled her out, and, soaked to the skin, she set out again through the steamy heat.

Presently they came upon a party of men and women who were on their way to N'dorko to sell their rubber. They exchanged greetings and went on towards the town. About half a mile farther on, however, they came to a great sheet of filthy water:

Our path went straight into this swamp over the black rocks forming its rim, in an imperative, no alternative, come-along-this-way style. Singlet, who was leading, carrying a good load of bottled fish and a gorilla specimen, went at it like a man, and disappeared before the eyes of us following him, then and there down through the water. He came up, thanks be, but his load is down there now, worse luck. Then I said we must get the rubber carriers who were coming this way to show us the ford; and so we sat down on the rocks a tired, disconsolate, dilapidated-looking row, until they arrived. When they came up they did not plunge in forthwith; but leisurely set about making a most nerve-shaking set of preparations, taking off their clothes, and forming them into bundles, which, to my horror, they placed on the tops of their heads. The women carried the rubber on their backs still, but rubber is none the worse for being under water.

The men went in first, each holding his gun high above his head. They skirted the bank before they struck into the swamp, and were followed by the women and our party, and soon we were all up to our chins.

We were two hours and a quarter passing that swamp. I was one hour and three-quarters; but I made good weather of it, closely following the rubber-carriers, and only going in right over head and all twice. Other members of my band were less fortunate. One, finding himself getting out of his depth, got hold of a palm frond and pulled himself into deeper water still, and had to roost among the palms until a special expedition of the tallest men went and gathered him like a flower. Another got himself much mixed up and scratched because he thought to make a short cut through screw-pines. He did not know the screw pine's little ways, and he had to have a special expedition. One and all we got horribly infested with leeches, having a frill of them round our necks like astrakhan collars, and our hands covered with them, when we came out.

A few hundred yards beyond the swamp they saw brown huts. Mary led the way into the ramshackle village of N'dorko. Without a pause she passed through its one street, through the crowd of noisy, excited Africans, and, standing on a steep slippery bank, looked down upon the black, mud-laden waters of the Rembwe. Turning back to the village, she rejoined her men, for she had promised to pay them as soon as they reached the river and she knew that they were impatient of a moment's delay. She asked for Hatton and Cookson's factory:

'This is it,' said an exceedingly dirty, good-looking, civil-spoken man in perfect English, though as pure-blooded an African as ever walked. 'This is it, sir,' and he pointed to one of the huts on the right-hand side, indistinguishable in squalor from the rest.

'Where's the Agent?' said I.

'I'm the Agent,' he answered.

You could have knocked me down with a feather. 'Where's John Holt's factory?' said I.

'You have passed it, it is up on the hill.'

This showed Messrs Holt's factory to be no bigger than that of her own firm. Mary was worried, for clearly neither of these stores could provide the variety of goods needed to pay off her carriers. For the moment she put her men, and the agents, in a good humour by purchasing tobacco from one store and rum from the other and distributing these desirable commodities among her followers. Then, when she had taken up her quarters at the hut of her agent, and had it cleared of the noisy Africans who had pressed round her ever since her arrival, she asked her host if there was no bigger store anywhere at hand on the Rembwe. He told her that the main up-river store, under the charge of Sanga Glass, was only an hour's paddle away. A messenger was immediately sent.

Glass answered her call without delay. He appeared in a state of considerable astonishment, for no white man had crossed from the Ogowe for years, and no one had ever reached N'dorko after such a journey. He was a pleasant, well-educated African, who was eager to do all he could to help. By now it was night, but Mary could see that her men would be very disappointed if they had to wait until the next day. She therefore set about the task of finding out what they wanted. The trade dispute took place in the moonlit street, and although Glass was an expert at this kind of business, the carriers had not made up their minds until eleven o'clock. The last orders having been written out, Mary's baggage was packed in the agent's canoes, and she, the Ajumbas, and Kiva, who came to see that his fellow tribesmen's bundles were made up correctly, set out for Agonjo, where Glass had his store. On their arrival, the store was opened and the goods chosen.

All the men were satisfied with the exception of Grey Shirt, Silence, and Pagan, who found the Rembwe prices so little better than those of the Ogowe that they preferred to take a 'book' on Cockshut at his Lambaréné store rather than risk taking their goods back through Fan country. Mary thought they were wise.

In the morning Mary returned to N'dorko to say good-bye and to make a present of the rest of her own trade goods to her carriers. She 'had a touching farewell with the Fans . . . whom I hope to meet with again, for with all their many faults and failings, they are real men. I am faint-hearted enough to hope that our next journey together may not be over a country that seems to me to have been laid down as an obstacle race track, and to have fallen into shockingly bad repair.'

She now spent a few lazy, pleasant days at Agonjo with the factor and his friendly wife. Mosquitoes there were in swarms, and the house was infested with rats, but vexations of this kind did not worry Mary. She was comfortable, and secure, and she relaxed after her trying fortnight in the Great Forest. She soon learnt, however, that the life of even an established trader such as the one at Agonjo was full of alarms and dangers. Either he or his assistant had to be constantly on guard, for the African who sold him a few logs of ebony during the day would often try to take them back at night, especially if it was inky black, or pouring with rain, or if a tornado was raging. The successful trader had to win the reputation of being a 'devil-man'. He must be

K

inflexible with regard to prices, always master within his own stockade, and completely without fear in his dealings with the neighbouring tribesmen. Mary was delighted when she learned that the Fans immediately recognized her as a 'devil-man'.

She was particularly interested in the trade in ivory. She studied it, and found that, compared with this trade, the quest for gold sank into a parlour game. A common way of collecting a tooth, and the easiest, was to kill the man who owned it. To guard against this, the owner often hid his ivory, and said nothing about it until a trader appeared. Because it had been kept in this way for years, some ivory was quite brown by the time it was sold. Another, more public way of acquiring it, was from elephants, and Mary had first-hand experience of the way the Fans set about this:

I am bound to admit that their method of hunting elephants is disgracefully unsportsmanlike. A herd of elephants is discovered by rubber-hunters or by depredations on plantations, and the whole village, men, women, children, and babies and dogs turn out into the forest and stalk the monsters into a suitable ravine, taking care not to scare them. When they have gradually edged the elephants on into a suitable place, they fell trees and wreath them very roughly together with bush rope, all round an immense enclosure, still taking care not to scare the elephants into a rush. This fence is quite inadequate to stop an elephant in itself but it is made effective by being smeared with certain things, the smell whereof the elephants detest so much that when they wander up to it, they turn back disgusted. I need hardly remark that this preparation is made by the witch doctors and its constituents a secret of theirs, and I was only able to find out some of them. Then poisoned plantains are placed within the enclosure, and the elephants eat these and grow drowsier and drowsier; if the water supply within the enclosure is a pool it is poisoned, but if it is a running stream it cannot be done.

During this time the crowd of men and women spend their days round the enclosure, ready to turn back any elephant who may try to break out, going to and from the village for their food; their nights they spend in little bough-shelters by the enclosure, watching more vigilantly than by day, as the elephants are more active by night, it being their usual feeding time. During the whole time the witch doctor is hard at work making incantations and charms, with a view to finding out the proper time to attack the elephants. In my opinion his decision fundamentally depends on his knowledge of the state of poisoning the animals are in, but his version is that he gets his information from the forest spirits. . . . When, however, he has settled the day, the best hunters steal into the enclosure and take up safe positions in trees, and the outer crowd set light to the ready-built fires and make the greatest uproar possible, and fire upon the staggering, terrified elephants as they attempt to break out. The hunters in the trees fire down on them as they rush past, the fatal point at the back of the skull being well exposed to them.

When the animals are nearly exhausted, those men who do not possess guns rush into the enclosure, and the men who do, reload and join them, and the work is then completed. One elephant hunt I chanced upon at the final stage had taken two months' preparation, and although the plan sounds safe enough, there is really a good deal of danger left in it with all the drugging and ju-ju. There were eight elephants killed that day, but three burst through everything, sending energetic spectators flying, and squashing two men and a baby as flat as a botanical specimen.

The subsequent proceedings were impressive. The whole of the people gorged themselves on the meat for days, and great chunks of it were smoked over the fires in all directions. A certain portion of the flesh of the hind leg was taken by the witch doctor for ju-ju, and was supposed to be put away by him, with certain incantations in the recesses of the forest; his idea being apparently either to give rise to more elephants, or to induce the forest spirits to bring more elephants into the district. Meanwhile the carcases were going bad, rapidly bad, and the smell for a mile round was strong enough to have taken the paint off a door. Moreover there were flies, most of the flies in West Africa, I imagine, and—but I will say no more. I thought before this experience that I had touched bottom in smells when once I spent the outside of a week in a village, on the sandbank in front of which a portly hippopotamus who had been shot up-river got stranded, and proceeded energetically to melt into its elemental gases; but that was a passing whiff to this.'

Though Mary found Agonjo so full of interest, and was in no hurry to return to civilization, Sanga Glass was deeply concerned because he was unable to find the means to ship this unusual form of merchandise to the coast. She offered to go down the Rembwe in any canoe that was available, for the river looked sluggish and harmless enough after the swift-flowing Ogowe. The agent was firm, however; nothing but a large sailing canoe would serve the purpose, for below the mouth of the Rembwe, where it was joined in the Gaboon estuary by two turbulent streams, the 'Como and the Boqué, the water was rough, and a small craft might well be swamped.

When matters thus appeared to have reached a deadlock, there entered upon the scene a character who captured Mary's imagination the moment she saw him. He called himself Captain Johnson, though his name was Obanjo. He was immaculately dressed in a huge sombrero, a spotless singlet, and a suit of clean, well-fitting dungarees. It appeared that he had heard of Glass's dilemma. He had almost completed the construction of a large canoe that would be just the thing in which to take Mary to Gaboon. He had therefore come to talk business.

12

WITH BLACK TRADERS ON THE REMBWE

OBANJO came on the scene suddenly and with a great deal of commotion. He dashed up the verandah, clapped Glass heartily on the back, and flung himself into a chair. Mary studied him with interest. His every movement was dramatic, and calculated to create the impression of a reckless, rollicking skipper. But she thought that beneath this façade she perceived very different qualities: determination and resource were evident in every line of his face. Here was a man whom she would engage without a moment's hesitation if she were planning another dangerous journey through the bush.

After she had been introduced, and had talked to the trader for a few minutes, Mary left the two men to reach agreement on the price to be paid for her safe conveyance to Gaboon. This was eventually settled, after the lengthy haggling without which no African trade deal is completed, and she was told that she was to be ready in the morning to board the canoe for her journey downstream.

Obanjo arrived in a fine-looking craft, made from an immense hardwood tree, with a mast and a gaff, on which was bent one of the most flimsy-looking sails that even Mary had ever seen. It was an old bed quilt, which must have seen years of service and which looked as though it would blow to pieces in the first fresh breeze—in spite of the fact that it had been patched with pieces of its skipper's old dungarees. Across the stern of the craft, flush with the gunwales, a staging of bamboo had been begun. When completed, with a canopy of palm thatch above, this platform would provide a very comfortable cabin, about five or six feet long: unfortunately, however, only the plain bamboo cross-pieces were in position when Mary went aboard, and though she made a couch on it with her various belongings, she

was to find it a very precarious resting-place when they reached
the rough water at the mouth of the Rembwe.

She was led to hope from the bustle, and shouting, and
general air of brisk seamanship which attended their departure,
that Obanjo proposed to make a long passage on this first day.
She knew the African character too well, however, to be greatly
surprised when, after only four miles, their craft nosed its way
alongside a small village, and its master went ashore in search of
cargo and additional crew. The villagers celebrated the arrival
of the trader in fine style, and he did not return until two in the
morning. He had acquired cargo, crew, and a small canoe to
serve as a tender.

During this first spree, Mary remained aboard, but on many
subsequent occasions she joined her 'bold, bad trader' and his
villainous-looking crew ashore. Obanjo was very fond of rum,
and sometimes got very drunk, but he never failed to treat his
passenger with respect—indeed his respect sometimes savoured
of idolatry. Fortunately his crew lived in such dread of him that
even when they were drunk they took no liberties.

On this first night, by the time Obanjo had stored the cargo
and had a meal, it was four o'clock. A brisk breeze had sprung
up, and, when they pushed off and hoisted the sail, the canoe
made steady progress with wind and current to help her. Obanjo
sat at the helm, but it was obvious that he wanted to join the
rest of his crew who were noisily sleeping amidships. Mary
offered to take his place, and when he had put her through a
test in practical seamanship and found her fully qualified, the
captain willingly surrendered the helm to her, and, lying down,
immediately fell asleep.

Now she was alone with the river and the black mangroves.
Her canoe stole past slime lagoons, and towards the shadows of
great trees which at first alarmed her, for she mistook them for
mud flats. For some time she avoided them, but at last realized
what they were and steered straight through them. Forward
rose the dim outline of her sail 'idealized from bed-sheetdom to
glory', and below it glowed the tiny cooking fire, a spot of warm
colour contrasting with the pale, cold light of the moon. She
had grown to love Africa's hills and its forests, its exotic flowers,
and even the surf that shone white along its coasts, but at no
time had she felt such an intense pleasure as now, when she

steered her dugout canoe, with its sleeping Africans, along the great, black, winding pathway of the sluggish Rembwe.

She preferred to sleep during the day, when the sun laid bare the monotonous drabness of the river scenery, and to take the tiller at night, when the land through which she glided was mysterious and fascinating in the kinder light of the moon. Only rarely, however, was her sleep uninterrupted. Along the banks were a great number of villages, built on clay mounds imposed on the sandy spits which stood out like islands amongst the ooze of the mangrove swamps. Though the canoe drifted past these at night, during the day Obanjo religiously tied up at each one in search of cargo. This practice, and the thread-bare condition of the sail, made their progress so slow that Mary claimed she had set up a record in the length of time she took to reach the Gaboon.

Since she was in no hurry, she enjoyed herself enormously during this leisurely cruise. At one village, where Obanjo possessed a wife and a flock of goats, she witnessed a first-rate, slapstick comedy. The trader wished to ship his goats to Gaboon, where they would fetch a very good price, and as she lay on the bamboo staging aft, trying to sleep, Mary was awakened by a startling series of yells and drum-beatings. Turning, she saw the skipper, his crew, and a number of helpful villagers trying to catch these goats. First the whole flock of goats appeared, and tore violently across the open piece of ground in front of the landing place. Two minutes later Obanjo and his helpers made their appearance, running at full speed in pursuit. For some minutes all she could hear was the sound of the chase; then the goats appeared once more in full flight, followed by Obanjo and his company. She and some of the villagers who were not engaged in the business cheered the pursuers on. This chase, which reminded her of a fight she had once seen on the stage between the armies of Macbeth and Macduff, save that it was better produced, with more noise and more supers, caused her a great deal of amusement.

While she was still enjoying this spectacle, she heard a well-modulated, evidently educated voice saying in perfect English:

'Most diverting spectacle, madam, is it not?'

She turned in surprise and saw standing on the bank by her canoe 'what appeared to be an English gentleman who had from some misfortune gone black all over and lost his trousers and been compelled to replace them with a highly ornamented tablecloth. The rest of his wardrobe was in exquisite condition, with the usual white jean coat, white shirt and collar, very neat tie, and felt hat affected by gentlemen out here. Taking a large and powerful cigar from his mouth with one hand, he raised his hat gracefully with the other and said:

'Pray excuse me, madam.'

I said, 'Oh, please go on smoking.'

'May I?' he said, offering me a cigar case.

'Oh, no thank you,' I replied.

'Many ladies do now,' he said, and asked me whether I preferred Liverpool, London, or Paris.

I said 'Paris; but there are nice things in both the other cities.'

'Indeed that is so,' he said; 'they have got very many decent works of art in the St. George's Hall.'

I agreed, but said I thought the National Gallery preferable because there you saw such a fine representative series of works of the early Italian schools. I felt I had got to rise to this man whoever he was, somehow, and having regained my nerve, I was coming up hand over hand to the level of his culture when Obanjo and the crew arrived, carrying goats. Obanjo dropped his goat summarily into the hold, and took off his hat with his very best bow to my new acquaintance, who acknowledged the salute with a delicious air of condescension.

'Introduce me,' said the gentleman.

'I cannot,' said Obanjo.

'I regret, madam,' said the gentleman, 'I have not brought my card-case with me. One little expects in such a remote region to require one; my name is Prince Kakaga.'

Mary apologized for being without her cards, and gave him her name and address. Obanjo was ready to set out, and the black gentleman having said good-bye in the most courteous manner, the canoe was pushed out from the bank. When they were out of earshot she learned that he was a Mpangwe who had at one time been agent for a big European firm at Gaboon but was now trading on his own account.

As the canoe glided quietly along on this same afternoon, two smaller canoes, each paddled by a young boy, shot out from the bank and made for them. The boys jumped on board, and after a few words with Obanjo, one of them carefully sank his boat, while the other turned his adrift. Mary thought little of this incident until their own small canoe, which had been astern with a crew, trawling for fish, came plunging through the water at a speed she had never seen it make before. The men on board were terror-stricken, and as they approached barely found breath to shout: 'The Fan! The Fan!' When they had overtaken the dugout, they scrambled over the side and flung themselves into the bottom of the boat.

Obanjo fired questions at them. They said there were thousands of Fans, armed with knives and guns, coming down the Rembwe with the set purpose of killing all on board their canoe. When the rest of the crew heard this news they too flung themselves into the bottom of the boat. But Obanjo was not a man to be afraid of anything:

'Take the rudder!' he shouted to me, 'take her into the middle of the river and keep the sail full.'

It occurred to me that perhaps a position underneath the bamboo staging might be more healthy than one on top of it, exposed to every microbe of a bit of old iron and what not and a half that according to native testimony would shortly be frisking through the atmosphere from those Fan guns; and moreover I had not forgotten being previously shot in a somewhat similar situation, though in better company. However I did not say anything; neither, between ourselves, did I somehow believe in those Fans. So, regardless of danger, I grasped the helm, and sent our gallant craft flying before the breeze down the bosom of the great wild river (that's the proper way to put it, but in the interests of science it may be translated into crawling towards the middle).

Meanwhile Obanjo performed prodigies of valour all over the place. He triced up the mainsail, stirred up his faint-hearted crew, and got out the sweeps, i.e. one old oar and four paddles, and with this assistance we solemnly trudged away from danger at a pace that nothing slower than a Thames dumb barge, going against stream, could possibly overhaul. Still we did not feel safe, and I suggested to Ngouta [who had, not surprisingly, decided to accompany Mary rather than return with the Fans through the forest] he should rise up and help; but he declined, stating he was a married man. Obanjo, cheering the paddlers with inspiring words, sprang with the agility of a leopard on to the bamboo staging aft, standing there with his gun ready cocked to face the coming foe, looking like a statue put up to himself at the public expense. The worst of this was, however, that while Obanjo's face was to the oncoming foe, his back was to the crew, and they forthwith began to re-subside into the bottom of the boat, paddles and all. I, as second in command, on seeing this, said a few blood-stirring words to them, and Obanjo sent a few more of great power at them over his shoulder, and so we kept the paddles going.

Presently from round the corner shot a Fan canoe. It contained a lady in the bows, weeping and wringing her hands, while another lady, sympathetically howling, paddled it. Obanjo in lurid language requested to be informed why they were following us. The lady in the bows said:

'My son! My son!'

In a second, three other canoes shot round the corner full of men with guns. Now this looked like business, so Obanjo and I looked round to urge our crew on to greater exertions and saw, to our disgust, that the gallant band had successfully subsided into the bottom of the boat while we had been eyeing the foe. Obanjo gave me a recipe for getting the sweeps out again. I did not follow it, but got the job done, for Obanjo could not take his eye and gun off the leading canoe, and the canoes, having crept up to within some twenty yards of us, poured out their simple tale of woe.

It seemed that one of those miscreant boys was a runaway from a Fan village. He had been desirous, with the usual enterprise of young Fans, of seeing the great world that he knew lay down at the mouth of the river, i.e. Libreville Gaboon. He had pleaded with his parents for leave to go down and engage in work there, but the said parents, holding that the tenderness of his youth unfitted him to cope with Coast Town life and temptation, refused this request, and so the young rascal had run away without leave and with a canoe, and was surmised to have joined the well-known Obanjo. Obanjo owned he had (more armed canoes were coming round the corner), and said if the mother would come and fetch her boy she could have him. He for his part would not have dreamed of taking him if he had known his relations disapproved.

Everyone seemed much relieved, except the *causa belli*. The Fans did not ask about two boys and providentially we gave the lady the right one. He went reluctantly. I feel pretty sure he foresaw more kassengo (or punishment) than fatted calf for him on his return home. When the Fan canoes were well back round the corner again, we had a fine hunt for the other boy, and finally unearthed him from under the bamboo staging. When we got him out he told the same tale. He also was a runaway who wanted to see the world and, taking the opportunity of the majority of the people of the village being away hunting, he had slipped off one night in a canoe, and dropped down river to the village of the boy who had just been reclaimed. The two boys had fraternized, and come on the rest of their way together, lying waiting, hidden up a creek, for Obanjo, who they knew was coming down river; and having successfully got picked up by him, they thought they were safe. But after this affair boy number two judged there was no safety yet, and that his family would be down after him shortly; for he said he was a more valuable and important boy than his late companion, but his family were an uncommon savage set.

We felt not the least anxiety to make their acquaintance, so clapped heels to our gallant craft and kept the paddles going, and as no more Fans were in sight, our crew kept at work bravely. While Obanjo, now in a boisterous state of mind, and flushed with victory, said things to them about the way they had collapsed when those two women in a canoe came round the corner, that must have blistered their feelings but they never winced. They laughed at the joke against themselves merrily. The other boy's family we never saw and so took him safely to Gaboon, where Obanjo got him a good place.

This incident resulted in the mouth of the Rembwe being reached sooner than at one time had seemed possible. At this point their clumsy craft became difficult to handle, for the waters of the Rembwe, 'Como, and Boqué were met by the rising tide, and the travellers found themselves contending with a swirling, unpredictable set of currents. They made poor progress. Because Obanjo's cargo had been dropped carelessly aboard, the canoe had developed a marked list, and in the rough water Mary found it impossible to keep to her place on the bamboo aft. The canoe rolled in the choppy seas and also developed a frightening lurch, which occurred at irregular intervals. Mary's belongings, loaded on the stern, were hurled into the water at the first kick of the canoe. Obanjo swore furiously, and even Mary regretted her lack of adequate language. To make matters worse, at the first puff of wind that reached them the counterpane-sail came away from its spar and spread itself over the crew. Now the canoe, yielding to the tide, jogged backwards towards the bank, swinging round and taking aboard a great deal of water. Amongst Mary's stuff floating around them was a basket to catch souls in, given to her as a parting gift by one of her most valued friends, a witch doctor, all her toilet requisites, her black bag, which held all her blouses, and various miscellaneous articles which she had collected in her travels.

Obanjo once more showed his quality: he hastily grabbed the black bag and bullied the rest of the crew into retrieving every single article that had gone overboard. It was now nearly time for the sun to set and as they had all seen enough of the estuary for the time being, he allowed the canoe to drift back into the Rembwe, where he moored for the night.

Early in the chilly, dank morning, their flimsy sail was hoisted once more and they set out to cross the estuary. By nightfall they had sailed the nine miles from the south to the north shore and anchored off Dongila. Mary was invited to spend the night at the Roman Catholic Mission, but she felt too tired to be able to face an evening in company, and declined. Instead, rolling herself in her blanket, she stretched herself on the bamboo staging and was soon sound asleep. At about midnight the tide turned, the canoe swung round viciously, and she was jerked into the water. Swimming round the craft, she scrambled aboard and in the inky darkness changed her wet clothes. Then she slept again, but on the bottom this time.

The next day they coasted along the northern shore to Glass. Mary was delighted, but a little apprehensive, when she saw Hudson awaiting her on the pier. After greeting her, he said that he had heard of her adventures. He made it very clear that he did not approve. When he had received news that she had left Lambaréné, he had reckoned that if she came out of the Great Forest at all, she would reach the Rembwe at Agonjo. Accordingly he had sent a surf boat with a good crew to that place to bring her downstream. This boat must have passed them while they were dodging up some creek in search of cargo. Mary was very grateful for Hudson's kindness, all the more because it was he alone who had made it possible for her to see the Ogowe. She told him how much she had enjoyed herself and how valuable his help had been, 'but he persisted in his opinion that my intentions and ambitions were suicidal, and took me down the Woermann Road, the ensuing Sunday, as it were on a string'.

Many of Mary's friends made it plain on her return that they believed she had simply been used by the black traders and hunters with whom she had journeyed for their own selfish purposes. They had taken her from one village to another as a 'circus turn'; in her company they had entered towns where the price of rubber and ivory was low, towns which they would otherwise never have dared to enter. When they had got into trouble, they had expected her to pay their fines, or in some cases their old trade debts. She was honest enough to own that there was a grain of truth in their argument.

Certainly Obanjo had found her a great help in his trading, as well as a most trustworthy lieutenant. Just as the Fans had been eager for her to stay with them and go elephant hunting, so he now invited her to join him in a trading venture up one of the neighbouring rivers into Spanish territory. When she asked him how she would profit from this expedition, he replied with true logic:

'What for you come across from Ogowe? You say, see this country. Ah, I say you come with me. I show you plenty country, plenty men, elephants, leopards, gorillas. Oh! plenty thing. Then you say where's my trade?'

She was forced to admit that trade was not her chief object, but declined to go with him on the grounds that, for the time being, she had seen enough men, elephants, and gorillas. Also she preferred to go into wild districts under the French flag. Even so, she did not state that she would never go with him again; as late as 1896 she was considering entering into this bizarre partnership, though she had quite made up her mind that she would at least insist upon a more courageous crew:

Picture to yourselves, my friends, the charming situation of being up a river surrounded by rapacious savages with a lot of valuable goods in a canoe and with only a crew to defend them possessed of such fighting mettle as our crew had demonstrated themselves to be. Obanjo might be all right, would be I dare say; but suppose he got shot and you had eighteen stone odd of him thrown on your hands in addition to your other worries. There is little doubt that such an excursion would be rich in incident and highly interesting, but I am sure it would be, from a commercial point of view, a failure.

13

CORISCO AND THE GREAT PEAK OF CAMEROON

THOUGH little mention has been made of Mary's serious work during her journeys among the Africans of the bush, it must not be assumed that all the time had been spent simply in travel. At every village she came to, the chiefs and the old people had been encouraged to talk. Special efforts had been made to get to know the witch doctors. The pursuit of the 'wild African idea', as she called it, was exciting, dangerous, and far more satisfying than big-game hunting. Back in Gaboon, she was eager to talk to Nassau, who could help her to understand some of the beliefs and practices that she had learned of at first hand. Even when she returned to England she received long letters from him, full of information about the religious ideas of the Bantu tribes amongst whom he had lived so long.

On her arrival on the West Coast her mind had been full of the deductions of every book on ethnology, German or English, that she had read in the previous fifteen years. Tylor's works, and those of the German anthropologists, had been studied, and in Frazer's *Golden Bough* she thought she had found a key to the underlying idea of native custom and belief. After her field-work she was forced to admit that this was not the case; some, but not all, of her facts could be fitted into the ready-made pattern, and the inconvenient exceptions could not be ignored. Nassau agreed that there was frequently no apparent link between the primitive African ideas and those of other religions, and that until more work had been done, no sweeping generalizations could safely be made.

Before he had come to Gaboon, Nassau had established his headquarters on the island of Corisco, some twenty miles by sea from the estuary. Mary was intrigued by his account of the island, with its Benga population and its inland lakes full of fish. It was clearly her duty to go over and investigate. The missionary was helpful, lending her his little schooner, the *Lafayette*, with his head man, Eveke, as skipper. Mary was delighted when she saw it, and, even though its African crew was the motley collection of riff-raff usually to be found on the Coast, she decided to sail on the next day.

The tide was under them and the wind was astern when they left Glass early the next morning. With the wind in its great white mainsail, so different from the counterpane of Obanjo's dugout, the yacht raced through the waves towards the open sea. At the mouth of the estuary the wind freshened, and they ran through the big seas in a splendid if somewhat alarming manner. Mary loved the sea, and was enjoying this exhilarating sail when she suddenly noticed that Eveke was happily sailing by the lee. In another second the boom swung violently across and, striking her a glancing blow, knocked her into the bottom of the boat. There she decided to stay, making herself as comfortable as she could with her collecting case as a back rest. All her faith in her skipper had gone.

She was not at all surprised to see the crew drink all the ship's water and go softly off to sleep. Her experienced eye noticed that the cargo was badly stowed, having been thrown in without regard to the balance of the boat, and she determined to have it shifted at the first opportunity. She was always finding fresh evidence of the African's utter failure to cope with the simplest mechanical operations. Unless he was under white supervision, he seemed incapable of getting a log into the water, or launching a surf-boat, without an enormous amount of pointless energy. Since Africa needed skilled labourers, Mary had come to the conclusion that a complete revolution was essential in the education provided by the mission schools. They must stop turning out clerks and train farmers, and craftsmen, and seamen.

Chancing to turn her eyes from the waves which rushed past, she saw to her astonishment that Eveke had lashed the helm and gone to sleep in the stern sheets. She got up from the bottom of the boat and took her place at the tiller. In spite of the fierce sun and the rough sea she felt a keen pleasure at being in command of her own craft once more. Africa had developed the latent desire for power which was the basic characteristic of this extraordinary woman. To satisfy it, she had fought the rapids of the Ogowe, defined the dangers of the Great Forest, and brought under her domination the most ruthless savages. This was the 'skylarking' which, once experienced, was to call her back to Africa and make the society of London dull and pointless.

She awakened Eveke when she made a landfall. He took over, roused the crew, and, after a series of most unseamanlike manœuvres, brought the yacht close up to the beach of Corisco and dropped anchor. Eveke had been born on this island, where his father, the Reverend Ibea, was the sole representative of the Presbyterian Mission. Mary was taken to his home, only to discover that the preacher was away on an evangelizing tour on the mainland. His wife, however, was very kind, insisting on giving her visitor her own clean and comfortable bedroom, with a superb view over the Atlantic.

Here she stayed for the next few days, waiting until the women of the island were ready to set out on their annual fishing trip to the lakes. She spent the time in solitary rambles, on one occasion getting lost, and on another finding herself followed by a jeering, spitting, sand-throwing band of children. They followed her with shrill cries of 'Frenchy no good! Frenchy no good!' An albino boy of about fourteen, with his head and arms thrust through an old sack which was his only garment, led this mob. Mary decided to teach these children a lesson. Pretending to be tired and feeble, she rounded a rocky point and there lay in wait. Round the corner after her came the yelling pack, led by the albino, straight into her arms. The leader left her without his sack and very much the worse for wear, and the girls who had spat and thrown sand at her were given a sharp reminder that good manners pay in the long run.

When the women were at last ready to set out, Mary went with them, and saw them plunge into the shallow water and scoop up fish by the basketful. The fish were disappointing: instead of the unknown specimens which she had hoped for, they turned out to be mud-fish, of which she already had a surfeit.

On her return she met Ibea, back from the mainland. He proved to be a splendidly built, square-shouldered man, a pure Benga, full of energy and enthusiasm. He spoke with great animation of his tribe, which was one of the oldest on the Coast. Formerly they had dominated all the surrounding regions, making war on their neighbours, hunting elephants, serving as crews on whaling ships, and capturing Africans to sell to the slave-traders.

Now there were hardly two thousand of them left, and these, he told her with regret, were poor in physique and unadventurous in spirit.

The decay of the coastal tribes was a matter of great interest to Mary. She asked for Ibea's opinion regarding its cause. He put it down to infant marriage and rum. Mary promptly pointed out that the latter at least had been plentiful during slaving days, and he was forced to admit that the present indolent life of the Coast was a more probable cause. As a Christian minister he felt it his duty to think that it was for the best that the old, blood-thirsty, warlike, Benga spirit was broken. Mary thought otherwise, and felt sure she detected a note of regret in his voice for the past glories of his tribe.

Her long talks with him confirmed her in her conviction that the thin veneer of white culture which the coastal African acquired was harmful. Her considered opinion was that the worst enemy to the existence of the African tribe was the man who came to it and said, 'Now you must civilize, and come to school, and leave off all those awful goings-on of yours, and settle down quietly.' For, since the African is teachable and tractable, the tribe often did so, and the women and some of the young men were happy and content with the excitement of European clothes and frequent church services, but the older men and some of the bolder young men soon got bored with these things and with the irksome constraints. Then they began to drink far too much rum, or to mope themselves to death, or to return to their native customs. The end was now worse than the beginning.

The African treats his religion much as other men do; when he gets slightly educated, a little scientific one might say, he removes from his religion all the disagreeable parts. He promptly eliminates its equivalent Hell, represented in Fetishism by immediate and not future retribution. Then goes his rigid Sabbath-keeping, and food-restriction equivalent, and he has nothing left but the agreeable portions: dances, polygamy, and so on; and it's a very bad thing for him.

On August 8th she set out for Glass, though there was a high wind and the sea frothed and boiled on the rocks with which Corisco Bay is studded. On Eveke's advice, she waited for slack water, then, saying good-bye to the missionary and his wife, she boarded the *Lafayette*. With her went an African woman whom

L

she had promised to land at Gaboon. Once more the luggage had been carelessly thrown into the boat, and she insisted that it should be properly stowed before they left their moorings. A lively scene followed, in the course of which Mary jumped forward, as she thought on to a bundle of the crew's clothes; it turned out to be the passenger's husband, however. He groaned loudly and demanded some compensation, but she pointed out brusquely that he came 'at shipper's risk'. The crew worked hard, but to little effect, for there were no lockers or cabins on the schooner, and the cargo, which included a lively ram, was not easy to pack away in an orderly fashion.

When at last they were ready to go, Eveke sailed the *Lafayette* clear of the land, and then Mary took over again. The wind was still from the south-east; the sheets were hauled tight, and the little yacht charged gamely over the rough seas, throwing up sheets of water which the wind blew back on to the crew as they chattered, and ate, and, for brief moments, slept. Not until the mainland was reached did Eveke take the helm again. They plunged on, just outside the line of surf that thundered all along the coast, until nightfall. Suddenly the wind dropped; Eveke ordered the sweeps to be manned, and they made an exciting dash through the breakers and beached their craft on a sandy spit of land. Here, they were protected from the full force of the rollers by two rocky reefs, and, having waded ashore and stretched their cramped limbs, they returned to have a meal and to get what rest they could on board.

The men used the mainsail and its boom to rig up an awning for themselves, and offered to make a shelter for Mary with the jibsail, but she preferred to sit by the rudder, watching the black, heaving sea, and the flying foam. She saw the mist come creeping out from the land, sending long arms towards the surf, and in the end enveloping the yacht and its crew. Now and then she dropped off to sleep—only to be startled into wakefulness either by the yacht dragging her anchor and bumping into rocks, or by the groans and cries of pain which came from under the awning when the ram became restless and its sharp horns came into contact with the sleeping men around it. Three times, with a plantain bush as weapon, she silenced one of the crew, whose high, quavering snore penetrated the noise of the surf and roused her to fury.

When the morning came, grey and cheerless, she awoke the

men, the boat was pushed off, the sail hoisted, and they set out to round Cape Esterias. By mid-day they had reached it, but the wind and tide were so foul that they were forced once more to beach their craft. A nearby village saved Mary from the discomfort of spending another night aboard, and though it was still early, she was soon asleep on a sack of seaweed on the floor of the house which one of the villagers had lent her.

On awakening, she visited the Roman Catholic Mission under the wing of a most attractive young African woman who made it her business to see that the white visitor was taken care of. The Father in charge entertained her, though they could not talk together, neither knowing the other's language. He insisted on giving her bread, sugar, meat, and oranges from his frugal store, and she returned to her house to have

a square meal and sugar in my coffee, thanks to the missionary, and so to bed, as Mr Pepys would say. I am sure, by the way, Mr Pepys would like Agnes, she is quite his style of beauty, plump and pleasant; I don't expect he would care for my seaweed bed though, unless he had been broken in to it by African travel, for Mr Pepys had great ideas of being comfortable in a conventional way.

On the next day she made presents to Agnes and to the owner of her house, who refused any payment, and made her way to the shore. She met the local lunatic, an enormous, jet-black negro, who, fortunately, was quite harmless. In her travels she had seen many such, although among some tribes it was customary to kill all who showed signs of madness. She was glad to find that the Benga, with whom she had been staying, were more humane, giving food and shelter to the afflicted ones and chaining them to trees only when they were dangerous.

At sea again, she had a frightening experience:

We get out through the breakers and hoist our mainsail and beat along among the rollers, rolling ourselves like mad as the heavy waves sweep broadside on under us. Just off the Cape itself we have to run almost out of sight of land, to get round a rock reef; I am bound to admit that the consequences of this spirited display of seamanship are not encouraging. A terrific marine phenomenon exhibits itself suddenly off our weather bow, at a distance of fifteen to twenty feet. My first opinion is that it is the blow-up of a submarine volcano, not because I am a specialist in marine volcanic methods, having never seen one out of a picture-book, but this is very like the picture-book, waves, and foam, and flying water. In another second it explains itself completely, for out of the centre of it springs aloft the immense fluke of a great whale, as high as our mainmast. It swings round with a flourish and then comes flop down on to and into the broken sea, sending sheets of water over us and into the boat. We bale hard all, and stand by for another performance, but, to my intense relief, we see the whale blow a few minutes later a good distance off, and then have another flourish—a most charming spectacle on the horizon.

My crew then say as they take the baling easier, it is a common affair in Corisco Bay just about now, for it is the courting time for whales. I don't come again into Corisco Bay in canoes or small craft while any of that wretched foolishness is going on. They also tell me that the other day four people coming from Cape Esterias to Gaboon in a canoe were drowned, all hands, and they think they must have fallen in with this whale; certainly if a small canoe had been as close as we were it would have had a bad time of it, for with us the mainsail protected us from a lot of water coming on board. Goodness knows, however, we had enough, and did some brilliant baling.

Soon after this they reached the estuary and raced for home with the wind on the beam. They put in at the guardship, where the medical officer demanded a clean bill of health. While they were explaining that it was impossible to get one, since there was no Spanish official on the island, the *Lafayette*, tied up to the guardship, managed to get her topmast up the tap of a cistern. When they had been ignominiously extricated by the crew of the bigger ship, they shoved off, hoisted their mainsail and made a dash for Hatton and Cookson's Wharf. Mary was glad to return to comfort and pleasant company, for she was bruised and jaded after her sea cruise.

Here she remained for several weeks, continuing to study native religion and law and adding to her collection of specimens; then, with great regret, she said good-bye to her English and French friends and boarded the *Niger* for the first stage of the return voyage. Though the Germans, with whom she claimed kinship, were her favourite race, she had been forced to admire the spirit and efficiency shown by the French in their West African lands. Her dream, never to be realized, was to see British territories on the West joining hands with those on the East to form a great belt across Africa from which trade goods would drain down to the coasts and enrich both the African producer and the English manufacturer. The French, by their drive from their colony in Senegal towards the Nile, were already making this more difficult, but she bore them no grudge for their expansionist policy; she only regretted the lethargy of British statesmen in allowing these lands to slip from their grasp.

The *Niger* called at Cameroon, and, as she approached, Mary was again confronted with her great temptation—the magnificent Mungo Mah Lobeh—the Throne of Thunder. It had attracted her on her first voyage on the *Lagos* in 1893, and although there was neither fish to collect nor fetish to study, she landed in Cameroon to climb this mountain. At Victoria she made preparations for her expedition and was ready to set out by September 20th. Several mountaineers, amongst whose number was Richard Burton, had scaled the Great Peak from the west; no one, with the possible exception of Roger Casement, had climbed it along the route which she proposed to take from the east.

The weather was fine when she left Victoria with a miscellaneous collection of Wei Weis, Ivory Coasters, Liberians, and two Africans of Cameroon who knew the mountain. Up to Buea, 3000 feet above sea level, the Germans had begun to build a road, for a few miles the party walked along it through superbly beautiful scenery. Soon, however, it came to an end, and they turned into the unbroken forest. Torrential rain now fell, turning the slippery bush path into a rushing stream. Hours of squelching through mud, scrambling over rocks, and wading knee-deep through running water, at last brought them to a long low hut where two African Bible-readers lived. Mary decided to spend the night here.

Soaked through and shivering with cold, she was in a most miserable state. Soon she hated the sight of the mission teachers, who stood about, and smoked, and spat, and made themselves thoroughly disagreeable. She had paid them well for accommodation for the party, and at last managed to get the room to herself. News of her arrival had spread, however, and soon the hut was thronged with neighbouring tribesmen. She was kind to them, gave them rum, and ushered them out. A few moments later she was disturbed by a noise and, looking round, saw that the shutters had been pushed aside and the window was full of black heads. Even when these were firmly closed, the sightseers did not give up: bunches of them managed to edge their way into her room silently and she would turn to see rows of shining teeth and watching eyes.

In the next room she heard chattering and high-pitched laughter, and noted that one of her men, Kefalla, seemed to know a lot of entertaining, though highly scandalous, facts about the white residents of Victoria. But she must have sleep. First, she vaselined her revolver, for it had suffered from the rain, then she rolled herself in a blanket, and with two Bibles and two prayer-books bound in a pair of trousers as a pillow, stretched herself on the plank which served as a bed.

The next day's journey was worse: first one and then another of the travellers began to slip, lost control and fell full length, sliding down the muddy hillside on his belly. Mary had her turn, covering herself with mud from head to feet and arriving at Buea in such a sad, bedraggled state that the first thing that Herr Liebert, the officer in charge of the German garrison, suggested after a friendly greeting was a hot bath. But, just as she had refused to borrow kindly agents' clothes when she had arrived soaked and shivering at their factories in the bush, so she now declined this well-meant invitation: 'Men can be trying! how in the world is anyone going to take a bath in a house with no doors, and only very sketchy window-shutters? . . . Thank goodness he has a table and a bench, and a wash-hand stand, made out of planks, for his spare room, which he kindly places at my disposal. . . .' Here she washed and changed into the driest of her clothes.

Mary thought nothing of living alone with naked cannibals for weeks; in fact she was amused and rather scornful when she heard of the American lady traveller who insisted on Africans putting on drawers before they were admitted to her presence. Yet she had all the primness which one expects from a Victorian woman in matters which concerned her own dress or conduct.

Herr Liebert was on the verandah when Mary reappeared. In spite of her tiring climb, she listened with genuine interest to his account of the recent capture of Buea by German forces, and to his description of his troubles in running this isolated village. She possessed a keen sense of humour, a matter-of-fact courage, and a calm reliance upon her own resources, all of which made her a welcome guest in the houses of lonely African traders and administrators. But it was her deep and instant understanding and sympathy which gave her power over all whom she met.

As she talked with Herr Liebert, vivid lightning flashed from dark clouds which had rolled down from the mountain, and suddenly a tornado burst upon Buea with a fury which made her wonder what would happen to her when she left the shelter of the town. But she had accepted the challenge of the Great Peak, and, after a good night's rest, rose at 5 a.m. and roused her men. All their arguments for waiting for another day were brushed aside, and with a sergeant from the garrison as a guide, the little party left the last outpost on the slopes of the mountain.

The guides and carriers in her party were a poor lot and she missed the lively, indomitable Fans badly. On her first attempt to reach the summit, they all deserted her, and she had to find her way back alone to the dreary, tentless camp which they used as a base. Ignoring their excuses, all palpable lies, Mary first silenced and then shamed them with her flow of invective. Three of them she sent back in disgrace the next morning, and then prepared to set out once more.

A tornado descended on them, however, and the attempt had to be abandoned on that day. When it had passed, the bundles were made up ready for an early start in the morning, and she tried to get some sleep.

September 25th. Rolled off the bed twice last night into the bush. The rain has washed the ground away from under its legs, so that it tilts; and there are quantities of large longicorn beetles about during the night—the sort with spiny backs; they keep on getting themselves hitched on to my blankets; and when I wanted civilly to remove them they made a horrid fizzing noise and showed fight—cocking their horns in a defiant way. I awoke finally at about five o'clock soaked through to the skin. The waterproof sheet has had a label sewn to it, so it is not waterproof, and it has been raining softly but amply for hours. I wish the camp bed had had a ticket sewn on, and nothing but my profound admiration for Kaiser Wilhelm, Emperor of Germany, its owner, prevents me from making holes in it, for it sags in the middle, and constitutes an excellent rain-water cistern.

She had to drive her Africans hard on this day. As they climbed higher on the mountain, the cold clutched and numbed them; and it was only the spirit of their leader that prevented them from lying down to die in the cold, sleety rain. Her bones ached with the cold, and her teeth chattered in her head, yet, when they reached some trees, she had the strength to wrap each carrier in a blanket, administer a tot of rum, and get a fire going. When her men had recovered a little, she made them light two more fires, cut wood and place it near the flames to dry, and warm up some food for themselves and her. With a hot meal inside them, and their pipes glowing, the men cheered up and set about building covers, made from wet blankets, for the fires. Then they curled themselves up and slept. Mary, afraid that one of them would catch fire, tried hard to keep awake, and, wrapping herself in her two sodden blankets, sat down upon the food box and leant her back against a tree. Twice when she dozed, she rolled off into the fire. Her men pulled her out before she was burnt or had put the fire out.

On the next day, September 26th, in bitter weather, Mary reached the summit of the Great Peak. Her men failed again: only two reached the face of the peak; one, Xenia, she left three-quarters of the way up, the other, Bum, stumbled on beside her.

When we are some 600 feet higher, the iron-grey mist comes curling and waving round the rocks above us, like some savage monster defending them from intruders, and I again debate whether I am justified in risking the men, for it is a risk for them at this low temperature, with the evil weather I know, but they do not know, is coming on. But still we have food and blankets enough for them, and the camp in the plain below they can reach all right, if the worst comes to the worst; and for myself—well—that's my affair, and no one will be a ha'porth the worse if I'm dead in an hour. So I hitch myself on to the rocks, and take bearings, particularly bearings of Xenia's position, who, I should say, has got a tin of meat and a flask of rum with him, and then turn and face the threatening mist.

It rises and falls and sends out arm-like streams towards us, and then Bum, the headman, decides for the third time to fail to reach the peak, and I leave him wrapped in his blanket with a bag of provisions and go on alone into the wild, grey, shifting, whirling mist above, and soon find myself in at the head of a rock ridge in a narrowish depression, walled by massive black walls which show fitfully but firmly through the mist.

I can see three distinctly high cones above me, and then the mist, finding it cannot drive me back easily, proceeds to desperate methods, and lashes out with a burst of bitter wind, and a sheet of blinding, stinging rain. I make my way up through it towards a peak which I soon see through a tear in the mist is not the highest, so I angle off and go up the one to the left, and after a desperate fight reach the cairn— only alas! to find a hurricane raging, and a fog in full possession, and not a ten yards' view to be had in any direction. Near the cairn on the ground are several bottles, some of which I suppose the energetic German officers had emptied in honour of their achievement, an achievement I bow down before, for their pluck and strength had taken them here in a shorter time by far than mine. I do not meddle with anything, save to take a few specimens and to put a few more rocks on the cairn, and to put in among them my card, merely as a civility to Mungo, a civility his Majesty will soon turn into pulp. Not that it matters—what is done is done.

Only twenty-eight people had reached the summit before her, but she found cause for pride only in the fact that she had got her men up so high and back again without a casualty: 'but as they said I was Father and Mother to them, and a very stern though kind set of parents I have been'.

On the 28th, after two days of dangerous and exhausting travel, she stumbled back into Victoria, taking great care to arrive after nightfall so that her conventional, though kind, host, von Lucke, should not be shocked by the sight of her tattered, mud-stained clothes.

Her journeys in her beloved West Africa were nearly at an end. Von Lucke managed to dissuade her from making the passage from Victoria to the Rio del Rey, and from thence into Calabar, by canoe. He convinced her that during the tornado season such a journey would be suicidal folly: two out of every six canoes which set out had been lost with all hands. Instead, he promised her a passage on the *Nachtigal*, the guardship which served as the Governor's yacht. While she waited for it to arrive, she spent pleasant days walking in the country around Victoria, or in exploring the bay by boat.

She studied the German administration and found much to admire. Later she was to defend the government of Cameroon against charges of undue severity towards the African. The traders interested her. She witnessed the last stages of an amusing tussle between a defaulting Cameroon trader and his creditors.

Now according to African law, if you take a man's life, or for the matter of that, his body, dead or alive, in settlement of a debt, your claim is satisfied. You have got legal tender for it. I remember coming across a demonstration of this law in the colony of Cameroon. There was, and still is, a windy-headed native trader there who for years has hung by the hair of loans over the abyss of bankruptcy. All the local native traders knew that man, but there arrived a new trader across from Calabar district who did not. Like the needle to the pole, our friend turned to him for a loan in goods and got it, with the usual result, namely, excuses, delays, promises—in fact anything but payment. Enraged at this and determined to show the Calabar traders at large how to carry on business on modern lines, the young Calabar trader called in the Government and the debtor was gently but firmly confined to the Government grounds. Of course he was not put in the chain-gang, not being a serious criminal, but provided with a palm-mat broom he proceeded to do as little as possible with it, and lead a contented, cheerful existence.

It rather worried the Calabar man to see this, and also that his drastic measure caused no wild rush to him of remonstrating relations of the imprisoned debtor; indeed they did not even turn up to supply the said debtor with food, let alone attempt to buy him off by discharging his debt. In place of them, however, one by one the Cameroon traders came to call on the Calabar merchant, all in an exceedingly amiable state of mind and very civil. They said it gave them pleasure to observe his brisk method of dealing with that man, and it was a great relief to their minds to see a reliable man of wealth like himself taking charge of that debtor's affairs, for now they saw the chance of seeing the money they had years ago advanced, and of which they had not, so far, seen a fraction back, neither capital nor interest. The Calabar man grew pale and anxious as the accounts of the debts he had made himself responsible for came in, and he knew that if the other debtor died on his hands, that is to say in the imprisonment he had consigned him to, he would be obliged to pay back all those debts of the Cameroon man, for the German Government have an intelligent knowledge of native law and carry it out in Cameroon. Still the Calabar man did not like climbing down and letting the man go, so he supplied him with food and worried about his state of health severely. This that villainous Cameroon fellow found out, and was therefore forthwith smitten with an obscure abdominal complaint, a fairly safe thing to have as my esteemed friend Dr Plehn was absent from that station, and therefore not able to descend on the malingerer with nauseous drugs. It is needless to say that at this juncture the Calabar man gave in, and let the prisoner out, freeing himself thereby from responsibility beyond his own loss, but returning a poorer but wiser man to his own markets, and more assured than ever of the villainy of the whole Dualla tribe.

In Calabar she was grieved, yet amused, by the way the Presbyterian missionaries refused to take into account African ways of life. She found it was customary in the best African circles for young girls to wear a trailing cloth to which their spirit souls—all the tribes she met thought that each child had its own soul, a second soul which was pure spirit, and a third soul which lived in some animal, reptile, or bird—could attach themselves. Since this was a pagan custom, the stern-faced Presbyterians made it a rule that no girl with a trailing cloth should enter their schools. A war followed between parents who were profoundly shocked at the idea of their daughters having no tails, and missionaries equally shocked at the idea of their having them. Presbyterian prejudice fought African respectability.

Mary met a young girl in Victoria who had been taught at the mission school. She asked her what she was learning:

'Ebberyting,' she observed with a genial smile.

This hurt my vanity, for though I am a good deal more than twelve years of age, I am far below this state of knowledge; so I said, 'Well, my dear, and if you do, you're the person I have long wished to meet, for you can tell me why you are black.'

'Oh, yes,' she said with a perfect beam of satisfaction, 'one of my pa's pas saw dem Patriark Noah wivout his clothes.'

I handed over to her a crimson silk necktie that I was wearing, and slunk away, humbled by superior knowledge.

It was from first-hand encounters such as these that she came to the conclusion that the teaching of some of the missionaries was of little benefit to the African.

Eventually the *Nachtigal* dropped anchor off Victoria; Mary made herself presentable in the only dress which had survived her long stay in Africa, and went aboard to meet the Governor. He confirmed the offer made by his deputy to take her to Calabar, and, after a few more pleasant days in Ambas Bay and on the neighbouring islands, she found herself transported in state to the English colony. Sir Claude and Lady MacDonald had left for home, but she was entertained by friends she had made there earlier in the year. She made a point of paying a visit to Miss Mary Slessor before she finally embarked on the *Bakana* for England. 'Skylarking and study' had ended. Ahead lay power, and reputation, and a grim fight against impossible odds.

14

THE RETURN

WHEN the *Bakana* docked on November 13th, 1895, Mary was no longer a nonentity. Government officials, traders, and missionaries had felt the impact of her powerful personality and news of her impending return had preceded her. Reporters were there to meet her when she landed.

She was not very communicative. Only to Reuter's representative did she give a résumé of her travels and adventures. She had important things to say about Africa and she had no intention of making the same mistake as Du Chaillu had made on his return. Thus she took great care to say nothing of her more startling experiences; gorillas, leopards, and elephants were barely mentioned. She simply stated she had passed through little-known parts of South West Africa, and when pressed to give more details, mentioned that there was, of course, plenty of big game in those regions and that some of the tribes with whom she stayed were cannibals. She tried to give the impression that she had rarely been in danger.

Most of the daily papers gave the better part of a column to careful and fairly accurate accounts of her experiences and the object with which she had made the journey. The *Daily Telegraph* went further, however, and acclaimed her as a champion of women's rights: 'almost more wonderful than the hidden marvels of that dark continent are the qualities of heart and mind which could carry a lonely English lady through such experiences as Miss Kingsley has "manfully" born'. Their columnist declared that she was striving for the 'emancipation of the sex', but warned others that she 'ought not to be imitated by any lady of less robust constitution and firm resolution than she had exhibited'.

Mary had no intention of allowing these comments to pass unchallenged. She was no 'new woman', nor did she take the least interest in the emancipation of the sex. Throughout her travels she had been careful to avoid any hint of masculinity; indeed, at times she had been almost prudish. She wrote immediately to the *Telegraph*: 'I do not relish being called a "new woman". I am not one in any sense of the term. Every child I meet tyrannizes over me, and a great deal of time I ought to give to science goes in cooking etc. I do not think travelling now lays one open to this reproach.'

She was generous in her praise of the traders and officials who had helped her:

I just puddled round obscure corners and got myself immersed in catastrophes . . . they have hauled me out of rivers with boat-hooks, they have given me passage in their river steamers, though doing so for them meant sleeping under the saloon table, they have sent provisions up country after me.

In order to show how dependent she had been on the male sex, and to put an end to some of the sensational stories which were beginning to be told in the more sensational papers, she promised to publish her journals.

By 1895, when Mary returned to England, a great change had taken place in men's attitude towards the empire. Thirty years earlier it had been the declared policy of the Government to avoid any extension of British territory overseas. Even Disraeli, who is so often looked upon as the champion of empire, had expressed the opinion to Lord Derby in 1866 that the colonies should be left to defend themselves; that the African Squadron should be recalled, and that the settlements on the West Coast of Africa should be abandoned. When this policy proved impracticable, particularly in Africa, it was very reluctantly that men such as Gladstone had taken action. Disraeli made a great show of being an ardent imperialist, and spoke in high-flown language of the splendour of Britain's imperial future, but he did very little during his six years of office to extend the empire: the route to India had been secured by the purchase of almost half the shares of the Suez Canal, and Cyprus had been acquired by diplomacy. Now, in the 'nineties, Britain was eagerly competing with France and Germany in West Africa: territories in the Niger valley, which Britain might have occupied without opposition at any time after the discoveries of Mungo Park in the first quarter of the century, had become a cause for dissension among these three powers. So great was the danger of armed clashes, which might lead to war in Europe, that the Berlin Conference was convened, and spheres of influence were delimited. Public opinion supported those English statesmen who were determined that Britain should get her share in the 'scramble for Africa'.

A number of factors contributed to this new concept of empire. The writings of the new imperialists, Sir Charles Dilke, Sir John Seeley, and J. A. Froude, had been partly responsible; for, though holding widely different views, all stressed in one way or another the important part played in Britain's development by her lands overseas, and asserted that it was her duty to be the leading spirit of an empire from which her greatness had arisen. The competition of Germany and America in the world's markets had made British industrialists appreciate more fully the benefit of vast areas under the Crown, where their goods could be sold without prohibitive tariffs and from which raw materials could be brought back for the mills and workshops at home. The travels of Livingstone, 1853 to 1873, had aroused an interest in Africa unrivalled since the day when Park had returned from his heroic exploration of the Niger; while Stanley's accounts of his travels, from 1869 to 1893, had painted a picture of powerful states and fierce warriors which stirred the imagination of young and old. When, finally, there appeared a poet writing on imperial themes who possessed the art of appealing both to the uneducated and to the middle classes, the revolution was complete. Some men came to see British possessions and dominions overseas as an historical necessity; others conceived of them as a source of profit; while to most of the remainder the adventure of Kipling's far-flung empire made a powerful emotional appeal.

Mary was fortunate to find yet another change. By tradition the Colonial Secretary played a very minor role in national affairs, and the post was assigned either to a young politician with little influence, or to a peer. In 1895 Joseph Chamberlain, acknowledged to be the most powerful personality in British politics after the retirement of Gladstone, had astonished all his friends by choosing this post in Lord Salisbury's ministry. He at once interested himself in colonial development. West Africa, which had been acquired reluctantly, and shamefully neglected, was bound to attract his attention. He regarded it as part of an undeveloped estate, in which money must at first be spent lavishly in order to bring profit and honour to the mother country. He set about building railways; he enabled the colonies to borrow on favourable terms; he encouraged the investment of British capital in colonial enterprises; he provided funds for research into tropical diseases. Under his direction an attempt was made to reform colonial administration, and to introduce some uniformity throughout the empire in place of the chaos which prevailed when he took office. Moreover, he took up the French challenge and prepared to support British claims by force if necessary. Men's attention, then, was directed to Britain's imperial future, and not least in her African dependencies. More important still was the awakened interest in the peoples who inhabited the vast, unknown regions of Africa.

In December 1895 Jameson, supported by Chamberlain and Rhodes, made his abortive raid into the Transvaal; Lugard had won the 'race to Nikki' for the Royal Niger Company, and had forestalled the French in their attempt to seize control of Borgu; an armed force was engaged in following up his success by a campaign against the slave-raiding Emir of Nupe; and an expedition was on its way to deal with Prempeh, the king of Ashanti, whose Golden Stool at Kumasi was still washed by the blood of human sacrifices in spite of the treaty signed with Sir Garnet Wolseley twenty years previously. No traveller had ever returned from Africa when it was more in the public eye.

It is not surprising that the firm of Macmillan, which had published the works of Charles Kingsley, should invite his niece to write an account of her travels for them. She accepted gladly; she had a great deal that she wished to say about Africa, and she needed money to enable her to return and continue her studies. In the midst of household tasks she set to work sorting the 'rag-bag of miscellaneous information' contained in her diaries and notes. The thread of narrative she determined to keep as thin as possible: African religion, law, and customs were to be her main theme; trade and industry subsidiary but still important. Her own adventures she regarded as of no consequence, but she had to relate some of them to prove that she had been in West Africa and was speaking of a country she knew personally.

Meanwhile her return had inspired the *Spectator* to publish an article on 'Negro Future'. The writer said that the total impression of her story, as of nearly all African stories, was that of a people abnormally low, evil, and cruel. 'There is no corner of Europe, Asia, or America,' he declared, 'where that tale of the villages, in which human limbs are regularly exposed for sale as meat, would not produce a shudder of horror, and so far as geographers know, there never has been one.' He went on to assert that it was in Africa that the lowest depths of barbarism had been reached, and that the evil nature of the African was a problem that the European must study and solve if the vast continent were to be governed in security and peace. All European powers had failed so far, he claimed, and he advocated a system of government 'steady and kindly' which treated the African as a child to be turned into a man. He strongly opposed any form of self-government.

Mary was roused. The exaggerated stories of her adventures were damaging the cause she had very much at heart: the establishment of a system of government which would be least injurious to African institutions. No restraint was evident in her reply. First, she repudiated the accounts of her travels which were appearing, then she struck out at the missionaries, whom she held largely to blame for the contempt and horror with which the African was regarded in Great Britain. 'In mental and moral affairs the African is by no means as strikingly inferior as he is in handicrafts: he has both a fair sense of justice and honour, not much worn by daily use, and very easily eliminated by a course of Christian teaching; but it is there, and if you know the way, you can rouse it, and make it work,' she wrote in a letter to the *Spectator*.

She declared emphatically that the African was not deliberately cruel, but that, in a land where there were no prisons, workhouses, or hospitals, treatment of criminals and sick persons was bound to be ruthless by European standards. In the matter of sacrificial rites, she argued that one should try to understand the underlying idea before condemning too harshly. She denied the assertion that the African was a drunkard, and claimed that his 'so-called friends, the Protestant missionaries', made him out to be one in order to explain to their supporters at home why they had produced such poor results. Lastly, she had a word to say about cannibalism: 'I dare not openly defend his cannibalism and will only remark that the true Negroes, the natives of the Niger

Delta, for example, are *never* culinary cannibals, but always do it from religious motives.' She admitted that this was not the case with Africans of Bantu stock, but declared that 'whenever you find among them a cannibal tribe, you will find a superior tribe, like the Fans for example'.

This last extraordinary statement, not surprisingly, led some to accuse her of defending cannibalism. Reference was made to her 'singular letter' by St. Loe Strachey, the editor of the *Spectator*, and the missionaries showed how incensed they were by her unprovoked attack. Though in the numerous lectures she gave and articles she wrote during the next four years she learned to use judgement and restraint in controversy, Mary never retracted one word of these first allegations against the Protestant missions on the Coast. She was absolutely convinced by what she had seen, that by removing the fear of immediate retribution for evil-doing and putting in its place the concept of punishment in some future existence—punishment, too, which could be mitigated by repentance—the missionaries had opened the way for vice, and crime, and dishonesty among their converts. Far too many of the rogues, cheats, and liars whom she had met on the Coast had been Christians.

Meanwhile Mary had sent her collection of fishes, insects, and reptiles to Gunther at Kew, and he reported on them most favourably. Notable amongst the specimens was one absolutely new fish brought from the Ogowe, which he named after her; also six modifications of known forms; and one fish which delighted the specialist, for only one specimen of its kind had ever been seen, and that had been brought from the Nile forty years earlier; one new snake; one lizard for which the British Museum had been waiting for ten years; and altogether forty-three different species of fish which were valuable for distribution to other museums. Gunther's praise delighted Mary, more especially as he was eager for her to undertake another expedition.

A great deal of her time was now spent on her book. Writing came easily to her, and the happiest moments in England were spent pen in hand. The 'at-homes' and the dinners to which she was invited held no attraction. She was still, in her own opinion, an outsider—one who watched the game and was distressed to see people sitting together, calling one another by their Christian names, when a short time before they had been abusing one

M

another in different company. She preferred to be with rough bush traders, or lively straightforward Africans.

Her first, and most important, task was to get the chapters on fetish right; after that she was sure all would be easy. In this she was fortunate. On a visit to lecture at Liverpool, she met again Forshaw, an old African trader whom she had first met at Calabar in 1893. He was, perhaps, the most useful critic she could have had, for he was one of the only two white men who had been admitted to the great Secret Society of Egbo, which dominated the negroes of the Oil Rivers. He agreed to read her work, and Mary was jubilant when he found no fault with it.

Literary agents, editors, and societies now invited her to write or to lecture: 'there is simply nothing like feeling a dilapidated idiot for bringing down intellectual work on one,' she wrote to her publisher, 'and one monthly magazine after another now are asking me for articles, pointing out carefully, that it will be good for my book'. She agreed with them and, in spite of the protests of her friends, she undertook a great deal of work, especially as a lecturer. At first she found this a strain, for she was completely without experience of public speaking. She soon gained confidence, however, and satisfied most of her audiences with a mass of information interlaced with racy anecdotes, all told in lively and colloquial fashion.

She was now in a position to give expression to the ideas of empire which she had, in part at least, learnt from her father. Any undeveloped land she regarded as legitimate spoil for the conqueror. Africa, especially, needed a paramount power which could establish peace, suppress barbarous practices, put an end to the traffic in slaves, and protect the trader. The soldier had his part to play. War was to her no evil thing if waged in a good cause. All she demanded was that 'tiger justice, tempered with mercy', should be administered and that the conqueror's honour should never be tarnished.

To follow Mary in her lecturing tours during the years that she spent in England after her second expedition would be a pointless task even if it were possible. Yet so much of her time and energy were spent in this way that the nature and scope of her work is worth study. She travelled the length and breadth of the British Isles to address learned societies, colleges, and schools. A considerable income was made from fees, which seem to have varied between five and ten guineas. She was always prepared, however, to help a good cause by lecturing for nothing, and on several occasions raised large sums for the nonconformists. Her most important work was done at Oxford, for the Hibbert Trustees; at Liverpool and Manchester, where she spoke to the Chambers of Commerce; and at the Imperial Institute in London. Since she believed that once the British public understood the African, he would have justice, she never hesitated to accept invitations to lecture, even when she was hardest pressed.

Though she had no connection with any Christian church, many of her lectures were given to those interested in missionary work. She tried hard to combat the prevalent ideas—of the inherent wickedness and brutality of the black man—which returning missionaries had instilled in their English audiences, partly, in her opinion, to make their work appear more dangerous and difficult than it really was, and partly to satisfy their supporters who expected a stirring tale. At one meeting in 1898 she heard the ex-bishop of Sierra Leone condemning the negro for his lack of gratitude and for his failure to understand unselfishness in others. He concluded by stating categorically that the African mistook kindness for weakness, and by advocating rigorous discipline. Speeches of this kind she considered to be misrepresentation of the facts, bound to lead to hatred and injustice, and she set to work to give a truer and deeper insight into the African's character.

There is no doubt that Mary believed that the Church of England missionaries on the Coast did more harm than good, and she did not mince her language about them when she wrote to her personal friends. After the first few weeks in West Africa, she had declined to stay with them; and in 1898, when she was planning to return, she declared bluntly that never again would she darken their doors under any circumstances. She blamed them largely for the evil reputation of the traders in West Africa, a reputation which, in her view, was often not deserved; she herself had suffered from their horror of unconventional behaviour and the tales they told of her free and easy intercourse with black and white traders. Though she was too honest to accept their hospitality and then attack them, she had no scruples in accepting their invitations to lecture in England. There is a note of amusement in her reference to herself as a 'Mephistopheles' whose main object in talking to their supporters was to remove the illusions carefully fostered by their own missionaries.

As a professional, paid lecturer, Mary, while still concerned to give a true and sympathetic picture of life in West Africa, was naturally less eager to deal with controversial subjects. Typical of this group of talks is the one she gave to Cheltenham Ladies' College which provides the material for the account in chapter nine of her experiences in the Ouronogou country; or the one she gave to the Liverpool Geographical Society in which she described her visit to a Fan village far up the Ogowe in the Sierra del Cristal. She could be a lively and highly entertaining speaker when she ceased to be a propagandist, and she became so popular that by 1899 she was seriously taxing her strength. In a letter to her friend John Holt, in November of that year, she gave the following list of engagements: Friday, at York; Saturday, Newcastle, where she lectured to two thousand people in a draughty theatre; Monday, another lecture in Newcastle; Tuesday, Edinburgh; Thursday, Glasgow; Friday, Dundee; Saturday, Edinburgh again; Monday, Aberdeen; Tuesday, Glasgow again; Wednesday, Hawick; Friday, Birmingham. On Saturday she returned home.

She instructed her agent to book lectures for her in the big industrial towns of the Midlands and the North. She preferred them to the residential towns; she found Clifton so refined that she had to seek relaxation, after her lecture, in the company of a ship's carpenter living in the back streets of Bristol, whom she had met on her travels.

Mary was most in earnest when she was speaking of trade and politics in West Africa. The bulk of these lectures, however, were given after she had become a public figure, with the publication of her first book, *Travels in West Africa*, early in 1897. The views she expressed in them, and the battles she fought on behalf of the trader and the African, will be discussed in a later chapter.

Meanwhile every second of her time was taken up. Her brother Charles had returned from China—she had 'unshipped him, safe and sound', and brought him back to the little flat in Addison Road. But his presence meant more work, and when she was at home she spent far too much time looking after his comfort. He offered one piece of sound advice on the writing of her book: 'unless you can write in the grand style, you had better write naturally'. He helped her with a sketch or two and in a letter to her publisher she asks for one of these by 'that talented and fitful artist', her brother, to be included.

Two matters caused her a great deal of worry as the book neared completion. First, she was not satisfied with the maps which were available; they were not accurate enough to suit her. In the end she left them out, both from the first edition and from a later edition—even after there had been some criticism of a travel book without maps. To Macmillan she wrote: 'I can go on feeling I am the only African explorer who has *not* published an iniquitously inaccurate map.'

The other problem caused her considerable distress. Her old friend, Guillemard, whom she had asked to read her manuscript to make certain that she had made no mistakes when writing of scientific things, took it upon himself to act as a literary editor. He began to send to her long passages completely rewritten. She felt very strongly about this, for while she had no literary pretensions, she considered that her own writing made her meaning clear. Africa, with its smells, its loathsome diseases, its men, black and white, going about their business without regard to good taste or convention, had captured her imagination. Wandering, colloquial, and lacking in grammar and syntax her style might be, but by means of it she had somehow managed to show Africa as she had seen it. Guillemard, on the other hand, though grammatical and to the point, managed to take all the colour out of her narrative.

To Macmillan she stated the case plainly. She found it difficult to recognize her own book when the doctor had done with it; moreover, he had taken out all those things which, she was convinced, would appeal to the reader. She would have none of this 'Guillemardese'; out must go all the 'perhaps's, however's and Dear Readers'.

She was very tactful when she wrote to her friend: she suggested that the book had not enough literary merit for it to be worth his while to attempt to improve it. His corrections, she said, 'stood on stilts out of the swamps and gave a very quaint but patchy aspect to the affair'. She reminded him that she had asked him only for an opinion on scientific affairs, never dreaming that he would go in for detailed emendation of the script. Finally, she stated that she would sooner publish the work as it stood, since she had no literary reputation to lose nor any ambition to gain one. She had her way.

She had previously written to Lady MacDonald, who was now at Pekin, complaining of the amount of expurgation which had been thought necessary, presumably by her publisher. Never one who respected those in authority, Mary had been particularly hard on Governors, Consul-Generals, and bishops and it was these passages that had to be left out. One scene, in particular, she regretted having to suppress: it was a lively account of a quarrel on one of the Ogowe steamers between a bishop with a long, red beard and voluminous, white flannel petticoats, and the Governor of the Ogowe. The captain and Mary had to take refuge on the saloon table to keep clear of these two gentlemen who were rolling about on the floor of the tiny cabin 'in close but warlike embrace'. The fight went on in spite of the messages of peace she and the captain poured down upon them.

Though she found these restrictions tiresome, she yielded to her publisher. On one matter, however, she remained adamant. Macmillan's did not wish her to provoke attack by becoming further involved in the controversy which was raging at this time on the liquor traffic. When she had been on the Coast she had commented openly on the absence of drunkenness amongst the Africans. The traders, to whom she made the remark, said that others had noticed this fact before her but had carefully refrained from making it known when they returned home. They had dared her to mention it. She had already taken up the challenge in her reply to the article in the *Spectator*, but she was not satisfied with that. She insisted on including a long attack on the misrepresentations of the missionary party on this subject, in the section of her book which dealt with 'Trade and Labour in West Africa'.

By the end of 1896 she was very tired. She wrote to her friends about her everlasting colds and headaches. She seemed to have no time even for brief visits to those whom she was fond of. But the book was nearly ready for the press, Charles talked of going to Burma, and she could soon return to her South West Coast. She had seen quite enough of London; one last effort and she would be free to do as she wished. Such was her state of mind as she finished off the book which was to make her a public figure and a power in the land.

15

AFRICAN RELIGION

MARY KINGSLEY wrote and spoke flippantly about her adventures and when, on her return to England, she was drawn deep into controversy about the way in which West Africa was administered and reluctantly suggested a different system, she declared that the task was really beyond her powers. In her chosen field of study, African religion and law, however, she claimed to be an expert and was prepared to stand up to recognized authorities on anthropology like Tylor or Lyall if they disputed any of her conclusions. She was convinced that her pioneer work amongst the primitive peoples of the West Coast was of vital importance, and her dearest wish was to return to the Coast to carry it a stage further.

In her view it was impossible to judge West African institutions without first studying and understanding the basic principles of African religion, for, unlike the European, the African was influenced in every thing that he did by his religious beliefs. To be successful in war or trade, to preserve his crops, or protect his family, he had to be on good terms with the host of spirits who, he believed, were for ever interfering in his affairs. His religion consisted of a knowledge of this spirit world, and his customs and ceremonies arose from his idea of the best way to influence it in his favour.

Good administration, then, must be based on a sound knowledge of African beliefs. The work which she had begun must be carried on by trained anthropologists. African institutions must be understood before they were modified or destroyed. Any other course was fraught with danger, not only to the subject races but also to the imperial power. Africa might well become another Ireland if it was left to the kind of men sent out by the Colonial Office, for they knew little or nothing of the people they ruled and their main preoccupation was to gain promotion to another, healthier, colony.

In the first book written after her return, *Travels in West Africa*, Mary devoted over a hundred pages to fetish. Fuller details and explanation followed in articles, in lectures, and in her second book, *West African Studies*. It is clearly neither necessary nor possible to deal fully with the subject here, yet to make no attempt to give some idea of what Mary always regarded as her main contribution to the West African problem would leave a curious gap in the story of her accomplishments.

She wrote first of the African conception of God. She found that the religious ideas of the negroes who lived in the district from the Gambia to the Cameroons differed considerably from those of the Bantu tribes of the South West Coast. The beliefs of the latter were not nearly so definite, nor did they influence these men in their everyday lives to quite the same extent. Their great God, although he varied in name from tribe to tribe, was essentially the same amongst all the tribes from the Fans of French Equatorial Africa down to the Bihe south of the Congo. He was a non-interfering deity, so remote and disinterested that his influence was negligible. Having created man, plants, animals, and the earth, he took no further interest.

It was not so with the lesser spirits with whom the African believed the universe to be peopled. Their interest in human affairs was profound, and, since they were nearly all malevolent, means had to be found to drive them away or to propitiate them. Because they paid little heed to his frequent prayers to them to turn away, to leave him, his loved ones, and his property alone, the African had been forced to develop a cult whereby they could be understood, managed, and, on occasion, used. This cult is what the European calls witchcraft.

Mary concentrated her attention on these lesser spirits, and upon the methods used by the people of the South West Coast to circumvent their evil designs. She learnt that the spirits could never be trusted; that even an established medicine man might fall a prey to the very beings which he had previously controlled and used. She discussed them with Dr. Nassau of Gaboon, who was the greatest living authority on the religion of the Bantu tribes. He agreed with her that the origins of these lesser spirits were not clear, for some seemed to have come into existence through the authority of God, some to be self-existent, and a third group to consist of the souls of human beings who, although in another world, still retained their human wants and feelings. He attempted to classify the spirits: *Manu*, human disembodied spirits; *Abambo*, vague beings equivalent to our ghosts; *Ombwiri*, spirits like dryads, having a special habitat such as a rock, a promontary, or a tree; *Mionde*, the chief agents in causing sickness and in aiding or hindering human plans; and lastly two vague groups, one resembling the Lares and Penates of classical times, and belonging especially to one family, and the other consisting of those who enter into any animal body—usually that of a leopard. The last are sometimes the spirits of human beings, and the animal will then use its strength in the service of the 'possessor'.

All these spirits are limited in the nature of their power: none can do all things, and all are subject to proper human incantations though they cannot always be trusted to perform their allotted tasks. Only a medicine man can capture a spirit and imprison it in a charm. Mary made a careful study of this process. The medicine man who had been called in, after a great many ceremonies and other antics, induced the spirit to localize itself in some object belonging to the man who had ordered the charm. Antelopes' horns, large snail shells, large nut shells, and similar articles were often used for this purpose. Among the Fans, Mary discovered, the customary charm-case was in the shape of a little sausage, with an outer casing of pineapple fibre, filled with dung and other putrid substances. These were believed to attract the spirit and to induce it to leave its former abode and enter the charm. In addition, other materials were inserted which had relation to the work the spirit had to do. The nails, hair, or blood of the person whom the charm was to influence were thought to be potent ingredients, and if they could not be procured—no easy task, since every African was on his guard, and carefully buried or destroyed such things—parts of his clothing, such as his loin-cloth, which contained his sweat, had to serve. If the charm—variously called *ju ju, mionde, bian, larwiz,* or *gree gree*—contained a powerful spirit, its owner became a witch greatly to be feared by his neighbours.

Charms can be made for any purpose: to kill, to cause love, to protect a house, a canoe, or a weapon, or to ensure a good bargain with a trader. Sometimes they fail. The cause of failure, in the opinion of the Africans, is the unreliable nature of the spirit within the charm. Even if all the proper ceremonies have been performed and all the necessary gifts offered, the spirit may desert its owner. All he can do now is to purchase another charm from the medicine man and cut his losses by selling the useless *ju ju* as a curio to some white man.

There are only a few spirits which can be controlled and made to serve their masters. The others have to be placated by sacrifice and incantations. The value of a sacrifice bears a definite relation to the importance of the request made: for instance, a dish of plantains is thought adequate to induce a powerful spirit to grant a minor favour, but a much greater favour may necessitate the sacrifice of a human being. *Ombwiri* are often propitiated by quite small gifts: stones heaped by passers-by at the foot of a great tree, or a leaf thrown from a passing canoe towards a promontory, gratify the spirits inhabiting these things. Incantations either resemble the prayers of Europeans—though almost always their object is to induce spirits to stay away and to allow the African to manage his own affairs—or consist of cabalistic words and phrases handed down from their ancestors.

Believing as he does that the universe is peopled by so many malevolent spirits, the African is forced to turn to his medicine man for protection and advice. The life of negro and Bantu is dominated by a profound belief in witchcraft and its effects. Death is nearly always regarded as a direct consequence of the witchcraft of some hostile human being who acts by means of spirits over which he has obtained control. He may use his power either to 'witch' something out of his enemy or to 'witch' something in. In the former case, witches sometimes made money by trapping a man's soul, which leaves his body and wanders about while he sleeps. When they have caught the soul, they tie it up over the canoe fire and its owner sickens as the soul shrivels; unless he is prepared to buy it back from the witch, he dies.

Other witches, through sheer wickedness or because they are hired by a man's enemies, may entrap his dream soul in such a way that it is permanently maimed. In the bait which attracts the soul are hidden knives and sharp fish-hooks that kill it or damage it so severely that its owner sickens and dies. On one occasion Mary noticed that one of her Krumen was worried and was obviously sickening for some illness. On enquiry, she found that for several nights he had smelt the enticing odour of smoked crawfish seasoned with red peppers. The head man was called in, and he came to the conclusion that some witch had set a trap, baited with these delicacies, for the unfortunate man's soul. Accordingly for the next few days extraordinary precautions were taken to prevent his soul from wandering at night. When he lay down to sleep, he was completely covered by a blanket and his nose and mouth were protected by a handkerchief tied tightly round his face. After he had spent three or four most uncomfortable nights thus, he was judged to be safe. Certainly he recovered his spirits and his health.

Mary found that among the Bantu tribes it was more common to witch something into a man. She was convinced that more Africans died as a direct result of this form of witchcraft than from any other single cause. That poison, rather than an evil spirit, was the agent, seemed clear to her. Since the suspicion of witchcraft arose at almost every death, the witch doctor was called in and a post-mortem held. The body was cut open to find in the entrails some sign of the path of the injected witch. The witch doctor then set about finding the person responsible for his patient's death:

Then woe to the unpopular men, the weak women, and the slaves; for on some of them will fall the accusation that means ordeal by poison, or fire, followed, if these point to guilt, as from their nature they usually do, by a terrible death: slow roasting alive—mutilation by degrees before the throat is mercifully cut—tying to stakes at low tide that the high tide may come and drown—and any other death that human ingenuity and hate can devise.

The terror in which witchcraft is held is interesting in spite of all its horror. I have seen mild, gentle women and men turned by it, in a moment, to incarnate fiends, ready to rend and destroy those who a second before were nearest and dearest to them. Terrible is the fear that falls like a spell upon a village when a big man, or big woman, is just known to be dead. The very men catch their breaths, and grow grey round the lips, and then everyone, particularly those belonging to the household of the deceased, goes in for the most demonstrative exhibition of grief. Long, low howls creep out of the first silence —those blood-curdling, infinitely melancholy, wailing howls—once heard, never to be forgotten.

The men tear off their clothes and wear only the most filthy rags; women, particularly the widows, take off ornaments and almost all dress; their faces are painted white with chalk, their heads are shaven, and they sit crouched on the earth in the hut, in the attitude of abasement, the hands resting on the shoulders, palm downwards, not crossed across the breast, unless they are going into the street.

Meanwhile the witch-doctor . . . sets to work in different ways to find out who are the persons guilty of causing the death. Whether the methods vary with the tribe, or with the individual witch-doctor, I cannot absolutely say, but I think largely with the latter.

Among the Benga I saw a witch-doctor going round a village ringing a bell which was to stop ringing outside the hut of the guilty. Among the Kabindas (Fjort) I saw, at different times, two witch-doctors trying to find witches, one by taking on and off the lid of a small basket while he repeated the names of all the people in the village. When the lid refused to come off at the name of a person, that person was doomed. The other Kabinda doctor first tried throwing nuts upon the ground, also repeating names. That method apparently failed. Then he resorted to another, rubbing the flattened palms of his hands against each other. When the palms refused to meet at a name, and his hands flew about wildly, he had got his man.

The accused person, if he denies the guilt, and does not claim the ordeal, is tortured until he not only acknowledges his guilt but names his accomplices in the murder, for remember his witchcraft is murder in African eyes. It is not just producing the parlour tricks of modern spiritualists.

If he claims the ordeal, as he usually does, he usually has to take a poison drink. Among all the Bantu tribes I know this is made from Sass wood (sass = bad, sass water = rough water, sass surf = bad surf etc.) and is the decoction of the freshly pulled bark of a great hardwood forest tree, which has a tall unbranched stem, terminating in a crown of branches bearing small leaves. Among the Calabar tribes the ordeal drink is of two kinds: one made from the Calabar bean, the other, the great ju-ju drink Mbiam, which is used only in taking oaths.

In both the sass-wood and Calabar bean drink the only chance for the accused lies in squaring the witch-doctor, so that in the case of the sass-wood drink it is allowed to settle before administration, and in the bean that you get a very heavy dose, both arrangements tending to produce the immediate emetic effect indicative of innocence. If this effect does not come on quickly you die a miserable death from the effects of the poison interrupted by the means taken to kill you as soon as it is decided from the absence of violent sickness that you are guilty.

The dread of witchcraft and its consequences made life in most African villages dark with fear and murder. It was no uncommon thing for ten or more people to be killed for one man's sickness or death. Throughout vast regions outside the control of

European administrators Mary Kingsley estimated that the death-rate exceeded the birth-rate because of this wholesale slaughter.

The African witch doctor was not concerned solely with dealing with spirits; he also practised more mundane methods of medical treatment. Some went in for surgery and their technique resembled that of European doctors up to the seventeenth century. Mary tells the story of one man who had been accidentally shot in the chest by another on the Ogowe: the native doctor who had been called in made a perpendicular incision into the man's chest, extending down to the last rib; he then cut diagonally across, and actually lifted the wall of the chest and groped about among the vitals for the bullet, which he successfully extracted. Of course no anaesthetic was used. The patient died. On another occasion she saw a minor operation. A man had broken his left arm; the doctor drove a piece of bamboo through the flesh and muscles from his wrist to his elbow, wrapped the arm in plantain leaves and bound it round tightly with bush-ropes. When she met the man several months after the operation, his hand and arm were quite useless and were withering away. In view of these heroic methods of African surgeons, it is not surprising that the Africans of the French Congo travel for hundreds of miles to place themselves under the care of Dr. Schweitzer at Lambaréné.

After describing the frantic efforts of Africans to prevent their relations and friends from dying by forcing pepper up their noses and into their eyes, or by propping their mouths open with sticks, or by yelling at the tops of their voices—all efforts to persuade the soul to return—Mary wrote of what she had found out about funeral ceremonies and burial customs. The subject is too long to deal with here except to mention that burial varied from the cannibalistic methods of the Fans to a form very similar to our own among the Igalwas and M'pangwe. In those regions in which she travelled she found it a common practice to destroy the bodies of those who had malevolent souls, or of those whose souls after death persisted in returning to inhabit new-born babies.

Even after a man is dead and his slayer has been found and punished, his widows must remain in a state of filth and abasement until after his soul-burial is complete, a business which may take six months. They are forced to sit only on the ground, to eat only a little coarse food, to watch in the hut after the body is buried, and to provide from their own property for the entertainment of all the friends of the deceased who come to pay him the last compliments. It is rare for the wife, or even the sons, to inherit the property of the head of their family: more commonly it goes to his eldest brother, probably, Mary thought, with the purpose of keeping the wealth of the 'house'—i.e. the estate—together. If it were allowed to pass into the hands of weak people like women and children, this would not be the case.

The spirit of the dead man, after a certain period, goes to the underworld. The tribes that Mary encountered had different ideas about this place. All agreed that there was no marriage there. Some races, such as the Tschwis and the tribes of Calabar, ensured a chief's happiness by killing a number of his wives and slaves so that he might be well served in his new home. This custom had the more practical merit of protecting him, during his life, against poison, for his wives, knowing that if he died they would die too, were extremely careful to see that his food was wholesome. Mary heard the complaint that when European authorities stepped in and prevented the killing of wives and witches, no longer was an honest man's life or property safe.

Since some tribes believe that in the new land there are markets, towns, and all things as on earth, their dead have to be provided with wealth to keep up their position. When the killing of wives and slaves is prohibited, this takes the form of gold dust, cloth, and other forms of wealth. However, there are sometimes difficulties:

In the Delta there is no under-world to live in, the souls shortly after reaching the under-world being forwarded back to this, in new babies, and the wealth that is sent down with a man serves as an indication as to what class of baby the soul is to be repacked and sent up in. As wealth in the Delta consists of women and slaves I do not believe the under-world gods of the Niger would understand the status of a chief who arrived before them, let us say, with ten punchions of palm oil, and four hundred yards of crimson figured velvet; they would say 'Oh! very good as far as it goes, but where is your real estate?' The chances are you are only a trade slave boy and have stolen these things'; and in consequence of this, killing at funerals will be a custom exceedingly difficult to stamp out in these regions. Try and imagine yourself how abhorrent it must be to send down a dear and honoured relative to the danger of his being returned to this world shortly as a slave. There is no doubt a certain idea among the Negroes that some souls may get a rise in status on their next incarnation. You often hear a woman saying she will be a man next time, a slave he will be a freeman, and so on, but how or why some souls obtain promotion I have not yet sufficient evidence to show. I think a little more investigation will place this important point in my possession. I once said to a Calabar man, 'But surely it would be easy for a man's friends to cheat; they could send down a chief's outfit with a man, though he was only a small man here?'

'No,' said he, 'the other souls would tell on him, and then he would get sent up as a dog or some beast as a punishment.'

My first conception of the prevalence of the incarnation idea was also gained from a Delta Negro. I said, 'Why in the world do you throw away in the bush the bodies of your dead slaves? Where I have been they tie a string to the leg of a dead slave and when they bury him bring the string to the top and fix it to a peg, with the owner's name on, and then when the owner dies he has that slave again down below.'

'They be fool men,' said he, and he went on to explain that the ghost of that slave would be almost immediately back on earth again growing up ready to work for someone else, and would not wait for its last owner's soul down below, and also that a soul returning to a family, a thing ensured by certain ju-jus, was identified. The new babies as they arrive in the family are shown a selection of small articles belonging to deceased members whose souls are still absent; the thing the child catches hold of identifies him. 'Why, he's uncle John, see! he knows his own pipe.'

Mary witnessed encounters with apparitions, some of which were nature spirits, others human spirits—which exist before as well as during and after bodily life—and finally the spirits of material objects. One of the most frightening spirits, or class of spirits, of which she had first-hand experience, was known as Sasabonsum among the Tschwis, though he had other names in other regions. The spirit lived in the forest, usually under great silk-cotton trees at whose roots the earth is red. No African would make a path near such a tree, nor camp near one at night. Sasabonsum, who took the form of a giant, was the friend of witches, who often drew their power from him, and he delighted in attacking unprotected travellers at night, overpowering them, and either eating them or sucking their blood. Attempts were made to placate him by gifts of human victims in remote regions, or, where this was prohibited, of sheep and goats. While Mary was in Africa human sacrifices were still being offered to him by priests dedicated to his service in Ashantee and Dahomey.

Rarely did they travel at night without her companions encountering some apparition. They would stop dead in their tracks until the spirit had vanished, then they would advance slowly and examine with the utmost care the spot where it had stood. From the physical condition of the place they could tell what class of spirit had halted them: if they found only a log, a rock, or the branch of a tree, some inferior spirit had been there; white ash betrayed the presence of a medium-class spirit which had been destroyed by the magic they had thrown at it, or, at worst, one from which they could buy protection from the medicine man of the next town they entered; but if there were no traces of the spirit, then gloom descended upon the party, for they knew that they had been confronted by a powerful spirit which would undoubtedly do them harm. Unless they found a witch doctor with very potent charms to protect them, one at least of the party would become seriously ill.

It was Sasabonsum himself who caused the greatest terror amongst her followers; in the Cameroons, on the Calabar, and on the Ogowe this evil spirit made its presence felt. One side of the spirit was rotting and putrefying, the other sound and healthy, and her African porters believed that their lives depended upon not touching the unclean side. Usually they flung themselves into the bush at the side of the path when they heard or saw anything that looked like a man approaching; but sometimes the track was too narrow, being a mere ditch between smooth clay walls, or a narrow gorge between rocks. Then there was no means of avoiding the horrible apparition. It is not surprising that Africans refused to stir abroad at night or that they should prefer to spend their time dancing to the beat of the tom tom, or sitting in the village hut listening to the tales of their elders.

Mary found that the African believed that man has four souls: the soul that survives, the soul that lives in an animal away in the bush, the shadow soul (the shadow cast by the body), and the dream soul. If any of these souls was harmed in any way, the man to whom it belonged was in serious danger of dying. At the first sign of sickness the witch doctor was called in to decide what should be done. He might have to inject another dream soul into the sufferer, if his own had been trapped by an enemy, or he might order that offerings should be made to a bush soul that was causing trouble because it felt neglected; but if he diagnosed damage to the shadow soul or to the soul that survives, there was little he could do for the sufferer. The fact that many forms of illness were attributed to interference with men's souls by a witch was another cause for the fear and hatred of witches throughout West Africa.

Many witch doctors were among Mary's friends, and she had made a careful study of their methods and beliefs. She came to the conclusion that they believed in the underlying ideas upon which their practices were based. They made no claim to be infallible, but they could with truth assert that most of their patients recovered. She suspected that this was due either to the work of the village apothecary—who usually administered drugs before the witch doctor was called in—or to the fact that the African was far more prone than the white man to all kinds of nervous disorders which were best treated in the awe-inspiring and forceful manner adopted by witch doctors. On the whole, then, Mary thought they did more good than harm, since even their detective work in finding witches acted as a deterrent to murder by poisoning.

In the eighteen months that she spent in West Africa, Mary had discovered that the pagan African's concept of a good life differed basically from that of the races who have accepted a revealed religion. In West Africa, devotion to religion did not constitute virtue; in fact the man who was least mixed up in religious affairs was held to be the most virtuous. The African could gain the love and respect of his fellow men by being a good husband and father, an honest man in trade, and a just man in the council house. Only out of necessity did he take part in religious practices; he had to protect his family and his possessions from interfering spirits and from his enemies who might harm him through their agency. If he were a house father or a chief, he might have to go in for religion in a big way, for it was his duty to become the possessor of a *ju ju* powerful enough to protect his people from the spirits who brought plague and famine. His religious practices might make him feared and respected but they had nothing to do with virtue.

Mary was convinced, then, that the barbarous customs which she studied in West Africa were the result of the harsh conditions

N

under which the primitive tribes lived. All natural forces were their enemies, and to survive they believed that a constant and ruthless war must be waged against the spirits and the evil men who used them. Interference by missionaries and administrators who failed to realize or understand this basic fact would, in her opinion, upset the delicate balance of tribal life without seriously affecting the cult of witchcraft.

To substitute trained doctors for witch doctors in the vast territories which were being annexed to the Crown was a stupendous task—in 1949, according to available figures, there were less than four hundred doctors in Nigeria, with a population of over thirty million, and the proportion is still lower in French Equatorial Africa. To expect a few missionaries not only to convert millions of Africans to Christianity but also to induce them to abandon superstitious beliefs and to lead moral lives when the fear of immediate punishment was removed, seemed to be unrealistic. Better, she thought, to leave things as they were, rather than attempt to turn Africans into Europeans overnight.

Though many who have studied primitive peoples sympathetically have come to the same conclusion, it would seem that the counsel they give is one of despair. Conquering races surely have an obligation to raise the subject peoples from the morass of barbarism and superstition in which they often live, and to teach them the techniques of the modern world. The romantic view of the noble savage, left to develop his own culture aided by the anthropologist and the teacher, is in some ways further from reality than the dreams of the philanthropists. To make of West Africa a reserve might well be to condemn the African to stagnation and extinction.

16

A PUBLIC FIGURE

UNTIL the end of 1896 Mary Kingsley had been known only to the small circle of those interested in West African affairs. She had made a good story for the newspapers for a month or so after her return, and she had drawn large crowds to hear her lectures. If she had not written *Travels in West Africa* she would soon have been remembered only as another of the band of Victorian women who had already shown that they could shoulder responsible tasks. With the publication of this book she became a public figure.

Sales were remarkable for a volume of over seven hundred pages, containing long passages on fetish, trade, and the geography of West Africa—subjects which do not usually attract great numbers of readers. By the end of the year, when the publishers were planning a cheaper edition, Mary felt herself justified in refusing to leave out sections which they thought too controversial. To a friend she confided the fact that they had made three thousand pounds profit from the first edition, so she was under no obligation to them.

Many newspapers and journals printed reviews, and most of them were favourable, though the African expert who wrote for *The Times* wrote slightingly of it. One notice in particular delighted Mary. The redoubtable Bruce Walker, who had himself explored the Ogowe, wrote about her book in the *Athenaeum*. He had done more than anyone to discredit Du Chaillu when the latter had written of his adventures in gorilla land in 1861. Now he paid glowing tributes to Mary:

Miss Kingsley—humorous and even comical as her method often is—must undoubtedly be taken seriously. . . . Moreover she has the courage of her convictions, and spares neither government officials nor missionaries when she thinks that they merit censure, whilst she does not hesitate to bestow a due meed of praise on the often abused trader.

He was impressed by her knowledge of African religion and law, and declared that it was 'impossible to speak too highly of the chapters on "Trade and Labour", and "Disease in West Africa" '.

Mary had the greatest gift that a writer can have. She was an interesting character, and in every sentence that she wrote she revealed something of herself. This was no dull travel book, no catalogue of places seen, but an adventure in which every reader walked by her side. With unlaboured skill she led him into the disease-ridden swamps, or into the dark forest among poisonous snakes and gorillas, and imperceptibly brought him to think of the savage men who were her companions. Some of them were cannibals, none of them thought much of killing a man; but they had a sense of justice, they could be trusted and controlled. When she demonstrated that most of their savagery was the result of their environment, and of the powerful spirits whom they had to control or propitiate, even the most prejudiced reader began to doubt whether after all the African was 'half devil and half child'.

Though she wrote disparagingly of her own adventures, and invited her readers to laugh at them, no one could fail to realize that a deep purpose lay beneath her chaff. Neither the African nor the trader must be condemned unheard. She was eager to stand forth as their champion.

It was natural that she should be invited to lecture at Liverpool, the headquarters of the African merchants. It was in her talk to the Geographical Society of this city that she came down unequivocally on the side of the trader. In her opinion he was not the black sheep that the missionaries made him out to be. Rough he might sometimes be, but on the whole he was just, and honest, and, in nine cases out of ten, he protected and fathered the Africans whom he employed. When she had met some of these men on board ship, she had thought them heartless and cruel. Seeing them again among their employees, she had been surprised to find them sitting up at night with a sick African, or defending his rights against unjust officials. The best of them, such as Hudson, Forshaw, Boler, and Dunnett, went further and made a study of their customs and religion in order to understand them.

These men, too, were doing a work essential to England. She told her Liverpool audience:

A colony drains from the mother country yearly thousands of the most able and energetic of her children, leaving behind them their aged or incapable relations; whereas the holding of the West African markets drains a few hundred men only—only too often for ever; but the trade they carry on and develop enables thousands of men and women and children to remain safe in England in comfort and pleasure, owing to the wages and profits arising from the manufacture and sale of articles used in that trade. So I trust those at home in England will give all honour to men who are still working there, or who are lying buried in the weed-grown, snake-infested cemeteries and the pathless swamps of the Coast; and may England never again dream of forfeiting or playing with the conquests won for her by those heroes of commerce, whose battles have been fought out on lonely beaches, far from home or friends and often from another white man's help, with none of the anodyne to death and danger given by the companionship of hundreds of fellow-soldiers in a fight with a foe you can see, but with an enemy you can see only in the dreams of delirium which runs as a poison in aching brains and burning veins.

I may be regarded as unduly prejudiced in their favour by having known these men individually, but I assure you that the very mean opinion they have openly expressed as to my intelligence in going out there after beetles and fishes was enough to make even a naturalist like myself prejudiced permanently against them. Nevertheless, I own they have given me the greatest assistance, and it is owing to them and to their influence and power over the natives that I have been able to do anything worth the doing that I have done, and I have always found them men I was proud to be allowed to call friends and know were fellow-countrymen, for, as has been well said, 'of such is the kingdom of England'.

Mary went even further than this in her support of the traders. She was convinced that it was primarily upon the commercial men that the West Africans must rely for justice and prosperity. A flourishing and peaceful community meant good business for them: moreover, they were prepared to stand aside from the day-to-day government of the country, and to leave African institutions untouched provided that they were not too blood-stained for a white man to stomach. Neither the missionaries nor the Government officials could do this: the former, in Mary's view, overlaying native savagery with a 'thin veneer of rubbishy white culture', and the latter, often through sheer ignorance, tampering with African law and custom in a way that was bound to lead to the breakdown of tribal life and authority, without putting anything else in its place. From 1897 until her departure for South Africa in 1900, she worked ceaselessly to persuade the Government to grant the independent traders a voice in the running of our West African colonies.

It is difficult to accept Mary's estimate of the worth of the trader. Wherever the home government has stood aside and left the development of primitive regions mainly in his hands, the African has suffered. By the 'eighties the Liverpool and Manchester firms were asking for the help of the Government in their struggle with the African middlemen, who tried to control all the trade of the Niger hinterland. When, partly to safeguard trade interests, protectorates were declared over large areas, it was only reasonable that the Colonial or Foreign Office should hold the balance between trader and African. The fact that, in Mary's opinion, this task was being mishandled was no justification for abandoning it.

It was in the interests of the trader to keep the West African permanently as a producer of primary goods which could be bought cheaply and shipped to the factories of Europe. Further profit could then be made by selling him manufactured goods from England. In this way both merchant and manufacturer benefited. While the trade on the Coast was in the hands of a great number of competing firms, the native producer could expect a fair price for his goods; but in the twentieth century most of these firms were absorbed by vast organizations and there was a serious danger that West Africa would become a source of monopoly profit. Any increase in the world price of primary products tended not to go to the African who brought them to the Coast, but to the foreign trader who could simply increase the price of the manufactured goods which the African was forced to buy. There would have been no question of 'the common sense and humane opinions of the English trade lords' (in which Mary placed so much reliance) preventing this exploitation. The African has had to look for protection to the Colonial Office which she so detested.

Some time in 1897 Mary met John Holt, the most remarkable of the Liverpool merchants who traded with West Africa. Beginning as an assistant to the British consul on Fernando Po in 1862, he had set up as a trader on his own account when his employer died, and had built up an impressive business. His own diaries show him to have been a hard-headed business man—he even drew up a formal legal agreement when he employed his brother to help him in his early years at Fernando Po—but he was completely honest, and a true friend to the African. There must have been some quality in this successful man which appealed to Mary. For three years she corresponded regularly with him, asked for his advice on all the most serious matters of policy, and on one occasion declared in a letter to E. D. Morel: 'I regard Mr Holt as my political leader, and am a nice nuisance to him; but I absolutely trust him, and I know the educated Africans look on him as the only man they can rely on.'

Africa has exercised a powerful attraction upon a number of gifted men. Mungo Park, after great hardships in his first expedition, gave his life in a second attempt to find the mouth of the Niger; Clapperton, a sick man, returned to the court of the Sultan of Sokoto where he died trying in vain to open up British trade; Richard Lander could not keep away from the Niger, whose course he had traced to the sea, and was killed there by Delta tribesmen who resented British interference with their trade; Livingstone, after years of tramping through bush tracks exploring the Zambesi, returned to die in central Africa, far from any white settlement; and in our own time Albert Schweitzer has, since 1913, abandoned his brilliant career in Europe to live as a doctor amongst the primitive Ogowe tribesmen. These men, and a host of lesser ones, cut themselves free from family ties, and lived bleak, comfortless lives. Mary, like them, had felt the fascination of Africa, and like them she had no personal life.

It is necessary, then, to write of the last years of her life rather as one writes of a prominent politician. The reader may like to know that the great man has a charming wife, or spends his leisure hours felling trees or painting pictures, but the real life of the man is so interwoven with affairs of national importance that an understanding of one is impossible without an at least superficial knowledge of the other. To understand Mary, it is necessary to know what was happening in Africa between the time when she returned home and her last voyage out to the Cape in 1900.

Mention has been made of the international rivalry in West Africa. The groups of Englishmen who resisted French and German claims were not themselves united. First, Sir George

Taubman Goldie, who controlled the Royal Niger Company, by vigorous action, and by the influence he exercised on the British Government, had countered every move made by the French since 1880. It was he who had sent Lugard in 1894 to make treaties and to show the English flag in the towns which the French were claiming, in what is now Nigeria. But this great man was detested by the independent traders of Liverpool and Manchester, and not without cause. The Powers who met at Berlin (1884–5) had declared that Great Britain should see that the navigation of the Niger was free to the traders of all nations. In 1886, however, this duty, with all other powers of administration, was passed on to the Royal Niger Company. In the words of Miss Margery Perham: 'To charge the Company . . . with the duty of ensuring freedom of trade . . . was rather like employing a cat to ensure the safety of mice.' In fact these powers were used by Goldie to enforce a virtual monopoly of trade for the Company, thus excluding the Liverpool men and giving them a real grievance.

Neither was there a united effort by the Government: at the Colonial Office Chamberlain was determined to resist the French, but parts of the West Coast came under the jurisdiction of the Foreign Office, where Lord Salisbury was more ready to compromise. Chamberlain appears from the first to have been determined to withdraw the charter of the Royal Niger Company, ostensibly because its resources were inadequate to open up the vast hinterland to trade, but more probably because he found Goldie too masterful for his liking. In 1897 he was prevented from taking this step only by the fear that the French might then refuse to recognize treaties made by agents of the Company with African chiefs in the disputed areas. Until a definitive treaty was signed, he was glad to use the rivalry between the chartered Company and the independent traders to bend both to his will.

Mary was a close friend of Goldie and his wife. Rarely, after 1897, did a month pass without her visiting their home. She stood up to this imperious, rather disdainful man, and it is clear from references in her letters that there was an unusually strong bond between them: she told Holt, 'we are like two savage animals on a small island, we each know we should be lonely if we got rid of the other'. Yet, while acknowledging that he had a greater understanding of Africa than any other Englishman, she crossed swords with him on a number of important issues. Because she believed that chartered companies were controlled too completely by one man, Mary was opposed to them. They were too risky: a great man, as she believed Goldie to be, might do good, but a man like Rhodes, whom she disliked, could do immense harm. Secondly, she was convinced that his views on the liquor traffic were wrong. He thought it was an evil thing, and had prohibited it through the territories which he controlled. He supported the Anti-Liquor Association which was trying to put an end to it everywhere. In this controversy he was supported by Lugard but opposed by Mary.

The attack on the trade in liquor was reopened by Lugard towards the end of 1897. In an article he described the demoralizing effect of spirits upon the African people. The independent traders resented this bitterly. Mary had succeeded in restraining them in their attacks on Goldie up to this time, but now she feared that they would say and write things—true and untrue—which could only increase the tension between the white men who worked in West Africa. To prevent this mud-slinging campaign, against the advice of her friends, she again came forward as their advocate, and replied to Lugard. She had not found the African an habitual drunkard: 'in the whole of West Africa, in one week, there is not one quarter the amount of drunkenness you can see any Saturday night you choose in a couple of hours in the Vauxhall Road'. In such a dank climate she thought some spirits were necessary, and if the African failed to get his supply from Europe, he drank his own, home-distilled alcohol, which was definitely dangerous to health. The claim of the Anti-Liquor Association that trade gin was poisonous she treated with scorn, for she had sent bottles from the principal exporters for analysis and found that the gin shipped to the Coast was of exactly the same quality as that drunk in England. Moreover, a bottle of gin was an extremely convenient trade article since, unlike most goods in Africa, it suffered neither from mildew nor rust.

The Liverpool men were jubilant. She had achieved her purpose: she had answered for them, and the personal attacks on Goldie and the missionaries had been prevented. But though she had taken her stand after long thought, Mary had a price to pay. All the men whom she most admired were arrayed against her: Goldie, Nassau, Kemp, Lugard, and a host of others. An unusual touch of bitterness creeps into her letters at this time, though it is directed against prejudice and humbug, rarely against individuals. It is 'smug, self-satisfied, lazy, sanctimonious *Times* believing England' that she inveighs against.

Her chief antagonist, Lugard, she met at Goldie's toward the end of 1897. Her first impressions were not favourable: 'a dreamy partisan of the missionary party, a very fine explorer and soldier I have no doubt, but a man who acts under orders, and does not think . . .' she wrote to Holt. He irritated her personally and she found him 'a strangely simple-minded creature . . . who put me in mind of one of my old ladies who said to me the other day, "Oh, it must be true, I read it in a newspaper." ' She considered that he had 'not an atom of an idea of the elementary laws of evidence'. He wrote long letters in an attempt to convince her of the justice of his case, but she preferred to judge by what she had seen. She wrote in reply:

Of course my experience is nothing to yours, but no one who knows me on the Coast will give me a good character for keeping out of bush villages or native quarters of coast towns—in the factories I have stayed at—I have always bribed the watchman not to start a concert on his bell and rouse the house when I came over, or through, the stockade after hours, and the amount of brilliant burglaries I have committed getting into my quarters which have been locked up by careful stewards when I have been down town o' nights should place my name alongside C. Peace's . . . I cannot help thinking I must have seen, going on as I did, something of the evils of the liquor traffic had it been so fearful and so prevalent. I have seen drunkenness of course here and there but very rarely. . . .

In her next fight, Mary had Lugard and Goldie on her side. Since her return from the Coast, she had reluctantly come to the conclusion that the permanent officials at the Colonial Office were ignorant, prejudiced, and idle. Though they controlled the administration of vast territories, they neither knew nor wanted to know anything about the customs or laws of the people whom they ruled. In Mary's view their policy threatened to dishonour England and to cause hatred and revolt where there could easily be loyalty and peace. Early in 1898 a rising occurred on the Coast, and Mary set out to prove that the African, and not the British Governor, had justice on his side.

The narrow strip of coastline, twenty miles deep and two hundred miles long, which had formed the British colony of Sierra Leone was extended in the nineteenth century to include great regions to the north. A formal Protectorate was declared in 1896, and the Governor, Sir Frederick Cardew, immediately prohibited all traffic in slaves and announced that from January 1st, 1898, a tax would be levied on every house in the Protectorate. The money was to be spent on a more efficient police force and on the general development of the country. The Colonial Office had agreed to these measures.

Mary of course approved of the suppression of the slave trade. The tax she regarded as bare-faced robbery. The Africans who were expected to pay it had voluntarily signed treaties with England—treaties which were now completely disregarded by the stronger party. When the chiefs refused to pay the tax, black troops were sent against them; they were flogged, imprisoned, and publicly humiliated. To the vast mass of Englishmen the rising that followed was simply another attempt by a barbarous people to resist lawful authority.

Mary considered it her duty to tell them the truth, and wrote to the *Spectator*. The English tradition, she argued, was to maintain African law when it was not too barbarous to be enforced by colonial administrators. This tradition was being ignored, and the confidence and loyalty of the West Africans undermined by the imposition of a direct tax of five shillings on every hut in the Sierra Leone Protectorate. African law made it clear that any property the occupier paid a regular fee for belonged not to him, but to the man to whom he paid the fee. The Government was thus, in African eyes, seizing property which it had promised in solemn treaties to respect. This act of robbery was the cause of the rising, not the wickedness of drunken slave traders.

She was not content to use only her pen to see that justice was done. She organized her party: the Chambers of Commerce of Liverpool and Manchester sent protests to the Colonial Office; Holt wrote to the *Spectator* in support of her arguments stating bluntly that he saw no need for the tax, and that he was not surprised that the Africans had objected to paying it. The Liverpool and Manchester men had important political connections and Mary began to use them: she discussed with Holt the possibility of electing a really influential M.P. for Liverpool, a man whose protests could not be ignored even by Chamberlain. The question was raised in the House, and the Government was induced to set up a special commission of inquiry under Sir David Chalmers.

The Colonial Secretary had been made aware of Mary's influence. She was supported by all educated African opinion, and by a growing body of liberal-minded people in England. In March 1898 he sent for her. He was extremely civil and asked for her views on the hut-tax. Mary was hopeful, but cautious, for he said one or two things that struck the wrong note: 'I sit like a spider in my web, and everyone who has anything to say comes and tells me.' She told Holt that she was convinced that up till that moment he had listened only to the permanent officials. Yet he was interested in what she had to say, and their talk covered topics very near to her heart: methods of improving health in West Africa by building sanatoriums, introducing a nursing service, improving drainage. He discussed means of improving trade and ways of inducing the Africans to work harder. The interview ended with his asking her to suggest other ways of collecting revenue.

The moves and counter-moves of the next two years are too intricate to follow here. Mary thought less of Chamberlain every month. She had been hopeful when he followed up the interview by writing to her and making it plain that he really wanted her opinion. But by May she was convinced that he was not seriously inclined to take her advice. To Holt she wrote: 'I am not going to be mixed up in his pettifogging ways.' He had asked her for an alternative method of administering the West African colonies, and she had, in the midst of her other work, devised a scheme whereby the traders were to have a place on a Council for Africa. Convinced that he had no intention of implementing this, she declared that she would not send it to him; he could wait until he read it in her book.

Meanwhile Chalmers was investigating in Sierra Leone and Mary had word from her friends there that he 'was acting in a most judicious manner, keeping himself clear of all Government influence . . . [having] no connection with Government officials and not even a clerk to take down the evidence'. By November she was afraid that his report would 'never see the light', for the Governor, Sir Frederick Cardew, had not been recalled and she could only feel that Chamberlain was backing his policy.

By January 1899 Mary had given up hope of getting the hut-tax removed from the Protectorate. She still fought to prevent its extension to other parts of the West Coast, but her active participation in politics had disillusioned her: 'I am tired of politicians; how timorous they are, how deaf to anything but praise and pleasant prophecy.' She wrote to tell Holt how disgusted she was that 'men at the head of affairs should allow themselves to be led by such third rate amateurs as Kidd and Rhodes'. She had learnt her lesson, however. Since she still hoped to influence the men who controlled Africa she intended to remain ostensibly friendly: 'I play the opportunist game, [for] I am so anxious not to do harm to what is good in England.'

Chalmers' report was in the end published, though

all the horrors he reports fall on deaf ears. England's heart has had a case built round it by the misrepresentations of the missionary party, may the curse of Allah rest on them through all their generations, while England is drunk today with an imperialism England of yesterday prepared.

She had been hard hit and she poured her heart out to Holt, the only man she knew who was deeply and genuinely devoted to Africa: 'I am so utterly lonely in this fight' (for Holt alone had supported her throughout); 'all the rest will turn on me any minute if it suits their advantage.' The Liverpool traders had made their peace with the Colonial Office when they found that order had been restored in the Protectorate and that trade had not suffered; Chalmers had died on his return to England—more through grief at the reception of his report than through the evil climate of Sierra Leone, according to his wife—and none of Mary's relatives or intimate friends was interested in Africa.

Mary had not been solely concerned with the hut-tax controversy during these years. Relations between the English and the French in West Africa had become very strained by the end of 1897. The success of the British expedition to Ashanti had enabled them to advance from this base towards the Niger. It was at this point that Chamberlain, distrusting the Royal Niger Company, intervened. He formed the West African Frontier Force and offered the command to Lugard. He ordered him to beat the French at their game of steady infiltration and the establishment of military posts in disputed territories. Lugard had worked under Goldie, and it was with reluctance that he undertook a task which both he and his friend thought was doomed to failure. Goldie persuaded him to do so only because he preferred someone whom he could trust in charge of the new armed forces in the Niger Company territories. Lugard obeyed Chamberlain's orders. Tension mounted and war seemed imminent. But Chamberlain had been right when he gambled on France's unwillingness to commit herself to a European war; he got his way and an agreement was signed in 1898 which gave England what today is Nigeria. Now he could safely revoke the charter of the Royal Niger Company, and take over vast territories to be administered by the Colonial Office.

Mary's dream of Nigeria and Uganda joining hands was shattered by the Anglo-French agreement. Mossi, in the hinterland of Ashanti, was signed away to the French; in return for the withdrawal of the French expedition from Fashoda, France was granted large territories between the Niger and the sea.

She had written articles, given lectures, and exerted all her influence to prevent this from happening. She was not surprised that she had failed, for decisions of such importance were made at the very highest level, and no single person without official position or the backing of a party could hope to affect the course of events. She was particularly distressed by two aspects of the settlement, and she did not hesitate to speak bold and dignified words of condemnation. One was the transfer of the Royal Niger Territories:

> Any student of Africa knows [she wrote] that the Royal Niger Company has been the only English institution in West Africa that France had any reason to fear in her great career of empire-making there. She, very wisely and perfectly justifiedly, wished the obstacle removed. She has got it removed. The whole of the negotiations of the recent Anglo-French convention constitutes a French triumph from start to finish.

She also regretted keenly the lowering of British prestige and the sullying of her honour, by her desertion of the King of Mossi after a treaty of friendship and protection had been signed with him. Lastly, she was convinced that the colonial administration was incapable of bringing justice and prosperity to so many million people about whose customs, religion, and way of life it knew nothing.

Until the moment she left for South Africa, she continued her attack on the Crown Colony system. She set out to prove that it was expensive in men's lives and in treasure—in one of her more bitter moments she told Holt that one good result of their wasting money in South Africa was that 'they won't have so much to throw away in making a mess of West Africa'. The Governors in West Africa had no expert council to advise them; they were controlled by an office in England which knew little of African affairs, and they were given no inducement to study native laws, languages, or ethnology. They were out of touch with African opinion, for they rarely came into direct contact with Africans, and their time was taken up with a mass of official business which was intrinsically valueless.

The unhealthy climate, the lack of a regular West African Service with good pay and prospects of promotion, and the failure of the home government to recognize and reward good, steady service, 'reduced on the local government official a fervid desire to get home to England, or obtain an appointment in some region other than the West Coast'. Thus no sooner did one of them get to know the country, than he was transferred to another region where he had to begin the business of learning all over again. No progress could be made under such a system.

Her conclusion was:

The desire to develop our West African possessions is a worthy one in its way, but better leave it totally alone than attempt it with your present machinery; which the moment it is called upon to deal with the administration of the mass of the native inhabitants gives such a trouble. And remember it is not the only trouble your Crown Colony System can give; it has a few glorious opportunities left of further supporting everything I have said about it, and more. But I will say no more. You have got a grand rich region there, populated by an uncommon fine sort of human being. You have been trying your present set of ideas on it for over four hundred years; they have failed in a heart-breaking drizzling sort of way to perform any single solitary one of the things you say you want done there. West Africa today is just a quarry of paving-stones for Hell, and those stones are cemented in places with men's blood mixed with wasted gold.

By the end of 1899 Mary felt she had failed utterly in all that she had set out to achieve.

17

LONDON, 1895–1900

UNTIL July 1898 Mary lived in Addison Road, into which
she and her brother had moved on leaving Cambridge.
There she looked after Charles, entertained her country
cousins and her friends from Cambridge, and there she was 'at
home' to many of her distinguished friends. If her neighbours
had been curious, they must have wondered at the strange assortment of men and women who found their way up the broad
stairway and disappeared for hours into the tiny flat. They might
have seen Sir Arthur Lyall, retired from the Council of India and
now interested in primitive religions. An anthropologist of
standing—the author of *Asiatic Studies*—he had written a review
of Mary's fetish chapters for the *Edinburgh Review*. Sometimes
a colonial bishop brought distinction to the neighbourhood;
sometimes a well-known publisher or a great merchant. But other,
more picturesque, if less respectable, figures might have been seen.
Hard-faced traders home on leave from Africa, bronzed sea-
captains renewing their acquaintance with their passenger, and
strangely dressed, dark-skinned West Africans were all made
welcome at 101 Addison Road.

For a year after her return from her second journey Mary was
busy writing *Travels in West Africa*, preparing lectures and giving
them, and keeping up a voluminous correspondence with anthropologists, journalists, traders, and West Africans. She had little
time left even for reading. What she had she seems to have spent
with Conrad's or Kipling's books, though occasionally she
turned to W. W. Jacobs for light relief. All wrote of men of
action: her sort of men.

Towards the end of 1896 her friendly publisher, George A.
Macmillan, gave her an introduction to Professor Tylor of
Oxford. She went to visit this distinguished ethnologist, met his
wife, and, as always seems to have been the case, became a friend

of the family. The details of their discussions on primitive customs do not concern us; it is enough to know that Tylor recognized the value of her work and grew to respect her intellectual qualities.

Sir Arthur Lyall, too, was prepared to argue with her on equal terms, and to listen to her views respectfully although they were sometimes opposed to his own. A correspondence had begun after his review; they had met and become friends. A letter she wrote to him in May 1898 shows how intimate she was with him and his wife, and how, after much discussion, he had been persuaded to accept certain of her opinions which did not fit in with his ideas of primitive beliefs in other lands:

I hope I did not weary Lady Lyall today by staying too long. I have been keeping away from her for a few weeks, fearing I might weary her by coming too often. A selfish thing of mine to come at all, but she is so restful and so pleasant to me whose home is in the valley of the shadow of death. I thought when I left Cambridge I had left that valley, but it was an error. It is evidently my home and I must reconcile myself to it, build my shimbec there and settle down, but it does me good to come out of it into Lady Lyall's sunshine. I need hardly remark your majesty need not bother your head over my ju ju. Now you have graciously permitted me to have a little Bethel of my own in W.A., I am happy and intend to have great times and drive out devils, vegetable spirits, and totemism, and deified ancestors.

She had many women friends. Miss Lucy Toulmin Smith, who had known her father well, often visited her, and criticized her writing—once describing it as 'good sixteenth century'. Her cousin, who wrote novels under the name of Lucas Malet, also offered her advice: she liked the descriptive passages in *Travels in West Africa* so much that she wanted more of them, even at the expense of action. Mary thought she was wrong and left things as they were. Mrs Roy, the daughter of the famous doctor, Sir George Paget, came to see her. She had been one of Mary's most intimate friends in Cambridge and had been her greatest comfort and help during her last wearisome years there. Her husband, who had been Professor of Pathology in the University, had died, leaving her nothing but debts, and Mary spent hours writing to her influential friends trying to find a post for her. Later, Mary came to be on intimate terms with Mrs J. Holt, and with Mrs J. R. Green. She was frequently to be seen in the drawing-room of the latter, holding animated conversations with the distinguished people whom Mrs Green loved to assemble there.

Dennis Kemp, the missionary from the Gold Coast whom Mary had met on her last journey, returned to England in 1897. He was the kind of man that she admired: strongly built, forthright, and deeply interested in the future of West Africa. Though she had been particularly kind to the Methodists, he had been grieved by her attacks on missionaries and wrote to her after the publication of her book. He suggested that she was hard and merciless in controversy. In her reply she tried to convince him that the humorous, bantering manner which she so often adopted, and which her critics described as 'coruscating wit', was not a sign of insensibility. On the contrary, she said that she felt so keenly that she was forced to hide her feelings from the world; otherwise she might be hurt and become embittered and so rendered useless in the fight.

It is from her letters to Kemp that we can get some idea of her religious beliefs. Brought up amongst agnostics, she still had 'an utter faith in God', which there was no need to prove by spiritualism. She did not intend to 'give it up and hand over the affair to Rome'. God, she believed, demonstrated himself through nature, and there was no place in her creed for any revealed religion nor for the preaching of any Christian church. She had no wish to convert anyone to her religion, for it was a gloomy one, and hard to live with.

Though Mary denied Mr Kemp's accusation of hardness there was some truth in it. She hated to be thought a philanthropist. She prided herself upon being a scientist who studied things as they were and who wanted to see West Africa governed by men who used the same approach. A letter to Stephen Gwynn is revealing:

There are not more than three people in all whom I dare let see them [her real feelings], for they are savage things that would make people, who have not got that sort of feeling inside them, shrink from me. There! That is the reason why I am what so many people call 'elusive'. When I am 'elusive' I know it and it is malice aforethought.

There is only one man connected with this West African affair who knows me and what I think entirely about it. That man is Sir George Goldie, and I know he thinks me a devil. We had a talk the other night concerning justice in the abstract, and the meaning of pain and misery,

and we found that, for all our seeming surface agreement, in underneath things we were absolutely different; and the humour of the thing
was he was the gentleminded merciful one.

On another occasion, writing to Holt, Mary said how surprised she was that Goldie should be so pleased to receive a
friendly letter from Liverpool, whose traders had fought him
bitterly. She went on:

he does not like to be hated, Rhodes don't care, I should not care a 2d.
damn if I had the friendship of you, Mr Jones, old Kohler of Berlin,
Plehn and Professor Tylor. I would take on the government of all
Africa, and simply laugh if the rest of the world slung mud and abused
me.

There can be no doubt that Mary Kingsley wanted power. She
was a dominating personality who had been constricted and
confined for thirty years. It was impossible to dominate George
Kingsley, he either fought back successfully or simply went away
on another cruise. The ingrained habit of subservience to her
mother never seems to have been broken, and her brother Charles
was a mere will o' the wisp. Nor, when her parents died, did Mary
see any hope of building a personal empire in Cambridge; so she
went to West Africa. There, traders, ships' captains, and primitive
tribesmen acknowledged her mastery; for the first time she had
tasted power and the taste was sweet in her mouth.

It has been shown how, on her return to England, she found
herself in a unique position. Often she told her friends that she
hated the power that lay in her hands; but she showed no signs of
letting it go. Apart from her efforts to influence Goldie, and
control the Liverpool and Manchester traders, she kept in close
contact with the 'Salisbury set'—as she called them—through her
father's friends the Pembrokes; she cultivated the acquaintance
of the French and Russian ambassadors; she was a frequent visitor
at the house of Reginald Antrobus, at that time head of the West
African Department of the Colonial Office, and by the Spring of
1899 she was trying to form a 'parliamentary party that you
[Holt] and I can more or less manage'. There is little doubt that
Mary's preoccupation with West African affairs, though deep and
genuine, was based on her knowledge that this was the sphere in

which she could meet the greatest men in the kingdom on equal terms.

Mary was so convinced that the policies she advocated were just and expedient, that her judgement of those who opposed her was often clouded. Though she learned to like Lugard, she had no good word to say for him, considering him futile as a politician, and wasteful and indecisive as an administrator. He was too much under the influence of the hated 'missionary party' to be supported in his African policy. She was equally biased when she came to give an opinion of Chamberlain: '[he] is not a strong man,' she wrote to Holt, 'only another lath painted to look like iron'. She persuaded herself that 'the Colonial Office forced him into a course of action he had not contemplated'. Her views on other, lesser men were equally startling. Cardew, who had imposed the hut-tax on the Protectorate of Sierra Leone, came to see her when he was in England, and attempted to justify his policy, arguing that the tax was essential, and that by means of it the African would be raised in the plane of civilization. Mary found him 'stupid, not wicked', and told her friends that 'he could live in an African Colony for a century and know no more about it than a policeman in the British Museum knows about cuneiform inscriptions'. Major Northcote, Commissioner and Commandant of the forces in the northern territories of the Gold Coast, also came to talk to her. Though she was friendly, and admired him as a brave and honourable soldier, she dismissed him as 'not highly educated', and so, incapable of understanding her viewpoint.

During this period when she was so busy with people and affairs, Macmillan invited her to write another book on West Africa. It was to embody her considered opinions, not only on life and customs and fetish, but on methods of colonial government. She felt that such a work was beyond her power. When she was writing of what she had seen, she knew that she could make her meaning clear, but she lacked confidence when she came to write of policy and administration. Yet, because she thought that outspoken criticism might lead to reform and prevent the squandering of lives and treasure, she undertook the task. It was with great labour and distress of mind that she produced *West African Studies*.

In addition to her other worries, Mary had personal and

domestic troubles in 1898. Early in the year she herself had been desperately ill with congestion of both lungs and threatened paralysis of the heart. Kemp had found her alone and at death's door and had told Macmillan, who had sent for Mrs Green, who was in Paris. It was left to these friends to nurse her back to health; her own relatives seem to have done little to help. A short time afterwards Lady Goldie, her dearest friend, died. Mary was deeply grieved and expressed her sorrow to Holt: 'I was very fond of her. She was a sweet gentle woman so unlike the majority of these fashionable, smart, foolish folk here who bore, weary, and disgust me with their airs of grandly good intentions. I feel I have lost something I can never have replaced.' Her sympathy went out to Sir George: 'I would do anything I could to cheer or rest him, he is so intensely internally wretched over the loss of his wife, to whom you know I was, and am, devoted. . . .'

In July she and her brother moved from Addison Road to a bigger house at 32 St. Mary's Terrace, Kensington. There she could entertain her friends and acquaintances in greater comfort, but the strain of moving tired her. She complained of being 'dead tired, with awful headaches'. Her brother was planning to go East again. While he was in England she felt 'tied by the apron strings'; he was still delicate and often inconsiderate—for he would disappear for days without letting his sister know where he was, although he well knew that she would worry—and she could not help showing her delight at the thought of being free to leave England again. Her publisher received a warning that she might need an advance of royalties to pay for her next journey. But for Charles to make plans was one thing, and for him to put them into operation was another. His departure was indefinitely delayed.

Her book was finished by the end of the year, and was published early in 1899. Twelve hundred copies were sold in the first week. The forthright attack on the Crown Colony system made enemies for her, but there could be no doubt that it increased her influence. *The Times* alone, of the most important newspapers, printed no review. This was because, in her opinion, this paper was the mouthpiece of the Colonial Office; since they could find no colonial expert to tear her arguments to pieces, they preferred to ignore the book.

Rumours had already reached her that Miss Flora Shaw, who

wrote on African affairs for *The Times*, hated her and used all her power on the newspaper to discredit her. In February 1899 Mary met this influential woman, who was the friend of Goldie and Rhodes, and who, later, was to marry Lugard. Mary wrote to tell Holt that whereas the officials of the Colonial Office were 'just vexed, and bothered, and surprised that anyone should attack imperial administration', Miss Shaw 'was civil but in a smouldering rage with me, feeling much as a Presbyterian Elder would feel towards a Jesuit or *vice versa*'.

It is more than probable that Flora Shaw felt no love for Mary. On almost every African issue they were opposed. One supported Rhodes and his South Africa Company, the other distrusted him and had instigated the furious attacks made on the Company by the *Spectator* and the *National*—attacks which had led the Government to reconstitute its Board of Governors. Unlike Mary, Miss Shaw belonged to the 'missionary party', opposed the traffic in liquor, supported Cardew and the policy in Sierra Leone, and put her faith in Lugard when he was appointed Governor of Nigeria. Worst of all, she had a low opinion of the independent traders whom Mary had championed through thick and thin. She even travelled in Africa. There could be nothing but hostility between these two female African experts.

Throughout 1899 there was just as much work to do. An invitation was accepted to write a book to be called *The Story of West Africa*—described somewhat contemptuously by its author as a Board School textbook. Before it could be begun, however, a lot of reading had to be done. Bookshops were searched for ancient works on the Coast and soon volumes of Hakyluyt, Jobson, Leo Africanus, Labut, Bosman, and Barbot added to the confusion of her rooms. Mary might often be found in the small hours absorbed in one of these books.

As early as 1893 Charles Kingsley had planned to edit some of the writings of his father. His sister had urged him to begin— with no result. Now, in the midst of her other work, she undertook the task herself. *Notes on Travel and Sport* was completed before the end of 1899: its introduction provides most of the information that we have about Mary's early years.

Lecturing was not abandoned. Goldie and Jones urged her to go on with this work; in their opinion one lecture had more effect than half a dozen articles. This may well have been true, for she spoke to vast audiences—hundreds sometimes being turned away—and what she said was memorable. She was now an expert speaker, with a convincing array of facts and the most entertaining and persuasive manner.

Her interest stretched to everything that was concerned with Africa. She had met the French ambassador, and she used the opportunity to expostulate with him when France, copying the pernicious system established by King Leopold of the Belgians in the Congo, granted vast concessions to privately run companies and began to raise tariffs against English traders. E. D. Morel, at that time an employee of A. L. Jones, the Liverpool shipping magnate, had her support when he began his attack on the horrors of the Belgian Congo. Unhappily she did not live long enough to see his success in rousing world opinion against the beastliness of the royal methods of exploitation, for King Leopold's private dominion survived her by a few years. The Russian ambassador consulted her about France's equatorial colonies, and she was glad to be able to speak so favourably of them, for she admired the French and wanted to see a firm alliance between these two powers.

Plans were made to put aside a few hundred pounds to subsidize an African Journal, edited by three scientific experts in ethnology; Tylor was helped in his research into Bantu distribution; nor was her old friend Gunther neglected when he asked for her help at the British Museum. She allowed herself to stand for election on to the Council of the British Empire League, and was active in the Anthropological Society. Only once did she return a curt refusal when asked to help a worthy cause. The movement for the enfranchisement of women was just being organized. Members of the committee called on one who they thought was the living proof of the justice of their claims.

I refused to attend. They came down on me, four of them and no good looks to spare, to ask why I had never given any help or sympathy to the enfranchisement of women. I said because I thought it was a minor question; while there was a most vital section of Englishmen unenfranchised, women could wait. . . .

She assured Holt that she was far more concerned with gaining representation for the independent traders on a Council for African Affairs.

In the midst of all these activities, Mary was often lonely. Her letters to her friends have a deep undertone of sadness. She was convinced that she was cut off from the main stream of human experience. No more a human being than a gust of wind, with no individual life of her own, she felt that she lived vicariously in the joys, sorrows, and worries of other people. To those who allowed her to 'warm [herself] at the fires of real human beings' she was grateful, but she belonged to the non-human world and her people 'were mangroves, swamps, rivers, and, above all, the sea'.

Early in 1899 Major Matthew Nathan was introduced to her. He was an officer of the Royal Engineers who had served in Sierra Leone before being appointed Secretary to the Colonial Defence Committee under Chamberlain. At the time when he met Mary he had just been offered the job of looking after the administration of Sierra Leone during the absence of Cardew, who was returning to England to reply to the points made in Chalmers' report. Mary was always stirred by soldiers, and she was fond of Jews, who attracted her because of 'their dreamy minds, their hard common sense and their love for beautiful material objects'. She invited Nathan to visit her. When he came he proved to be sympathetic, deeply interested in West Africa, and eager to learn more. He was her own age, striking in appearance, intelligent, able, unattached to any other woman, and on the threshold of a distinguished career. For the first time since the death of her father, Mary became deeply and emotionally involved with a man.

Her friends were invited to meet him; his name cropped up frequently, and often irrelevantly, in her letters; as much time as possible was spent in his company; long letters were written even before he left England. Mary showed all the signs of a woman in love. She even lost her sense of proportion, as the following typical passage in one of her letters to Holt, written on a visit to her friend Mrs Antrobus, shows:

Another thing turned up which upset me; the Major Nathan who goes out tomorrow to take charge of Sierra Leone during Cardew's absence, is a valued friend of mine, he is one of those referred to in my family as 'Mary's Jews'. Well, as I am a living woman Mrs Antrobus said, 'Oh, Miss Kingsley, isn't it strange there is a Jew in exactly the same position in English affairs as Dreyfus was in French affairs!'

'Indeed,' I said.

'Yes,' said she, 'isn't it strange?'

'Jews,' said I, 'usually are.'

'We,' said she, 'are sending him out to Sierra Leone.' 'My Aunts and Uncles,' says I to myself— 'these people have got a maggot in their heads about Matthew Nathan.' So there is another worry for me, for I know he is the very tone of honour, and I should grieve if anything happened to him.

If Mrs Antrobus had made these remarks about any other man, Mary would have thought nothing of it, and, rightly, put them down as part of the light chatter which is to be heard in all such drawing-rooms. When they concerned Matthew Nathan, she felt a pang of apprehension.

The Major disagreed with her views on the Hut-Tax. She wrote to him, ostensibly to justify herself, in reality to let him know the place he occupied in her thoughts. He had suggested that her intervention had made things worse in the colony. After trying to make it clear why she thought it her duty to defend the African and the trader she went on:

It has not been forgetfulness nor indifference that has prevented my writing to you sooner, but just a despairing feeling that I cannot make you understand. As a general rule it is simply a matter of no importance whether anyone, from Joe Chamberlain to the dustman, understands me or no, but you are the exception, and I suppose, with the irony of fate, you don't care a row of pins about understanding me, while the others downright worry trying to do it.

Three days later she was writing again:

It would be so much easier to be cheaply cruel and cowardly, so much easier to lie by silence and save people's feelings, things it hurts me to hurt. But if I did it once, I could not look you in the face again, and I must be able to—it is the only thing worth having living or dead. I have never done one thing in my life that I cannot face you with. I never shall. If you did not exist I should not be dishonourable, I should be just hard and I should not care. There is no mortal reason why you should care one way or the other what I am. Sir George Goldie has to tolerate me because his wife loved me and he loved her and loves her. You have no such link, so I explain to you—but not to him. I am of no account to you and I know it. I don't revel in it or I should not write to you thus. . . .

P

When Nathan took up his duties in Sierra Leone, Mary wrote again to congratulate him on his handling of a difficult task; on his return to England she spent a great deal of time in his company; but beyond that the relationship did not go. He was a confirmed bachelor, and she had none of the art—even if she had the conscious wish—to persuade him to change his mind.

Only a few of her friends knew of her deep-seated discontent. In company she was gay, and her irrepressible humour made her a welcome guest. The *Spectator* had been one of the first papers to criticize her somewhat flippant comments on cannibalism. Its editor, St. Loe Strachey, however, soon realized that she was a serious student of West African affairs. His paper printed a very favourable review of *West African Studies*, and Mary wrote to thank him. A friendship developed between her and Mr and Mrs Strachey, and the latter, in her book *Loe Strachey and His Paper*, has described her at this period of her life:

Slender, upright, carrying her body with a curious stiffness, she looked, with her blue eyes, humorous mouth, and fair hair parted in the middle under a black velvet snood, less like an explorer than anyone I ever saw. . . . She had a brain masculine in its strength and in the breadth of its outlook, but she had also an unequalled sense of humour and was quite the most amusing person I ever met.

Mrs Strachey described her visits to the house at 32 St. Mary's Abbott's Terrace, Kensington. There she found a miscellaneous collection of books, journals, and mementos of Africa. The odour of blood-stained ju-ju idols assailed her nostrils as she entered the door and the sight of one particularly loathsome image, into which nails had been driven by those who wished their enemies to die, made her shudder.

The Stracheys often invited Mary to their house at Dorking. On one occasion Mr Balfour was there, and Mary talked most vivaciously to the future Prime Minister about white ants and their depredations as well as about more serious matters. Later, they invited her to meet Lord Cromer, home from Egypt. Mary had at first declined this invitation on the grounds that she had domestic duties, but, finding that she was free, she arrived just before lunch seated by the side of the baker. She was 'sitting very still in her little black bonnet, and conveying somehow the

impression of the figure-head of a ship'. Lord Cromer said afterwards that he had never met a woman who impressed him so
much as having the mind of a statesman. Mary too was convinced
of his ability, giving it as her opinion that no one should be sent
out as an administrator to our dominions unless he could show
a certificate signed by this great man.

Meanwhile the clouds were gathering in South Africa. Mary
had had enough of controversy. She was convinced that she had
failed in her mission. She decided to undertake another 'odd job'
where she could be of some real service to the fighting men for
whom she had so much admiration. As soon as war broke out,
she offered to go to the Cape as a nurse. With its customary
optimism, the War Office assured her that she would not be
wanted—the whole affair would be over in no time. In February
1900 a letter came advising her that she was wanted after all, and
without a moment's hesitation she prepared to sail.

Before she left, she made a last declaration of her faith in
a lecture at the Imperial Institute, on February 12th, 1900:

You may say it is quite impossible to inspire a national feeling of
devotion to England among coloured races. I do not pretend to know
Asiatics, but I know Africans of various kinds—and remember they
vary quite as much as Europeans—and I have no hesitation in saying
that the finest of all native African races, the true Negroes, whose
home-land is in West Africa from Gambia to Cameroon, can be made
as loyal and as devoted to England as the man in the street up
here, provided you do not make two mistakes in dealing with him
today. One mistake is giving him, unintentionally I am sure on your
part, an agrarian grievance. . . . Buying and selling him from people
from whom he thought you had the right to buy him never shook his
love for England; but go and take away his own land in his own home
country when you said you would not, in treaties and by word of
mouth for more than a hundred years; go and make him, without
consulting him, a tenant at will where he was once holder absolute,
and a trustee for his future generations in the bargain, and you will
give him an agrarian grievance; and how he feels about it he explained
in the Hut Tax War in Sierra Leone.

Then there is the other mistake you can make with him—I am
obliged to refer to it delicately because our American cousins caught
the disease very bad in their constitution. Instead of taking as model
principles those of the British Constitution, which I take it are Liberty,
Justice and Representation, they took those of the French Revolution,

Liberty, Equality, Fraternity. This is an unworkable thing because not in touch with facts; hence it is one of the most dangerous diseases a national constitution can catch, and it has a horrid eruption, humbug. You have got a nasty touch of it yourselves, but, for goodness sake, stamp it out; humbug is poison wherever found. Strong men up here may just sneer at it and consider it is necessary; but strong men in Africa—Negroes—won't look at it in that way; in their eyes it is breaking faith; and in their eyes it is a crime between man and man, that no bribe, no gift, nothing but blood can wipe out.

She concluded by boldly challenging those who had attacked her for being proud of ancestors who had been slave-traders and plantation owners:

I thank you for your toleration of me. I know I owe it to the name I bear; I know I owe all that is good in me, to the blood of my ancestors; my Imperialism is their Imperialism, rather out of fashion in late years, though they practically did much to make a great Empire for you to take pride in, they and their old comrades, the merchant adventurers of England. It is merely natural that I should have a strange taste for West Coast traders. They are the representatives of the old merchant adventurers, men for whom Sir Francis Drake, of honourable memory, went out and fought, greatly to the making of the power of this realm; and it is natural I should like Negroes. Sir Francis was always 'exceedingly gentle' to these people, and he burnt a Spanish town, and a big one at that, just because it had killed his favourite Negro boy. I like to live at peace within my own house, so I know it is safer for me to stick to the old Imperialism of Drake with its rigid beliefs in keeping your own honour clean. If I were to depart from that and preach certain doctrines in modern Imperialism, it's a warm reception I should get from my family and the old merchant adventurers when I arrived at where they are held now to dwell—Fiddler's Green. Goodbye and fare you well, for I am homeward bound.

18

'HOMEWARD BOUND'

MARY was not sorry to see England sink below the horizon as the *Moor*, the troopship on which she embarked, steamed out into the Irish Sea. The last four years had been exciting; they had brought her power and fame, and a great number of interesting friends. But she was desperately tired in body and spirit. She had so taxed her physical powers that she had suffered almost continuously from nervous headaches, neuralgia, and colds. She was disheartened by the results of her struggle with the Colonial Office.

The sea smoothed and revivified her. The soldiers were pathetically sick when the ship rolled in the Bay of Biscay, but Mary had not lost her sea legs. She even had time and energy during the voyage to write an account of the cruise of the *Hannibal* of London, in search of slaves on the West African Coast in the seventeenth century. Long letters were penned to her friends. But the soldiers were dull in comparison with her 'palm oil ruffians'. They had no stories of death in various guises, of white ants, or ju jus. She grieved to see them, living in squalid, overcrowded quarters, dressed in heavy flannel shirts and thick uniforms, wasted and ill long before the ship reached Africa. The danger of disembarking men in such a weak state in a land where enteric fever was raging appalled her.

One of her letters was addressed to the editor of *New Africa*, a journal published in Liberia. It gives her final judgement on the relationship between Englishmen and Africans:

I know there is a general opinion among the leading men of both races that Christianity will give the one possible solution to the whole problem. I fail to be able to believe this. I fail to believe Christianity will bring peace between the two races, for the simple reason that though it may be possible to convert Africans *en masse* into practical Christians, it is quite impossible to convert Europeans *en masse*. You have only to look at the history of any European nation—the Dutch, the Spanish, the Italian, the German—every one calling themselves Christians, but none the more for that tolerant and peaceful. Each one of them is ready to take out a patent for the road to Heaven and make that road out of men's blood and bones and the ashes of burnt homesteads. Of course by doing this they are not following the true teaching of Jesus Christ, but that has not and will not become a factor in politics. So I venture to say that you who build on Christianity in this matter are not building on safe ground. You cannot by talking about Christianity to the Europeans save your people. . . . I have had to stand up alone these two years and fight for African freedom and institutions, while Africans equally well and better educated in English culture have been talking about religious matters to a pack of people who do *not care* about Christianity at all. The Christian public up here will bring little influence to bear on preserving Africa's institutions. The public, be it granted, is a powerful one, but it has been taught that all African institutions are bad, and unless you preserve your institutions, above all your land law, you cannot, no race can, preserve your liberty.

When Mary arrived at the Cape she reported to the principal medical officer, General Wilson, and volunteered to help in any way he pleased. He sent her to Simonstown to nurse Boer prisoners who were dying of enteric fever by the hundred.

The men were in many cases from the army of Cronje, who had held out for a week at Paardeberg before surrendering to Kitchener's overwhelming force on February 27th. During this time the Boers had been living in trenches with dead men and horses, drinking polluted water. Caught unawares, the British authorities were quite incapable of dealing with the terrible epidemic of camp fever which followed. They did everything in their power: brandy, milk, eggs, even champagne, were lavishly supplied, but they lacked hospitals. When these were improvised there were not enough doctors and nurses to make them effective.

One doctor and two nurses comprised the entire trained staff of the Palace Barracks, taken over as a hospital, when Mary arrived. They welcomed her, for they had been worked nearly to death. More than a hundred patients were immediately placed under Mary's charge—'delirious, fretting strong men, every third man wanting a nurse to himself'. The *Palace* was a typical barracks, quite unsuited for a hospital: narrow iron bedsteads, with sackcloth sheets and mud-coloured blankets, stood in long lines in the bare, cheerless wards. Even when two doctors and three nurses joined, the staff was pitifully inadequate. The nurses were at work every minute trying to restrain those who were delirious, or struggling to get patients, whose lives depended upon quiet, back into the beds from which they had flung themselves in their agony. It was a bitter, losing fight with death such as Mary had fought before.

For two months she worked to bring order to the chaotic hospital. She succeeded to a remarkable degree. Dr. Carré, the medical officer in charge, reported to her friends in Liverpool that between them she and he had 'turned a mortuary into a sanatorium'. But she did far more than help to reorganize a hospital. In the indescribable stench, amongst swarming bugs and lice, she found time from nursing the pain-racked Boers, and from laying out their dead, to listen with sympathy and understanding to those who spoke of home and kindred, and of the land to which they were so passionately attached. To many she brought warmth and hope even in that desolate place. She had her reward: these strong men tried to show their gratitude by obeying her least command. They even forgave her for being an Englishwoman.

Towards the end of May she caught enteric fever from her patients. Her heart had never been strong, and it had been weakened by the severe illness of 1898. After an operation, she died peacefully of heart failure on June 3rd, 1900. She had made one characteristic request before she died: to be buried at sea. The affection and respect in which she was held was made plain by the way in which this last wish was gratified. Her coffin was drawn on a gun-carriage from the hospital to the pier at Simonstown; soldiers marched in escort; a launch carried it to a warship which put out to sea. Living she had been the embodiment of the bold spirit and honourable ambition which had driven Englishmen to seek renown and fortune in strange lands; dead, she had found the same resting-place as the greatest of her heroes, Drake.

Her death was mourned as a national loss. Every newspaper praised this great Englishwoman. One of the most moving tributes came from E. D. Morel, who sympathized with so many of her causes. In July he wrote, in the *British Empire Review*:

. . . As she lived so she died, doing good to the end. . . . In the sphere of usefulness which she had mapped out for herself Miss Kingsley cannot be replaced. Her grasp of the problems and necessities

of West Africa was profound. There is none whose collective knowledge of the country and its people equalled hers; none, at any rate,
who wielded the power of communicating such collective knowledge
to the world.

He then wrote of her fearlessness and moral courage in attacking the most powerful interests, and of her determination to
make the British public realize the potentialities of our West
African colonies. Two years later, in the introduction to his book,
Affairs of West Africa, there is a more personal note:

> Few women, I believe, have inspired all sorts and conditions of men
> with so intense a respect, so wondering an admiration. Few women
> are able, as Mary Kingsley was able, to draw forth, by the magic of her
> earnest personality, the best in a man. She was so unassuming, so
> unaffected, such a womanly woman in every sense of the word. . . . The
> truest, kindest, staunchest friend that ever breathed—such was Mary
> Kingsley.

The merchants of Liverpool and Manchester expressed their
sense of loss by founding a hospital for the treatment of tropical
diseases—an institution they knew well would have given her the
greatest pleasure; another group of her friends founded a *Mary
Kingsley Society for West Africa* to carry on the study of African
customs and institutions.

It is difficult to estimate the importance of Mary Kingsley in
the development of West Africa. Certainly she failed in all the
specific tasks she set herself: the traders have never won a place
on a Council for West African Affairs; direct taxation has become
general throughout the colonies; the study of African religion
and law has proceeded slowly and had little effect on those who
are responsible for administration. The 'missionary party' that
she opposed in such a whole-hearted way still flourishes and
influences public opinion. There is proof that many Englishmen
still find it difficult to take a detached, scientific view of African
affairs: the African remains for many a 'child' to be helped when
he is amenable to British rule, and a 'devil' to be ruthlessly sup-
pressed when he is not.

Yet the relationship between England and her West African
dependencies has changed profoundly in the last fifty years. In
1900 no one thought that Africans of the Gold Coast, of Ashanti,

or of Nigeria, would be capable of running a parliamentary democracy. That they have been allowed and encouraged to do so is at least partly due to the pioneer work of Mary Kingsley. Her blunt speech acted as a cathartic shock to the smug, Victorian Englishman. He was no longer allowed to feel he had done his duty by contributing a few shillings to mission funds, nor was his wife after she had spent hours making hideous dresses to cover African nakedness. Strange opinions had disturbed them:

Let him have gin if he wants it, he is no drunkard. We are in West Africa to trade and not to preach. I am absolutely for Secret Societies. Witch doctors, on the whole, do more good than harm. The cannibal tribes are the finest in West Africa. Domestic slavery should not be condemned off-hand. Polygamy is a necessary institution and its chief supporters are the women. Tiger justice, tempered with mercy, not philanthropy.

Under her attacks the wall of prejudice and horror which separated the English people from their fellow citizens in Africa was breached.

Mary was more than the champion of a cause or of a people. She has a place in her own right in the galaxy of famous Victorian women. Had she never gone to Africa she would inevitably have played a prominent part in some other sphere—she might even have led the movement for women's emancipation which she declined to join as a mere follower. Her great intelligence, dynamic energy, and high principles were bound to leave their mark on her generation.

'She had the brain of a man and the heart of a woman.' In these words Sir George Goldie summed up the qualities of one who challenges comparison with England's greatest men in judgement, courage, and breadth of understanding, but who yet possessed the sympathy and the tenderness of a woman. Mary Kingsley is surely unique amongst the distinguished women of her race: unknown in 1892, when her parents died, within eight years she won fame and power, which she used to influence the lives of millions of Africans. Yet today the deeds, the words, and the very name of this noble woman are almost unknown in the land of her birth.

INDEX

229

1°N

CORISCO I.

FRENCH
EQUATORIAL
AFRICA

C. ESTERIAS

LIBREVILLE

0°

Fan villages:
M'FETTA, EFOUA, EGAGA.
ESOON and N'DORKO
lay somewhere on dotted line

CAPE LOPEZ   BAY OF
CAPE LOPEZ

O·G·O·R·O·N·O·G·O·U.

OGOWE OF ALLABAR.

1°S